From
Carm Lewis

Welcome to the game . . .

Mah Jongg

Mondays

a memoir about friendship,
love, and faith

Fern Bernstein

Interior design by Tabitha Lahr
Cover design by Jessica Bell

Published 2019
Published by JAG Designer Services
Printed in the United States of America
ISBN: 978-1-7337585-0-5
E-ISBN: 978-1-7337585-1-2
Library of Congress Control Number: 2019904142

For information, email: fernhbern@yahoo.com

In loving memory of my mother, Carol.
Receiving your mah jongg set was *b'shert.*

Thank you to the following women for sharing a mah jongg game with me: Larrisa A., Paula B., Diane C., Fern C., Lauren C., Roz D., Eileen D., Ahuva E., Robin F., Ceil G., Yvette H., Miriam H., Jill H., Laurie I., Amy K.1, Amy K.2, Alana K., Debbie L., Mollie M., Lisa M., Stacey M., Marci P., Peggy P., Fern R., Judy R., Fern S-R., Bari S., Alison S., Pauline S., Robin S., Pam S., Lisa S., Debbie S., Jody S., and Vicki W.

Contents

Author's Note

*D*ue to my age and changing eyesight, I have chosen a larger font in consideration for other readers experiencing this mid-life phenomenon along with me.

I have also included some pictures in my book because the child in me misses seeing pictures in the adult books I read.

The players have changed since my lessons and early games due mostly to work schedules. Leigh has remained from the start. I have changed the names of the women I play with and other persons named in this book except for the clergy, my life coach, the Psychic-Medium, my husband, and three sons.

I have italicized the Hebrew, Sanskrit, and Russian words and given an English definition for each.

With those four points made and out of the way . . . *please read on!*

Life is a song—sing it. Life is a game—play it. Life is a challenge—meet it. Life is a dream—realize it. Life is a sacrifice—offer it. Life is love—enjoy it.
—Sai Baba

Prologue

*E*xcitement builds. I'm one tile away from calling mah jongg and winning. I know. It's just a game. But, don't we all like the thrill of winning regardless of how old we are?

Hope builds. It's his last chemo treatment. He is the unknowing player invited by the result of an MRI. We say, "Game on." We don't want to lose. A life is at stake, the life of my husband.

B'shert, elusive yet certain, knows all the outcomes.

What does this mean and how are these things connected? Let me explain. *B'shert* and mah jongg are two very distinct words in my adult vernacular. Each word comes from a different language, culture, religion, and part of the world. *B'shert* is a Yiddish word that means destiny. It is an enigmatic term that I hold sacred. My sheer existence balanced on the whim of *b'shert*, of my mother and father meeting, marrying and creating me through their union.

Mah jongg is a Chinese word that means sparrow. It is a tile game that originated in China two centuries ago, was brought to America in the 1920s, and became the rage along with flapper dresses, pixie haircuts, jazz, and the Charleston.

B'shert found mah jongg, or maybe it's the other way around. Perhaps it was through divine intervention or possibly through happenstance. Nonetheless, they have found one another and interlaced themselves in the universe.

Welcome to my story about *b'shert* and mah jongg and how they are threading themselves into the fabric of my life here in modern-day Long Island, challenging me to the game of life where I'm learning to appreciate the precious gifts of time, family, friendship, and love.

Love always; love all ways, for time has no guarantee.

Chapter 1

The Big Idea

I love Mondays. For the last five years, they always include mah jongg. Sometimes it's a day game, sometimes it's a night game, but it's always a serendipitous way I can spend time with women I really like. My story started in 2013. I was forty-six years old, happily married, and a busy mom of three sons, ages seventeen, fifteen, and nine. It was a typical hot and humid August weekday on Long Island. I was invited to my friend Sarah's pool club with my two other friends, Leigh and Hope. I looked forward to escaping the drudgery of laundry and other house-hold duties filling my domestic to-do list. We decided to have a leisurely lunch and lounge in the sun for a little while before our kids came home from day camp. Where I live, many children in the circles I travel in go to day camp or sleep-away camp. It was quiet and relaxing at her neighborhood pool club. There were no children splashing in the water or yelling, "Tag!" What I did hear were some women sitting nearby, chatting and laughing. What I noticed was that they were enjoying themselves immensely, engaged in a game of mah jongg.

For a brief moment, I was back in my childhood, remembering my mother and her friends playing this old Chinese game. My heart skipped a beat like it always does when I think of my mother. I miss her every day. Before my mom died five years ago, she gave me a few special things she wanted me to have. One of those special things was her mah jongg set. I have it in a closet, tucked away like a precious jewel. I remember thinking to myself as she handed the set to me, *I'll never play this game. Why is she giving it to me?* Little did I know . . .

Whoosh. Just like that. In an instant, I had an idea. Or maybe it was my mom's spirit whispering into my ear. I turned to my girlfriends and asked, "Is anyone interested in learning to play mah jongg with me?"

We glanced in the direction of the ladies playing nearby. Sarah smiled. "Yes!"

Leigh raised her eyebrows with interest. "My mom loves playing. I'm in, too!"

Hope already played weekly, and said, "You girls will love it. Definitely learn how to play and start a weekly game. You'll be happy you did."

We decided we would give it a try! How hard could

it be? I have a friend named Fran who is a seasoned player and knew she would be the perfect person to teach us. I texted her from my poolside lounge chair and asked if she would be interested in taking on the task. She texted back a few minutes later that she would love to teach us. She suggested four to five lessons to complete the course, and within a few minutes, we had succeeded in scheduling a date, time, and place. I was so excited! We were set to start our lessons with her in just a few days. This was the beginning of my love for mah jongg and the wonderful things that can happen when four women are destined to come together to play an old Chinese game, sitting around a table with four racks, 152 tiles, dice, and a mah jongg card.

Lessons in Patience

On Tuesday, we all met at my house to start our lesson. Fran brought her mah jongg set and prepared a printout for us. She also brought her friend Susan to help us learn in the makeshift mah jongg classroom in my kitchen. She emptied out two plastic trays filled with the mah jongg tiles onto the bridge table I bought for this auspicious occasion. I remembered that familiar click-clack sound of the tiles as they fell onto the table from when my mother used to play. As Fran asked us to turn all the tiles face up, she said in her calm and reassuring voice, "Ladies, be patient with yourselves as you learn. This is a game that requires skill, strategy, and luck."

We nodded our consent as we sat around the table. Despite her warning, we were eager to learn and ready to join the mah jongg craze that buzzed throughout Long Island.

"Let's start by separating the three different suits you see," said Fran. We got to work. We grouped the tiles into sections of Craks, Bams, and Dots. Done. Fran then had us group the Wind tiles: North, South, East, and West. Easy breezy. Next, we grouped the Flower tiles, then the Red Dragons, Green Dragons, Soaps or White Dragons, and lastly the Jokers. Task complete!

Fran then handed each of us our 2013 National Mah Jongg League card. We opened the blue trifold card and looked like deer staring into a car's headlights. There were combinations of letters, numbers, and colors typed on the card. These cryptograms were listed in categories. This card looked more like a secret code to decipher than a fun game. I began to feel frustrated and questioned my big idea of learning this game. What was fun about this? I felt like I was learning a new language. I was lost, confused, and overwhelmed. I looked at my girlfriends and saw them struggling along with me. *But* we remembered to use patience . . .

As we continued our next three lessons with Fran and Susan, we eventually decoded the letters, numbers, and colors and created hands on our own. That was a huge accomplishment! We learned how to deal and replace a

Joker. We reviewed how to do the Charleston, the sequence of passing tiles. It was a dance of the tiles that we all had two left feet with at first.

We laughed a lot, and both Fran and Susan had the patience of saints. After four mentally challenging lessons, we finally grew more comfortable and confident, and we were able to transform a jumble of tiles into a justifiable winning hand. Fran and Susan shadowed our games in lesson five, helped us through moments of confusion, and confirmed if someone miraculously and hesitantly called, "Mah jongg?"

Fran and Susan would exclaim in excitement, "Yes! You did it! Hurray!"

I think they were just as thrilled for each of us as we were when we called mah jongg during those lessons. Their method of teaching had worked. They took us to the finish line. They set us up with the foundation and knowledge to maintain our own game.

Our fourth player was a friend of Leigh's. She stayed in our games for six months, until she started working full-time. We had a few different special women join our games over the next two years as our fourth player, but I've noticed mah jongg players sometimes change like the seasons. At our games, we were and still are patient and kind to one another. We learned in solidarity and through teamwork. Although mah jongg is a game of strategy, defense, and luck, where you play in hopes of winning against your opponents, we created a common code to keep a team spirit throughout our games, playing with kindness through tacit consent.

We were on our way to Mah Jongg Mondays in part from a whimsical idea while sitting at the pool, a little patience we all possessed, and with the help of great teachers named Susan and Fran.

Fran

Fran is one of the calmest women I know. I can substantiate that by the fact that we met in a yoga class. In addition to being calm, she possesses other wonderful characteristics that compliment that trait. She is positive, caring, compassionate, understanding, supportive, and honest. She has shoulder-length, dark-brown hair that accentuates her hazel eyes, which caress you when she gazes your way. Her smile starts to warm your heart before you know you are smiling back at her. She is five-foot-five, slim, and dresses comfortably yet stylishly. Due to a recent double hip replacement, she always wears comfortable and sensible shoes. Fran is married, with two children in their late twenties. She is beautiful both inside and out. We realized we shared some common things in our lives shortly after we met. We share a middle name. We both live at the same house number, but on different streets; we have the same wallpaper in our homes just in different rooms, and our dogs both have the same name of Coco. It was *b'shert.* The universe wanted us to meet, two yogis destined to be in each other's lives for reasons we would learn in the next few years. One would be so she could teach me mah jongg; the other reason we would both be shocked to discover in due time. She would be my mentor not only in mah jongg, but also my mentor in being a wise, strong, warrior caregiver.

Chapter 2

Growing Up

I grew up in a small New Jersey town called Cresskill. I lived in a split-level house with my mom, dad, and brother from 1968 until 1990. My parents were both teachers—my eccentric dad taught physics and chemistry in New York City, and my stoic and creative mom was a gym teacher before becoming a special education teacher. She became a stay-at-home mom after she gave birth to my brother. I joined the family a year and a half later in 1967, adding to my mother's career change from a teacher of other people's children to the teacher of her own flesh and blood. We lived a typical middle-class American life; had more than enough but never too much of anything. We never lived above our means and never felt the need to keep up with the Joneses.

Ever since I was a baby, we summered on the east end of Long Island in a quaint town called Greenport. My grandfather, William, built a modest home on waterfront property about seventy-five years ago. I never got to meet him. He passed away when my mother was seventeen, but he also passed down the legacy of a summer retreat which would provide his daughter the opportunity to create her own future family memories with her children. Indeed, just that happened, and both my brother and I came to love and appreciate this home and our summers in Greenport. We eagerly returned every year, from late June through Labor Day, until I was thirteen years old.

My grandmother Esther shared her home and her late husband's legacy every summer with us, where we created sun-kissed summer memories. Busy summer days were filled swimming in the jewel-blue calm water of the Peconic. My brother and I would make sand castles as sandpipers hopped along the shoreline nearby. I became acquainted with the music of the beach as a child. I listened to the sea-song of the water as the waves rhythmically met with the shore, creating a soothing and relaxing sound. We would dig a large hole, jump in, and lay in the expanse while the other one filled in the sand around our body leaving only our head uncovered. We would wiggle our bodies to try to move the sand away, to free ourselves from the sandy tomb, laughing together under a blue sky with tufty clouds of wizard-white drifting by. Echoes of squab-bling seagulls added to the symphony on the beach. These were the sounds of nature. The ice cream truck would provide man-made music. We would hear the approaching melodic chimes of the ice cream truck and excitedly run to our mother, asking for money, then run over to the parked paradise-on-wheels, hopping on alternate feet to make the wait bearable on the hot pavement, as we awaited our turn to order our cold and sweet summer treat.

My mother made a friend at the beach, and her four children, my brother, and I would spend endless hours together each summer. This became a lifelong friendship for both women until their deaths forty-five years into the future. My mother led aquatic activities: fishing, water skiing and sailing, while my father was the land-based activities leader by taking us biking or strawberry picking. Quiet summer nights were occupied with television, board games or reading. When I turned ten years old, I started listening to music. I liked the Bay City Rollers, Journey, and John Denver. I'd see Shelter Island's silhouette as I sat on the back porch of our summerhouse under an ebony sky filled with stars so brilliant, they drew my eyes heaven bound. I would gaze at the distant lights calling to my heart. I have always found the night sky mystical, alluring, and mysterious.

Two of my mother's friends from New Jersey would come out for a weekend every summer. One would bring her mah jongg set. I would hear the tiles clacking together as they were being mixed, the women's chatter and laughter filling the air. I'd hear the words Bam, Crak, and Dot being called out as they played their game. Then I would hear someone call out in excitement, "Mah jongg!" It was *b'shert*. The universe wanted me to listen to these strange yet innocuous words being spoken. My mother and her friends were destined to play mah jongg at our summerhouse exposing me to a game I would come to play and love, but not for thirty-five years into my future.

My Father, the Renaissance Man

We can't pick family, but we can choose how to navigate family relationships. I've come to that realization with maturity. I look at life as a vast, ongoing class; the earth our classroom, friends and family members being both classmates and teachers. My spiritual view on relationships is that they are experiences we encounter as lessons for our soul. Maybe these lessons are *b'shert*. Just maybe we're meant to meet someone or be born into a family to learn life lessons from that someone. Sometimes these lessons include karmic debts on our earthly journeys.

My relationship with my father is one that I struggled with for many years, especially as a pre-adolescent and young adult. Although I longed to have a close relationship with him, regrettably, he was not available as I had needed him to be, which resulted in a great deal of sadness and hurt. After nineteen years of marriage, my mother chose to divorce my father. I was thirteen years old. As a child and teenager, I couldn't understand some of his behaviors, choices of words, or selfish actions. I was left with scars both in my mind and in my heart. Growing up, I saw very little of his side of the family except for his mother and father, my grandmother and grandfather. He had a sister, who was married with two children close in age to my brother and me, and who lived on Long Island, but who we hardly ever saw.

As a more emotionally-attuned adult, I notice that time has healed some of my wounds, forgiveness comes easier to me, and I can appreciate my father and his uniqueness. I know he loves me in his own way. Our current relationship consists of daily phone calls and multiple texts with inexplicable emojis. I'll get a text, "Call me!!!!!!" along with the following emojis or text icons: Ferris wheels, barber poles, lightning bolts, piles of poop with eyeballs (you know the one I mean), clowns, lips, Jewish stars, and hearts in different colors of the rainbow. Instead of one inclusive text with these all included, I receive a separate text with each icon or emoji. My phone dings in succession ten times. This is what I come to expect every day now, but it does make me smile. My seventy-nine-year-old father is an avid texter, and I think it's great he connects with technology.

My father is a very intelligent man. He taught physics and chemistry to high schoolers. He has a Ph.D. in Science Education and reads the *New York Times* cover to cover every day. He immerses himself in the cultural arts offered in New York City. He has season tickets at the Metropolitan Opera House, and he enjoys attending the ballet. He attends both on and off-Broadway theater productions and goes to a myriad of city museums and local concerts, both big-ticket performers like Madonna as well as new-age music and jazz. He took me to my first concert as a teenager. We saw Queen with the amazing Freddy Mercury. My father nicknamed himself the Renaissance Man. It is a title he has earned. As a teenager, I wished he enjoyed being a father as much as he enjoyed being a Renaissance Man.

My dad loves that I play mah jongg and calls almost every Monday when I'm playing to say hi. He is especially fond of Leigh, nicknaming her Miss Flower Child, and frequently asks how she is. Over the years, Leigh and my dad have been in each other's company at family functions at my house or temple events with me, and they seem to genuinely enjoy each other. Leigh is intrigued by my father's sometimes-bizarre behavior.

Here's one memorable example: Five years ago, Leigh and I went to visit my father in the East Village in New York City where he lives. We took the Long Island Rail Road then a subway downtown. We met up at a favorite restaurant of mine on St. Mark's Place. My dad was wearing slacks, a button-down shirt with an orange tank top underneath (he usually gets warm and likes to dress in layers), square-shaped sunglasses, an orange baseball cap, oodles of multi-colored Mardi Gras beads around his neck, and orange and yellow rubber bracelets on each wrist. This has become his signature look. Although he is color blind, he has a colorful personality, and it seamlessly carries over into his choice of clothing and accessories.

Our hellos went smoothly. That was the only real communication my father had with me that day. Throughout lunch, I noticed he only conversed with Leigh. *Hmmm, this is odd,* I thought. I kicked her under the table to get her attention. She was well aware of his behavior. I would ask him questions, and he would respond looking at and speaking only to Leigh. I felt invisible. I was growing frustrated. I was mulling over options of how to handle this irritating and isolating situation. I decided I needed to leave as soon as possible. I couldn't accept his behavior toward me.

At one point my dad said, "Miss Flower Child, you need to tell my daughter her father is fragile both physically and emotionally."

I said, "Dad, I'm sitting here at the same table with you. You can tell me."

He glared at me through his icy blue eyes and sneered, "I'm not talking with you right now! Miss Flower Child can tell you what I'm saying. She's a smart woman."

Leigh gently kicked me under the table, and when I looked at her, she nodded like she had this under control. Thank God I was in her company. She is very understanding. I proceeded to take out my phone to keep busy until lunch arrived. When the food was served, I was relieved our mouths were occupied with eating, filling the void of conversation that I was facing. Thankfully my father had to go to the bathroom after he finished eating. As he walked away, I could see the bright yellow socks he was wearing show in between the space of his sneaker and the pant hem.

The second he was out of earshot, I said, "Oh my God. I'm so sorry you have to go through this. I didn't know he wasn't going to speak with me. I wouldn't have come in to see him."

Leigh had just one thing to say, "Fern, how the hell did you turn out so normal?"

I asked for the check while my father was in the bathroom. When he returned, I said that I had to go and that lunch was over.

He checked the time, looking at the watch on one wrist, then the watch on the *other* wrist, a watch with Hebrew letters on it.

"See! I wear this every day along with the Jewish Star you gave me too, my dear daughter!" he said enthusiastically.

"Great, Dad, glad you like and wear them both." Well at least he was speaking with me, but it was time to go, my patience had run out.

My takeaway and reframe of this father-daughter relationship is this: Life is always interesting and entertaining, and still sometimes challenging with my eccentric dad. My father's personality and behavior have contributed to how

I created a life for myself with a husband who provides me with a safe and loving relationship, who is consistent in his behavior and who is reliable and trustworthy.

Len

My husband, Len, and I met through mutual friends at a Halloween party in New Jersey. Unbeknownst to either of us, *b'shert* had finally crossed our paths. Little did I know that I would be meeting my future husband that night, he dressed as a samurai warrior. He wasn't aware the girl dressed as a French maid would be his future wife and would birth his three sons.

I was twenty-four, he was twenty-three, nine months my junior. He stood about five-foot-eight with a muscular and athletic build. He carried himself confidently. When we spoke, I noticed he had hazel-brown eyes. They were eyes that emitted warmth, joy, and a zest for life. We talked at the party for a little while and exchanged phone numbers before I left. I thought he was handsome, charming, and smart, but I wasn't interested in a relationship at the time. I had just moved back home from San Francisco, ending a year-and-a-half relationship with my boyfriend who lived there. I was getting over the break-up and focusing on rebuilding my life back in Cresskill. The company I had worked for in San Francisco had a location in New Jersey that I transferred to when I moved back home. As

I was settling back in, a new relationship was the furthest thing from my mind.

Len called. He called again. After the third message, I decided to call him back. He was persistent, I noticed. He asked me out on a date. I reluctantly accepted. We would be going out on Saturday night. I wasn't and still am not great with directions. He was late, but that was due to me. I sent him left instead of right, and he was lost in a neighboring New Jersey town. Cell phones weren't common in the 1990s, and so he stopped at a gas station to call me and get rerouted. He finally arrived, forty-five minutes later. I learned he was also very patient. I introduced him to my mom, and we then headed into Manhattan to go to a club and meet some of his friends. Our first date was fun, but I was in no rush.

On our fourth date, he took me home to meet his parents in Oceanside, New York. He and his parents are originally from Odessa, Ukraine, but speak Russian and identify as Russians. When I met them, I had to focus on what they were saying due to their heavy accents. They seemed to like me. My dating superpower was my religion. I am Jewish. He hadn't dated a Jewish girl before me. Being Jewish was very important to his parents, and they instilled that fact in Len as he started to date in college.

After dating for about a year, we decided to move in together in Bayside, New York, in a condominium his parents owned. We eventually got engaged, married about a year later in September of 1994, and decided to start our family a few months after our honeymoon. I got pregnant in the third month of trying to conceive. I was twenty-eight years old and not sure what motherhood had in store for me. I soon learned that I married an amazing partner and father. Len was a total hands-on dad when Jared, our firstborn, arrived on April 13, 1996. There was no diaper too challenging, no task too daunting for my energetic and goal-oriented husband. I was happy being a mom and enjoyed my little bundle of joy, but I felt isolated during the weekdays while Len was at work. I didn't have any mommy friends to share baby stories with or anyone who could answer some of my new-mom questions. I took strolls alone in our gated community while Len was working. I yearned for a friend. Luckily, *b'shert* had a plan all worked out.

Delilah

Delilah and I were two new moms living in the same condo complex in Bayside. We both needed companionship through a baby-based friendship. It was July, and we were both at the pool club with our infants and husbands. Her husband, Robert, spotted me, another woman his wife's age with a baby, and decided to walk over and introduce himself to my husband and me. He waved Delilah over, and our hopes were answered.

Our sons were less than a month apart in age. We were both in need of friendship that focused on our new status: first-time mother. We became instant friends, and we formed an inseparable bond.

The first thing I noticed about Delilah was her beautiful dark hair. It cascaded over her shoulders in thick dark brown waves. Her olive skin was sun-kissed, and her brown eyes emitted kindness and strength. She was five-foot-four and slim, remarkable for having a two-month-old baby. She was savvy, energetic, and enthusiastic. She projected goodness and vibrancy. She was someone you want on your team, in your corner, in your heart. Lucky me, that I met such an amazing human being. It was *b'shert*. The universe wanted us to meet, two new mothers destined to be in each other's lives for reasons we would learn over the years to come, one was so we could play mah jongg together, the other to endure different cancer journeys with our husbands, but not for at least twenty years into the future.

Delilah and I happily saw each other most weekdays with our infants. Life started to get into a groove . . . and then I got pregnant just after Jared's first birthday. When my period was late, I worriedly bought a pregnancy test. I opened the box, read the simple instructions, opened the wrapper uncovering the test stick, and then peed on the stick and waited. After a few minutes, I could see a very faint positive result. *It must be faulty,* I thought. The line didn't look like the one in the instructions or on the box. I went back to the drug store and bought four more tests just to be sure I had enough on hand. I took the second test, peeing on the stick and waiting again. Another faint line.

Hmmm . . . I better try another one. This time I opened a different brand. I had bought a few different brands while at the store, thinking maybe a batch from one brand could be defective. Another faint vertical "positive" line crossed the horizontal "negative" one. Time to get some help. I called Delilah in a panic and asked if I could come right over. I gathered my five (yes five!) pregnancy tests, scooped Jared up and put him into his stroller, and started my walk to Delilah's. She met me in the vestibule of her condo entrance. "What's wrong?" she asked.

I spread the pregnancy tests out on the table right there in the entrance.

"Look! I can't believe this! I can't be pregnant. I'm not ready for another baby!" I cried while giving Jared a bottle to keep him occupied during my crisis.

Delilah looked at each test and the ever-so-faint line showing a positive test result. "Fern, all of these can't be false positives. You are pregnant!"

This was *b'shert*, lovingly and mystically bringing two lives together, one life emerging within the other. The universe wanted this little zygote to be mine, whether or not I thought I was ready, and Delilah was the first to know. This little zygote nine months later grew into a baby. Alex was born on December 19, 1997, twenty months after Jared was born. I was reminded again that I married a caring, compassionate, supportive, and responsible man when Len hired a full-time mother's helper for me. Jared was an extremely energetic toddler who needed a lot of attention, and so our beloved helper, Molash, tag-teamed with me, sharing child-rearing duties. I never had more of a challenge in my whole life. I wasn't prepared for mothering and all its demands, but who really is? We get thrown into the trenches and do our best. I was blessed to have such a supportive husband, an incredible friend in Delilah, and a devoted helper in Molash. Len's parents also joined in to help us, often taking Jared for the weekend so they could revel in grandparenthood and I could revel in some extra sleep while Len helped with early morning feedings with Alex. Yes, sometimes it does take a village to raise children.

Our House

In 2000 when Jared was four and Alex was two we moved from Bayside to Melville, a Long Island town about twenty-five miles east of our condominium. The five-bedroom house was on an acre of land with a pool and basketball hoop. It was beautiful and more than I would have expected for our first home after leaving condo-living. We settled in, had the walls painted and decorated the rooms. The modern kitchen led into the family room, which overlooked the L-shaped pool outside. We got some new furniture for the boys' bedrooms and a couch for the family room. Our dining room, kitchen table and chairs, and a few other pieces of furniture came with us from Bayside. While unpacking boxes, I remember opening a box and finding my mother's mah jongg set. I placed it in the office in a cabinet where it would remain safe for five years.

Our third son Gabriel was born four years later, completing our family. Sadly, Molash couldn't move out with us to Melville, so I hired a loving woman named Emmy who helped me with the three boys. Len's commute was over an hour and a half in each direction, and he traveled about eight weeks a year. Emmy helped me keep my sanity by balancing the boys' schedules, housework, and homework. The boys went to preschool and eventually elementary school, and my life as a full-time mother filled every waking hour of my day. Life was good . . . until the fire.

I never thought as a child on our annual drive out from New Jersey on the Long Island Expressway to our summerhouse in Greenport, year after year, that I would be passing the exit ramp to my future home as an adult, married with three sons. I would live in that beautiful home for five years.

In December 2005, that house became engulfed in fire. Whoosh. Just like that. Fire, smoke, and the water to put them out would displace our family. We lost just about every material possession we had. But those destructive elements can't destroy a family's resolve. *B'shert* luckily had us out of the house when a spark turned into a flame that turned into a raging fire. Gabriel was nine months old and had he and I stayed home, we both would have probably been napping at the time the fire broke out. We would have woken up on the second floor with the house on fire and filled with smoke. Unbeknownst to us, the windows on the second floor weren't to code. I don't know how we would have escaped. This thought haunts me to this day. Instead, we were safely all driving in the car when we received a phone call from a frantic neighbor telling us our house was on fire.

What? We couldn't believe what he was saying. We turned around and headed back home not knowing what to expect. The road leading up to my house was closed off.

The fireman said to us, "Turn around. This road is closed due to a house fire."

I jumped out of the car, "Sir, that's *my* house that's on fire!"

I left the car and my family behind and ran in my high-heeled shoes around the corner to my house. Where's the dog? Oh my God, the dog! There were three fire trucks, police cars, and an ambulance at the scene. I stopped in the driveway looking at what was left of our house. A fireman came up to tell me a neighbor had our dog and that he was okay. I took a breath of relief for his safety. Then I took in a new breath filled with immense shock. I couldn't believe what I saw. Every window was broken open. Black charred marks scarred the skin of my house. I was speechless. I was frozen. I was homeless.

Len arrived with the children. We took them across the street to a neighbor's house, changed into old sweats they lent us, and walked into the remains of our home. The damage was extensive. The smell was overwhelming. I covered my mouth with my gloved hand. We walked amongst the wet, burnt, and smoky remains of our . . . everything. We literally only had the clothes on our backs. I noticed the electricity had shut off at 2:13 p.m. The clock on the oven marked the time our world would drastically change. We were then taken downstairs, to the basement. We were shown where the fire started by the fire marshal. The rug was soaked with water. Everything was burnt and black. I walked back upstairs and into each room. We never would sleep in these rooms again.

I vaguely remember walking through Target with a few friends that night. They helped me find underwear, sweats, shirts, socks, and sneakers for my family. I didn't have a nightgown, makeup, or makeup remover anymore. We lived in a hotel for the first six weeks after the fire and then rented a house for the next twelve months. We were homeless, but not helpless. I would learn through this devastating loss of personal possessions and displacement that Len and I were fighters. We were a solid team. We had resolve, strength, and perseverance. I felt if we could make it through this journey, we could handle almost anything life would throw at us. Little did I know, in ten years, life would wallop us again. Next time it would be an internal fire, the fire of cancer.

We had a focus and a mission. We were going to build a new home. We let the fire department use the house for a simulated fire training drill before the house was to be knocked down. They let me go in during this drill. I was horrified that I could hardly see through the simulated smoke. How would I have gotten out safely with my baby if I were home when the fire started? *B'shert* blessed Gabriel and me. The day of the fire we had a birthday party to go to in Brooklyn. Len told me to stay home, as the restaurant would be loud and noisy. He knew I wouldn't like the food and thought it would be difficult for me with the baby. We disagreed about Gabriel and me going with them. Something internal told me to go to the party. There are times in life when we believe in angels, divine intervention, or miracles. This was a defining moment for me. I made a decision that may have saved my baby's life and mine. We averted a horrible situation with an ending that thankfully never needed to be written.

We met with different builders and architects to review their designs and ideas. After we chose our team, we got to work on our labor of love. Framing to move-in date was nine months. Len and I helped in the planning of every inch of it. We decorated each room ourselves with Len's stylish eye from his experience in the textile field and my background in fashion, creating our own do-it-yourself interior decorating team. My new house is beautiful too, just in new beautiful ways.

Walk inside with me and let me show you what Len and I created, and how *b'shert* had a role in my house, too. I want to welcome you into my home and into the rooms where I spend the majority of my time. The kitchen is spacious, but ironic because I don't like to cook. The room has a Tuscan look with butterscotch-colored floor tile and traditional cream-colored wood cabinetry. The wallpaper of tan bricks with ivy and grapes peeking through covers the walls. The center island is spacious with two bar stools for countertop eating. There is a small sink there for convenience; something an avid chef would appreciate more than I. I make basic meals and wish I liked cooking more.

My kitchen also serves as a game room. This is the room where the girls and I learned to play mah jongg and where we still play on some current Mondays. There is enough room to set up a mah jongg table. My kitchen table's diameter is too big. We tried a game there once, and we each had to get up from our seats to pick a tile from the wall. Table size *really* does matter in mah jongg!

Having this exact kitchen is *b'shert*. About two years before the house fire, I received an advertisement with this same kitchen being displayed. I hung up the flyer inside a kitchen cabinet. I thought maybe one day we could remodel our modern kitchen and make it look like this picture. During the fire, the firemen pried the cabinet in which the advertisement was taped off from the wall and threw it on the kitchen table to get to the fire that was behind the wall. One day after the fire, when I returned to the house, still walking around in a shocked daze, I found the advertisement. It was still taped inside the cabinet. It smelled smoky, but I still slipped it into my purse. Once we started to rebuild, we called this very kitchen cabinetry company to get a bid and actually used them to make the same beautiful country kitchen I saw and fell in love with in the advertisement. That is some crazy kitchen karma.

I have another room to show you. This room was nick-named by a few of Gabriel's friends the "museum room," a.k.a. our formal living room. A tan velvet chaise lounge faces a creamy, marble-topped, antique coffee table. The ornately carved wood is painted gold. Masquerade ball face masks with feathers and glitter adorn the tabletop along with three candlesticks. Two grand Baroque-style chairs painted gold with black velvet upholstery face the table from the other side. This is one of the chairs I would be sitting in when I would receive a phone call from Delilah telling me about a terminal cancer diagnosis.

Above the fireplace is a giclée reproduction of a Wil-liam Bouguereau painting called *Evening Mood*. She is beautiful, a bare-breasted woman with dark chiffon bil-lowing in the wind around her subtle body. She glances downward, almost floating above the water; just her toes are holding her up like a graceful ballet dancer. Clouds of pink, grey, and blue are in the background. A crescent moon is visible in the left corner. She represents a woman of strength and beauty amidst a heavenly background. When I see her every day, she reminds me that beauty is fleeting, time is fluid, and we must gracefully move through life like a dancer in flight.

We have a black baby grand piano placed in the turret where Gabriel takes weekly lessons with Ms. Lena, his beloved teacher. He plays for Len and me as we sit in our Baroque style chairs, enjoying the music he has mastered. I have a second giclée by the same artist called *Abduction of Psyche* placed on the wall to the right of the piano. It is another sultry piece by Bouguereau where Cupid is embracing his love, Psyche, as he flies upward toward the heavens with her in his arms. It reminds me that love conquers all. Both giclées are framed in gold decorative wood frames, adding to the Baroque decor. There are floor-to-ceiling cream and black silk drapes adorning the windows of the turret, completing the room.

This is where I sit and write by the fireplace in the winter, or where I sit with guests. We've played mah jongg here a few times on some cold winter days, near the warmth and coziness of the fireplace. The ladies and I feel like we are in another time and place, and should be sipping champagne instead of water, and noshing on caviar instead of nuts and pretzels. It's interesting to see and feel that where we play mah jongg, the surroundings and mood of a room add ambience and variety to our game.

My *pièce de résistance* of the house is my bedroom, where I start and end each day. Double doors swing open into my personal sanctuary at home. On the right side of the door, a *mezuzah* is nailed in place. It is made of wood and is hand-painted in a golden cream color with the Hebrew letter *Shin* painted in between delicate flowers adorned with small rhinestones. The *mezuzah* welcomes me into my sanctuary and is a constant reminder for me that God is here, dwelling in my personal holy space. I imagine the *Shechinah*, the feminine aspect of God, residing in this space along with me. We are both tucked away from the masculine energy that fills the rest of the house.

This is a room that not everyone gets to see. It's filled with femininity and softness, and I'm grateful that Len agreed to let me decorate our bedroom like this. The carpet is pink floral tone-on-tone. Floral wallpaper of pink and yellow roses with light blue ribbons is above the chair rail, while off-white paint is below. I have a four-poster bed with ivory chiffon fabric draping at each corner and from post to post. My armoire, which is displayed with its doors open, is decorated with lacey brassieres, jewelry, and feathery boas draped on the door. Jewelry and my special things are strategically placed on the ten shelves inside the armoire.

In the turret, life-size bustiers are decorated with crinoline skirts and more lacey brassieres. Necklaces adorn these pieces, too. The turret also houses my writing desk, an antique-looking replica I found curbside that was being thrown away by a neighbor. I added a Pottery Barn floral fabric chair to coordinate with it. A corkboard I decorated with lace, silk flowers, and pink boa feathers hangs on the wall in front of the desk. When I'm writing, I can look up and see the important things I want to keep in view.

My life coach, Holly, suggested keeping a piece of paper displaying my core values in a place I would see daily. I chose to display them here on my decorated board. Those values are love, family, friendship, faith, gratitude, balance, and creativity. Seeing them daily reminds me of their importance. One of my favorite Hebrew prayers, *Shalom Rav,* is decorated on a piece of collage art I created. A picture of my family looks down at me with love. A picture of Oprah Winfrey glancing over her shoulder silently gives me iconic approval of my efforts in writing. Maybe one day she will read a book I have penned. A picture of women playing mah jongg is pinned up so I can glance at my favorite game being played, inspiring me to finish my book. My bedroom is my haven at home. Len knew I needed my sultry, feminine space in a house full of masculinity. This room is the essence of who I am at my core. It is my soul's home within my home.

Chapter 3

An Autumn Game

As my story continues, it is the autumn of 2016, and my friend Delilah has recently joined our game. Autumn is a beautiful season on Long Island. Gone are the hot and humid days of summer. I welcome the coolness that fills the autumn air and refreshes my skin as I step out each morning into a new day. This season slowly ushers in the quiet whispers of nature signaling to the squirrels to start to gather nuts and the birds to prepare for their southern journeys. The sun shines with less intensity, beckoning to the leaves on the trees to intrinsically shed the green of summer and to surrender to the tones of yellow, orange, and the fiery red of autumn. I can smell the season change as autumn starts to settle in. The air is different. It is less fragrant, as crisp temperatures ignite the end of the cycle of life for the annual flowers. Inside my house, the scents of orange, cinnamon, and pumpkin fill my home as candles burn or essential oil diffusers release warm and spicy aromas into the air.

September marks the start of a new school year in New York. It is a month of anticipation and excitement for both children and parents. My youngest son, Gabriel, was starting seventh grade. I teach beginner Hebrew and Judaica in the religious school to fourth graders and yoga to the preschoolers at my temple here in town. Each autumn reminds me that change and transition are part of life, but some transitions are harder than others.

Group text: Delilah, Rose, Leigh, Sarah
Me: Hi ladies! It's Mah Jongg Monday tomorrow; I'll host 11:30 a.m. Who's in?
Leigh: Me!
Rose: Count me in! I'll bake banana bread!
Delilah: I'll be there too!
Sarah: I'm excited I'm off from work! I'm in too!
Me: Awesome! See you all tomorrow!

Monday morning my iPhone alarm went off at 6:30 a.m. I opened my eyes, reached for the phone, and pressed the button to silence it. I start every morning while in bed with a prayer. I thank God for breathing my soul back into my body. I ask to be of service today, to make our world a better place by saying a kind word or doing a helpful deed. The do-good list is long, providing endless opportunities to make a difference in someone's life. Every day, this is my routine, including my morning mantra to "do good." It grounds my soul before I slide my feet out from under a warm blanket and step into my slippers and into a new day.

I started my regular weekday routine. I went to the bathroom, washed up, then headed downstairs to the kitchen to make a pot of coffee. I turned on relaxing music. No news to jolt me into the realities of a hectic world quite yet. Just calm and soothing music. I added water and coffee grinds to the percolator and waited for the smell of coffee to fill the kitchen. I took a favorite mug from the cupboard and prepared my morning caffeinated treat. With just a few sips, my day was off to a great start. I woke my youngest son Gabriel and helped him get ready for school. My husband, Len, and middle son, Alex, were getting ready for work. They work together at the textile business Len started with his father twenty years ago.

At approximately 8:45 a.m., the boys left by bus and by car and my mah jongg morning was mine. I practiced yoga for thirty minutes, meditated, showered, and tidied up the house. I always make sure the downstairs bathroom is clean for my mah jongg ladies. While living with three males, the bathroom can become a urinal war zone. I prepared snacks: cut-up fruit, salsa and chips, chocolate covered cashews, veggies, hummus, and water to drink. I gathered my disposable mah jongg party plates, which were pink and had the word Love written on them. I had matching napkins and used plastic utensils and cups. I'm all about easy clean-up when I host.

I took out my mah jongg table and put five chairs around it. The table is round and an upgrade from the square bridge table I first bought three years ago. Not only is it roomier, leaving space for drinks and phones, but also the tiles move around much easier during mixing. Next, I got the black velvet mah jongg bag with my name stitched on the outside in my favorite color, purple. Inside lies my peacock set with personalized Jokers. I meticulously chose this set after looking at a variety available at Where the Winds Blow, a popular online mah jongg company. I opened the two plastic containers housing the beautiful tiles, and I spilled them onto the table listening to them make that recognizable clicking sound that always evokes a sense of excitement and anticipation in me. The racks are clear white with pushers to help move the walls of stacked tiles out onto the table neatly. When the tiles sit against the racks they look so pretty, the teal colored peacocks facing out to the other players. The personalized Jokers have a rose and my name etched in golden ink into the white tile. I placed my 2016 mah jongg card in front of a rack, which now deemed it East. I turned on my iPad and searched for '80s music.

Rose arrived first, carrying the banana bread she made. We kissed hello, mah jongg excitement filling the air between us. I added it to the table with the other food. Rose put her jacket on the chair opposite me and placed her card down. Leigh came in next, greeting us both, kiss, kiss. She placed her jacket on the chair to my left and put her card down in front of the rack. Sarah came in next wearing a hat, her signature look. She took the seat to my right. Leigh, Sarah, and I have been playing together since Fran taught us. Sarah is an oncology social worker and recently started to go back to work part-time. Delilah had just started filling in for her. We like to play with five players in case someone can't make it. When we do have five players, the fifth teams up with one of us or they are the bettor.

We started mixing the tiles and setting up the walls against our racks to start the first game while we waited for Delilah to arrive. Mah jongg creates its own music with the sound of the clicking tiles. I noticed Leigh's nails were a pretty shade of fuchsia. I love to see the colors of manicures as we mix the tiles. I had a French manicure with Marshmallow, my signature look. Rose's nails were painted burgundy. Sarah's was a soft pink. We stacked the tiles by groups of two against our racks. I rolled the dice. They stopped, one revealing a two, the other a five. I counted out seven pairs, broke the wall, and started dealing. Each player received thirteen tiles. As the dealer, I got one extra tile to start the game. We caught up on each other's week as we racked our tiles.

The front door opened, and Delilah came in. She joined us in the kitchen, and we all greeted her from our seats. She looked like she had been crying. I stood up, went over and gave her a hug. I didn't need to ask what was wrong. I knew what was making her sad. I am closest to Delilah; we are kitchen friends, sharing our innermost feelings. We support each other within the depth of our friendship.

"I heard a song on the radio this morning that made me think of Robert. Some days are still harder than others for me to get through," she said.

I squeezed her hand reassuringly within mine and guided her to my seat at the table. Leigh got her a cup of water, and we huddled around her, waiting to listen and ready to offer support. Four sets of eyes connected around the mah jongg table, glances of unity for our hurting sister. Everyone knew what she had been going through. I hugged her tightly.

"I'm glad you came today. We're here for you," I reassured Delilah.

"Thank you," she said.

I broke our hug and let the girls have their turn comforting her next. Each woman went to support the sister in need of strength, compassion, and understanding.

"You girls are wonderful," she said as Rose gave her a

heartwarming hug. "I knew coming here to play mah jongg would help me feel better today. It gives me a reason to get out of bed on Mondays. It's a chore for me some days."

"Come sit with me, Delilah. We'll play this hand together," Sarah said.

It was comforting to have Sarah's knowledge and expertise in helping cancer patients and their families navigate through their personal journeys.

"I'll put a pot of coffee on for us," I said to the girls.

As I poured water into the percolator, my heart hurt for Delilah and her children, ages twenty, seventeen, and ten. I scooped the coffee grinds into the metal holder, snapped the lid on, and plugged it into the outlet. The sound of the percolator came to life, and the smell of coffee filled the kitchen. I sat down at the table and glanced at Delilah to make sure she was okay and ready to play. Sarah nodded my way, signaling to me that we could resume. We began the Charleston, passing tiles and building hands. Game one had begun as I placed the first tile onto the table, calling out, "7 Crak." We kept the conversation light, aware of Delilah's feelings. I knew her taking lessons from Fran and joining our group would help her in her mourning and healing process.

I was thrilled when she accepted the suggestion to take Fran and Susan's class. I called Fran and told her to keep Delilah under her wing and to put her with soft-spoken women for the lessons. She was happy to help and assured me Delilah would be in good and nurturing hands. I knew she would be; Fran is compassionate and empathetic. Now here we are with Delilah as part of our mah jongg game. She is healing, playing, and starting to live a little once again. I am proud of her, for her strength and for emerging through a world of hurt and loss. We noshed on food as we picked, racked, or discarded tiles, calling their number and suit as we each continued to vie for the winning hand. I was working on my favorite hand in Consecutive Run with the suit of Dots. As the game continued, I was one tile away from winning, and I was getting excited. Funny how I still get the same feelings I did as a child playing checkers or backgammon. There's a thrill in winning even in my late 40s. Sarah picked up a tile and discarded a 4 Bam. Rose called it exposing two other 4 Bams on her rack along with a Joker. She discarded a Red Dragon. Leigh picked a tile from the wall and racked her tile discarding a South. It was my turn. I picked a Flower. It was just the tile I needed.

"Mah jongg!" I called out as I smiled.

Transition

Delilah had lost her husband Robert less than a year before from pancreatic cancer. Transition became her "it" word. She transitioned from wife to widow, from co-parent to single parent, from happy to sad, from whole to shattered. I remember her calling me to tell me the news. I was sitting in my living room on the black velvet Baroque chair next to the fireplace. It was December 2015. She was crying, and I couldn't understand her at first. When I processed what she was saying through the sobs, I was frozen. Robert had a scan that showed the cancer was in his pancreas and liver. She said that, statistically, people don't live very long with this diagnosis. Her gut told her Robert had six months to live, but they were prepared to fight for each day. We made plans to meet at the diner a few days later. *B'shert* would reveal itself to me shaking me to my very core on that day.

We had plans to meet at Premier Diner in Commack. I wasn't sure I could eat, but I would order some food, push it around on my plate, and take it home. As I had my blinker on and about to turn into the diner parking lot my cell phone rang. I thought maybe it was Delilah telling me she was running late. Instead, it was Len's doctor's office. He had recently been diagnosed with chronic pancreatitis. Eating was painful. He was prescribed an enzyme to take with each meal, and it helped him tremendously. The doctor had Len do an endoscopy and sonogram to look at his pancreas a few days ago. They must be calling with the results.

"Hello?" I answered the phone.

"Mr. Bernstein, please," the voice said on the other end of the call.

"He is not here. I'm his wife, Fern. Can I be of help?"

"We need Mr. Bernstein to come in to see the doctor

to discuss his test result," the voice echoed in my ear.

I was now parked in a spot in the diner's parking lot although I didn't remember turning in.

I told the voice on the other end of the phone, "We are leaving in two days for vacation in Mexico."

The voice told me, "We need him to come in before you leave for Mexico. Could he come in tomorrow at 9:00 a.m.?"

I responded, "Yes, sure, but why can't the doctor speak to us on the phone?"

"I'm sorry. It's office policy. We'll see you and Mr. Bernstein tomorrow," the voice responded.

As I hung up, my mind went crazy with ideas of terrible scenarios. Len's pancreas must have a problem more significant than an enzyme deficiency. I was ten minutes late for Delilah although I arrived in the parking lot on time. I texted her that I would be right in, and I took a deep breath. I needed to compartmentalize fast. This conversation I just had must stay in this box over here in my brain. *Don't move and don't leak into my thoughts! I need to help my friend whose life was just turned upside down.* I took a deep breath and got out of the car. I pulled myself together and walked into the diner.

Delilah was at a booth already. I hugged her hello. She looked like she was holding it together, despite what she had learned only a few days ago. I knew she must be going through emotional hell. She had make-up on, which signaled to me she hadn't been crying this morning or since she applied it at least. She ordered matzah ball soup, and I ordered a salad, but we weren't here to eat, we were here to talk about life and death.

I looked into her eyes and said, "I'm so sorry that this is happening to Robert and your family."

As I held her hand, I felt her pain. Sometimes being empathic is hard, especially in moments like this.

My phone rang. I looked down. *Oh no. It's Len.* I picked it up but wouldn't tell him the doctor's office called and expected to see him tomorrow. I needed to be there for Delilah. He knew we were meeting for lunch and wanted to speak with her. I handed the phone over to her. I watched and listened to her speak with Len. *This can't be real,* I thought to myself. I wished this was a bad dream we would all just wake up from and get back to our normal lives. They spoke for a few minutes, and she handed the phone back to me. I told Len I needed to talk with him later and to please pick up when I called back. Our food came, but we couldn't eat. I let her talk, and I listened with an open and aching heart. She was going to lose her best friend, her lover and life partner. Their future was being cut short; their long and loving history would become cherished memories sooner than expected. They were planning on telling the children in a few days when their son came home from college for Christmas break. My chest tightened; sadness filled my body. I took on their pain envisioning those dreaded but necessary conversations.

I said, "I love you, and I'll be here to help you through this."

She said back, "I love you, too."

Welcome to the Game

I had my salad wrapped, and we walked out to the parking lot together. We hugged good-bye. She drove back to her husband with pancreatic cancer as I drove home to call my husband with the news we had to see his doctor tomorrow about his pancreas. I was numb driving home. Numb from the reality of Delilah's situation and numb from fear of what the doctor was going to tell us. I called Len and told him we had to go in to see Dr. Kaush to go over his recent test. Later I put in a call to the doctor. I couldn't wait for tomorrow morning. What a cruel thing to do to call a patient or their loved one and say you must come in to discuss your health, it's clearly serious, but we can't tell you on the phone. I hadn't heard back, so I called the emergency number around 8:00 p.m. that night. I left Len's information with the attendant on the other end of the line asking that the doctor please call me back tonight. I needed to know if he thought it was pancreatic cancer, damn it!

My phone rang five minutes later. "Hello?"

"Mrs. Bernstein, this is Dr. Kaush."

"Hello, doctor. I received a call earlier today that we need to come in tomorrow regarding Len's scan. Please, doctor, tell me something tonight, we won't be able to sleep, is it pancreatic cancer?" I pleaded for an answer.

"I can only tell you it is not, but we found something that needs to be addressed," he responded.

"Bless you, doctor, thank you for that answer. We will see you tomorrow," I said as I exhaled with relief.

I called Len with this news as soon as I hung up with the doctor. We were both relieved. Hopefully, we could get some sleep tonight.

Our sense of relief didn't last very long. The next morning, the doctor had us join him in his office. He showed us the recent scan of Len's pancreas and thigh region, which showed a sizable tumor in his iliacus muscle in his upper thigh. It appeared to be a sarcoma, which is a very serious and aggressive cancer. He recommended a surgeon for us to see as soon as we returned from Mexico.

We were just invited to a game of chance, the vicious and unyielding game of cancer. The scan's result was the unwanted invitation. We didn't know the rules, the language, or how to play. But we were in it and in it to win it. Somehow, we managed to go on vacation despite this scary news. Our world was jolted; we had shifted, moved into the unknown until we met with the surgeon. We didn't tell the children or Len's parents until we met with the doctor and had more information. We didn't want to cause everyone worry and felt that it was best for us to manage this on our own until we had more information.

We returned from Mexico on January 2, 2016. I wondered how this New Year would unfold. Everyone wishes one another Happy New Year! Would it be happy? People are filled with the anticipation of a clean slate, a fresh start, with renewed vim and vigor in striving for personal goals.

What did the New Year hold for Delilah and Robert? Time together? Making final family memories?

What did the New Year hold for Len and me? It would start with a doctor's appointment. We met with the surgical oncologist on January 6. He recommended robotic surgery to remove the tumor. We were newbies. We didn't know the cancer terms well, but I asked the doctor, "Don't you want to do a biopsy or a PET scan first before surgery?"

He responded, "No need; this looks like sarcoma, and this is the course of treatment."

We booked the surgery for January 21. Our first mistake was not getting a second opinion. The second mistake was having the surgery. It wasn't sarcoma. It was non-Hodgkin's lymphoma, and surgery can't remove this type of cancer. But chemotherapy does. Great, just great! After a five-day hospital stay and painful recovery, we saw an oncologist who specialized in blood cancers like non-Hodgkin's lymphoma. He recommended a PET scan. What a novel idea! I was hopeful that we had a doctor with insight this time. The PET scan showed Len had nine growths of cancer in different spots in his body. But, and it was a big but, since it is a slow growing cancer, they felt comfortable to proceed with a "watch and wait" plan.

"Excuse me? Watch and wait! Wait for what?" I asked the doctor.

"Until it displays signs of rapid growth. But this may stay indolent for many years," he reassured us.

Len was lucky in cancer terms, for now. He could

continue his everyday routine—work, gym, socializing, traveling—nothing would be different . . . yet.

Chapter 4

Fran's Phone Call

I received a phone call from Fran in February 2016. I remember exactly where I was, CVS in the cosmetics aisle. My phone rang, and I answered the call in my chipper manner.

Fran said, "I have something to tell you."

She sounded serious. My mind raced, wondering what was wrong. She stopped the inquisition in my mind by telling me, "Sam has cancer, osteosarcoma to be exact."

I listened as she told me about the battle that lay ahead for her son, who was only twenty-eight years old and engaged to be married. He would get strong chemo for a few months, then a complicated surgery on his leg to remove the bone where there was cancer, and have it replaced with a metal rod. He would have physical therapy to help him learn to walk with the rod in his leg and then more chemo in the following months. Her son's treatment plan was so much more complicated and hellish than Len's "watch and wait" phase. Sam's biopsy result was his invitation to the game, the game of cancer.

I stood frozen in the cosmetics aisle as I listened to my beautiful friend tell me what was happening. I said to her that I was there for her in any capacity she needed. She told me she would keep me posted, and I sadly hung up. My heart hurt for my friend. What lay ahead sounded painful both physically and emotionally for Sam. Fran, as his mother, couldn't fix this with her kiss like she could when he was a child. No Band-Aid or antibiotic ointment from aisle six in CVS could stop this aggressive cancer.

Their family banded together and rallied around him with tenacity and cohesiveness. They would take shifts in the New York City hospital so that every day a family member was with him. His fiancé, who was his angel here on earth, was by his side, a devoted and strong young woman.

This was all overwhelming, unbelievable, and frightening to me. Len was diagnosed in late December with non-Hodgkin's lymphoma. Robert was diagnosed in December, only a few days earlier, with pancreatic cancer. He was undergoing chemo and multiple surgeries to unblock clogged pancreatic ducts. Delilah shifted into survival mode and was all but living at the hospital. She was a courageous caregiver, wife, and mother, and my heart ached that she and Robert were faced with the end-of-life preparations so prematurely.

Fran displayed immense strength too, both as a mother and a caregiver to her son during his treatment. She was Sam's cheerleader, even as she watched her handsome son struggle through the side effects of chemo. His hair, skin tone, appetite, and energy were all affected, yet their strength was bigger than the cancer. Her positive attitude and sheer determination were the glue that held her family together.

Both of these women were teaching me how to be a fighter. Fran was my mentor not only in mah jongg, but also in being a wise and strong woman, and a warrior caregiver. This is the *other* reason that the universe wanted our lives to intersect at yoga many years ago. As we stood next to each other on our yoga mats in Warrior One pose, *b'shert* knew we would take that pose off the mat and into the cancer world as we endured the journey cancer laid in front of us with our loved ones.

Time is precious, yet elusive and fleeting. We can grab threads of it to create memories or re-live feelings, but we can't grab onto it or hold it still. Mah jongg helped me through this difficult time of sorting through a myriad of cancer feelings, most which lead to the king of them all . . . fear. Although Len was in a "watch and wait" phase for now, knowing what Fran and Delilah's loved ones were going through was hard to hear about or see when I would visit with Robert and Delilah. My weekly mah jongg games gave me structure, something positive and enjoyable to look forward to and were a mental break from worry and sadness. The mental stimulation of the game occupied my brain for a few hours every Monday. Although I couldn't create calm from the chaos of cancer, creating a hand out of the chaos of random tiles gave me direction, focus, and joy. Mah jongg was a beacon of light during the winter of 2016, leading me through the cold and darkness of this Long Island season and into the warmth and renewal of spring. Other sources of strength for me during this time were my religion, deep faith and sisterhood.

Judaism

I was born into the Jewish religion. My father grew up in an Orthodox household. He was a first-generation American son born to Polish immigrants. His family kept kosher, and my grandfather was a kosher butcher in the Bronx. My father became a *bar mitzvah* at age thirteen. My mother grew up in a more relaxed Reform Jewish home. Her family didn't keep kosher, and she didn't attend religious school, but her family observed the High Holy Days of *Rosh Hashanah* and *Yom Kippur.* They also celebrated *Passover* and *Hanukkah.* Both she and her parents were born in the United States. My parents decided to stay within the Jewish Reform movement when they married. We were members of a synagogue in Tenafly, New Jersey. Although my brother attended religious school, I was not offered that option, much like my mother before me. At eleven years old, I asked if I could please attend religious school and learn more about our religion and study to become a *bat mitzvah*. I had a calling to my religion, a deep yearning to know more and connect with my Judaism. My parents agreed to send me. I was late to the game. Most children start in earlier grades, so I had some catching up to do. I did so happily and enjoyed my experience learning the language and traditions. I believe this was *b'shert*, my destiny with religion and my formal introduction to God.

I loved attending Friday night Shabbat services with my parents. Communal prayer filled the walls of the sanctuary, and I became aware of it filling my heart as well. Music gave prayer movement and wings to fly on. I learned for the first time what it meant to have my soul nourished by prayer.

I became a *bat mitzvah* the month before I turned thirteen. I read from the *Torah* and helped to lead the service with my partner Amy. We shared the *bimah* and became Jewish adults together on March 29, 1980. After the service, my grandfather, Phillip, cut the *challah* while saying the *Motzi* (blessing over bread) and my family and friends were off to celebrate with me at a local venue. I was one of three Jewish children in my middle school class. I was one of the two *bat mitzvahs*, and Jeff Wolfman was the only *bar mitzvah*. Crazy but true—just three Jews.

Judaism still holds an essential place in my life. Although at my wedding we used a house rabbi from the venue because we weren't affiliated with a temple, shortly after we were married, I joined a temple in Great Neck. I would meet an associate rabbi there named Rabbi Susie Heneson Moskowitz, who is now the head rabbi at Temple Beth Torah where I am currently a member. After a lapse of affiliation, I felt called back to my Judaism and temple life. For the time I wasn't connected to a temple, I always kept my private conversations and silent prayer with God. Our relationship was sacred to me. God was like a holy parent for me.

I started to attend Shabbat services again after I was married, but I went alone. Len wasn't interested in formalized religion. It was a calling that I'm glad I answered. I was reconnected and to this day Friday night prayers and music lift my spirit and fill my heart with faith, grace, meaning, and love.

I don't limit my Judaism to Shabbat services or High Holy Days. I take adult education classes with Rabbi Susie. I volunteer with friends. I teach in our religious and nursery schools. I am on the board of trustees, and I am the president of our Sisterhood. Temple life is important to me. I find many holy moments through my temple experiences. Mah jongg has now become another layer of my Jewish cultural heritage as it is played by so many Jewish women in my Long Island world. Most of the women I play with are Jewish, members of the same tribe, but mah jongg is trans-cultural and is played worldwide by people of all religions and faiths. Judaism with all that it offers me spiritually, religiously and socially still nourishes my soul all these years later.

It was *b'shert* yet again. The universe had me meet an associate rabbi that would in five years work at the same temple I would join after moving to Melville with my family. She would become one of my greatest teachers in life. She would teach me about Judaism, Torah, prayers and rituals, holidays, Mussar, *Rosh Chodesh*, and yoga. Her years of teaching me would give me the foundation to teach the children in our religious school. She would help guide me to become a lay leader on the board of trustees and as our Sisterhood president. *Ani moda lach*, I thank you, Rabbi Susie.

My Two Sisterhoods

As president of my temple's Sisterhood, I enjoy creating events to bring women together. Some of those events include *challah* making (the delicious braided bread made for Shabbat), a meditation class run by my yoga master, Mah Jongg Madness, Ladies' Night Out/Shopping Night with vendors, Summer Swim, author events, and a book club named The Living Room to name a few. The Living Room runs two or three times a year, and we choose books with a Jewish theme or connection. Rabbi Susie usually runs these discussions at the home of a congregant, creating a more intimate and warm setting. I love reading and writing, and I often thought to myself during these discussions that I would love to have a book I've written discussed at a book club one day. But first I have to finish one. I've started a few. Maybe what I'm writing now is the one . . .

I'm also the leader of our mah jongg group. It just sort of happened by default. I send out our group texts to the ladies, making sure we have four players, and I figure out who will be hosting. My mah jongg group is a sisterhood too. The temple Sisterhood has Judaism, connection, and community outreach as common threads for its members. Aside from the game itself, my mah jongg sisterhood's common threads are creating bonds and a social connection, and most importantly offering and receiving support to and from women who are honest and trustworthy.

I was never in a sorority in college. I wasn't interested in the shenanigans of rushing and pledging to be accepted into a particular group of young women. I was never in a tight-knit group of ladies before mah jongg. I like the word sisterhood to describe our group of mah jongg-loving sisters. I'm blessed to know the women in my mah jongg sisterhood with whom I share conversation, time, and games each week. We learn from each other as women, mothers, daughters, wives, and friends. We share what's going on in each of our lives; we celebrate accolades and milestone events. We always have fun and laugh together. Sometimes one of us will cry. We help a sister if she's facing a problem, and we're there to listen if ranting or venting is needed. Being a woman isn't an easy task, but, then again, being human isn't easy either.

Our little Long Island mah jongg sisterhood is part of a larger group of mah jongg-loving women. In 1937, a group of thirty-two Jewish women formed the National Mah Jongg League, which today has over 350,000 members. These original women decided to standardize the game by creating consistent rules and publishing yearly mah jongg cards with new hands. I love the fact that each year the NMJL donates the proceeds from the sale of their cards to charitable organizations across the United States. The league also answers questions about rules, they settle disputes, help with replacement tiles, and they have an online store for some "Mahj" sweatshirts, sets, and other fun items. Mah jongg is popular with so many women that its own sisterhood organically formed, and I'm proud to be a part of it!

Super Soul Sundays

As much as I love Mah Jongg Mondays, I also love Super Soul Sundays. Oprah Winfrey created a platform to help viewers expand our minds through insightful and thought-provoking interviews. Her program nourishes my mind and body and lifts my spirit. I have watched (and rewatched) her interviews with men and women who have opened my mind and heart to new ideas and have expanded my spiritual awareness. Amazing people like Jack Canfield, Maryanne Williamson, Gary Zukav, Michael Beckworth, Carolyn Myss, Maya Angelou, Deepak Chopra, Brené Brown, and Glennon Doyle Melton have helped me walk through a gateway of learning and growth. She also interviewed the author Elizabeth Gilbert, whose book *Eat, Pray, Love* would help me on my journey in the months to come. Oprah held the key and unlocked the gate. These Super Soul episodes fed my soul Sunday after Sunday. I learned, grew, and became more aware of my soul's purpose here on earth. I also learned how to be open to the lessons in front of me every day, with every experience and with every person I meet. Oprah taught me about journaling and creating a vision board. *Of course*, she is on my vision board. No other person or celebrity has touched my life in such an expansive way.

Joel Osteen nourishes my soul on some Sundays too. His sermons are moving and uplifting as he offers hope through faith and inspiration. He opens my eyes to see grace in everyday moments and helps me believe in miracles. I know. He is an Evangelical preacher. I'm Jewish. But what he says and how he says his weekly sermons resonates with my soul. I've read some of his books, and I even went to see him at an event at Yankee Stadium years ago with my dad. The music was amazing. Now I'm hooked on contemporary Christian music because of uplifting lyrics about hope, faith, love, and family. These lyrics teach us about the struggles and hardships that God and faith can help us overcome. Joel Osteen and Oprah Winfrey are both blessings in my life.

These are some of the things and people that nourish my soul. I choose only to have positive, uplifting, nurturing and loving people in my inner circle. Fran once shared with me the different types of friendships that exist, something Holly, our shared life coach, taught her. There are the "street people," to whom we're cordial and with whom we discuss light subjects and exchange pleasantries. Then there are the "porch people," who we're closer to and with whom we can share more personal experiences; yet we still hold them at somewhat of a distance. Then there are the "kitchen people," the people with whom we share our intimate feelings; who know our struggles and are aware of what's going on deep within our lives. I'm blessed to have several women and a few men in my life who are my "kitchen people." We have each other's backs. We share our hearts with one another. We are honest, brave and real. My mah jongg girls are my kitchen people. It's part of the closeness our games create. Yes, mah jongg nourishes my soul too. Bam to that blessing!

Chapter 5

Flower Power

Spring is my favorite season here in the Northeast. It's a time of renewal and rebirth. The somber grey skies of the long winter are replaced with a blue canvas backdrop where cotton white clouds create ever-changing sky art as they move and morph as the breeze gently guides them on their journey. Gone is the snow, uncovering blankets of sleepy green lawns. Buds appear on tree branches, nurturing the unborn leaves like babies in a mother's womb. They will eventually unfold and fill the empty branches with color, depth, and volume. Nature starts to come to life in late March and early April. The Flower tiles of mah jongg remind me of this season. Perennials start to bud and bloom. Crocuses are the first brave flowers to awaken our senses in early spring displaying colors of purple, white or yellow. Tulips come out in spring's full glory, letting us know we are in store for months of color, warmth, and renewal.

Group text: Leigh, Sarah, Rose
Me: Hey there ladies! Hope everyone is having a great weekend. Tomorrow is Mah Jongg Monday. Who's in and who can host?
Rose: I'll host, how's 11:30 a.m.?
Leigh: Sounds good, I'm in!
Sarah: See you all then.
Me: Great, thanks for hosting, Rose!

We arrived at Rose's house, which is in a large gated housing development. Her home is warm and inviting. She had set up the mah jongg table in her living room/dining room area. Snacks and drinks were out on the dining room table for us. As I filled my snack plate, I noticed a decanter and a set of flutes in cobalt blue with gold paint on them displayed in her breakfront. They are called Bohemian glass and are very popular among Russian Jews, and my mother-in-law gave me some similar ones about twenty years ago. I like the Russian connection Rose provides for me. I have no other personal inlet to this culture except for Len and his family. Rose is closer in age to me than my mother-in-law, and we share more interests and time together than I do with Len's mom. Rose's husband shared part of his childhood with Len and his brother Anton after they moved to Forest Hills. She is also a window into Len's youth for me.

We all chose a seat and took out our new 2016 mah jongg cards. Each spring a new card is printed by the National Mah Jongg League. This creates buzz, excitement, and anticipation in the circles of mah jongg players. Rose took out her new set. It is quite beautiful and unique. The tiles are plastic but look like brown wood with roses on them. How apropos! The racks are cherrywood and complement the wood-like tiles. We turned the tiles face down and started to mix them. I noticed the colors of nail polish as eight hands stirred the tiles inside the square the four racks make. Leigh's nails were painted a bright pink ushering in the spring season. Rose also had a pink shade on her nails, Sarah's were a soft baby blue color, and I had a French Manicure. *Oh, the pampered hands we each have,* I thought to myself. These are the hands of Long Island women whose days are filled with domestic duties, carpooling, and part-time jobs for a few of us here at the table except for Rose, who works as a full-time psychologist. Sarah is starting to work more shifts at the hospital and let us know she will sadly be leaving our regular games in the fall. We are sad for our mah jongg game, but very happy for her as she loves what she does helping patients and their families.

I am often reminded that there are women around the

world who aren't able to take three hours out of their day to play a game with friends. Nail polish isn't something they think about. I am aware of the privileged life I live and the comforts that come with that. I am grateful for the house that I live in, the food, clothes, and car that we can afford in my household. Sadly, the world is filled with women faced with poverty, adversity, and restraint.

We are lucky women indeed. I think silently how lucky Rose has been with her health and also with the medical care she has received here in the United States. Some women aren't afforded the same medical care where they live.

We stacked nineteen pairs of tiles along our walls. Rose rolled the dice and dealt out the tiles. We caught up on events in our lives. We talked about where our children are going to camp this summer; one to sleep-away, three to the town camp and Gabriel who is going to Usdan, a local camp for the arts. Leigh's children have outgrown camp at eighteen and twenty years old.

"Ladies, how lucky are our children that they can go to camp?" I asked.

"I never went to camp," laughed Rose.

"Me neither, but my summers were fun in Greenport till I was thirteen," I said.

"I went to sleep-away camp for four years and hated it. I never felt like I fit in," Leigh sighed.

"I went to sleep-away camp and loved it! I cried every summer it was over," Sarah shared with us.

We are four women with four different pasts sitting

around a table in Long Island sharing our yesterdays, our todays and, I hope, our future Mondays. *B'shert* brought four lives together, converging our paths around a table every Monday, providing us with connection and friendship thanks to mah jongg. I look at mah jongg as social security; it creates a social opportunity for gaming, talking, and connecting. Just like poker creates bonds for men, mah jongg is the sister gaming opportunity for women.

We racked our tiles and got busy organizing them into common suits and numbers. I was lucky I got a Flower when dealt my tiles. I stack my Flowers on the left side of my rack, something Fran taught me to do when I had my lessons with her. I love the Flower tiles. Just as spring is my favorite season, this is also my favorite mah jongg tile. Some flower tiles have a season etched next to a number. Number one is spring, two is summer, three is autumn, and four is winter. Mah jongg is timeless and seasonless. It can be learned and played at any time in one's life. I started learning in my mid-forties.

I looked at my tiles and searched for a hand. I also had a bunch of 1s in different suits, and I decided to try a Like Numbers hand. We passed tiles through the Charleston. Rose started the game by discarding a 9 Crak. We took our turns picking, racking, and discarding tiles. As the game progressed, I just needed a 1 Bam to win. We were almost down to the final wall. Anticipation was building for me. Leigh picked a tile and discarded a 4 Dot. Sarah picked next, racked the tile, and discarded a South. It was my turn, with six tiles left in the wall I picked. Yes! It's the 1 Bam!

With mah jongg moxie, I burst out, "Mah jongg, ladies!"

"I was one tile away," Leigh said with disappointment.

"My hand has been dead for a while. I was just playing defensively," Sarah said.

Rose exposed the Winds hand she was playing. She was a few tiles away from a concealed hand. "Oh well," she sighed.

We all lay our tiles on the wooden racks, exposing the hands we were playing.

"I subbed in a game with my mom and two of her friends on Friday," Leigh said as we put the tiles in the center of the table and turned them face down.

"How was it?" Rose asked.

"They are very experienced and play fast. It took all my concentration to keep up with them," Leigh admitted. "It's much different than how we play. I haven't seen my mom play since I moved out after college. It was nice to connect with her through mah jongg. We've never played together before."

Leigh set off a memory of the first time I subbed in a game.

Subbing

A few months into playing, my friend, Hope, texted to ask me to sub in her game. I hesitated but agreed after Hope assured me she would tell the other two players I was new to mah jongg. She also told me she has an electric mah jongg table that is fun to play on. I'd never heard of an electric mah jongg table, and of course, I was intrigued.

An hour after I committed to subbing, I started to worry. *I'm out of my league*, I told myself. *I'll slow them down and frustrate them.* I called Fran, looking for reassurance. She told me I would do fine. She suggested I study the hands on the card, pick and rack every tile during the game and to play defensively by looking at the other players' exposures to see what hand they might be playing. I wrote down her advice and thanked her. She assured me everyone is nervous when they sub for the first time.

A few days later, it was subbing day. I arrived at Hope's, and she introduced me to the other two women who were in the kitchen getting snacks and drinks. We walked into the living room, and there it was, the coolest mah jongg table I had ever seen! I didn't know this even existed! The pedestal tabletop was square and covered in dark grey felt with plastic trim around the edges. In the center of the table was a circle with a dome made of plastic. Inside the dome were two dice. There were some buttons outside the dome, which would make the table come alive, I would soon see. The four walls were already set up neatly. We each took a seat, and Hope pushed one of the buttons, and the dice popped around inside the dome. As I watched, it brought me back to my childhood when I played the game Trouble.

When the dice stopped, one displayed a two and the other a six. Hope counted eight tiles, broke the wall, and started dealing. I had butterflies in my stomach and tried to remember Fran's suggestions. I decided I would avoid any hand needing too many pairs or any concealed hand. The women started chatting, but I was busy focusing on my hand. I couldn't have a conversation quite yet. I racked my tiles, grouping them in suits and pairs. I noticed the weight of these tiles. They were heavier than mine. I assumed they had magnets inside which added to their weight. I had been dealt a few Winds and decided to see what I would get in the Charleston. Luckily, I had filled in three more Winds after we finished passing through the Charleston. Hope started the game, discarding a tile. We picked, racked, and threw tiles as the game progressed. While their pace was much faster than mine, I focused on playing as fast as I could without making a mistake.

As the game continued, the woman across from me had exposed four 8 Craks and a Joker. She was playing a Quints hand. I was so happy to spot an opponent's hand! The woman to my left and I had yet to expose any tiles. Hope had an exposure on her rack, but I couldn't figure out her hand yet. On my next turn, I luckily picked up a Joker. We were getting down to the last wall. I was holding my own despite my questionable skill level, then the player across from me picked and called, "Mah jongg!"

We all exposed our hands, and then Hope and her

friend paid the winner. This was new to me. We don't "play and pay" in my game yet. I took out my wallet and luckily had spare change. We each paid her eighty cents, double the card amount because she picked the winning tile. Hope pushed a button on the table, and the center circle rose, creating a hole. The other women began to push the tiles into the abyss. I joined them and did the same. When the table was cleared of tiles, Hope pushed another button, and the circle descended to meet the tabletop. I could hear the tiles moving around within the table, followed by a click-clack sound, and within seconds an opening appeared in front of each of us. Miraculously, pre-stacked walls rose and presented themselves neatly in front of each player. Then the openings closed back up. This was amazing to watch! What a fun table!

We moved on to games two and three. During the third game, the player to my left picked a tile from the wall on her turn and was about to discard it. I noticed this tile could be replaced for the Joker in the exposure on Hope's rack.

I cleared my throat, and said, "Are you sure?"

She realized her mistake and replaced the Joker.

The player sitting across from me said, "Why did you say that? You shouldn't help other players."

Reality check. She apparently played by a different set of rules than I did. She was very serious about winning.

"This is how we play in my game. Don't worry, I won't make that mistake here again," I replied. Ouch.

We finished the game and played one more. My goal was to focus on the pacing of the game so that I wouldn't slow them down.

I actually won the last game and impressed myself. I was hesitant calling, "Mah jongg."

They confirmed I had indeed won. *Pay up, ladies!*

It was a twenty-five-cent hand I won. I realized it is fun to play for money, especially when you are the winner! I decided to ask the girls in my game if they wanted to start to play for money as well.

After I got home, I texted the girls about my first subbing experience and the automatic mah jongg table, which they also found intriguing. I texted them about the Joker debacle and shared that I was still feeling the sting from the woman's comment. They were all supportive and said they would have done the same thing that I did by helping the other player. I realized then how much I loved my mah jongg group. There was a sense of safety and security, friendship above winning, and camaraderie over competitiveness.

I was proud of myself for getting through my first game of subbing with seasoned players, and I was thankful that Hope gave me the opportunity to sub. This experience boosted my confidence in my mah jongg skills, and I was glad I went. Plus, I got to play on the most "mah-jelous" electric mah jongg table ever! I texted Hope to thank her. I sent Fran a text too, telling her that I got through my first subbing experience, and even won one game. Of course,

I described the electric mah jongg table. She texted back how proud she was of me. I replied that she taught me well, adding a few mah jongg tile icons from my iPhone keyboard. I was officially part of the mah jongg craze on Long Island and loved it!

Rose

Back to my game at Rose's. After our fifth game, I told the girls that it was time for me to leave so I could meet Gabriel as he came off the school bus. We all thanked Rose for hosting, disbanded in our own directions, leaving behind our latest Mah Jongg Monday memory.

As I drove home from Rose's, I thought back to when we first met. I was dating Len, so it was about twenty-five years ago. Len and I were visiting with his parents at their home in Oceanside. Len's parents are from the Ukraine, what was part of the former USSR. Len's brother Anton, his friend Sasha, and Sasha's girlfriend Rose were over Len's parents' house, too. They were also from the USSR, and I remember everyone speaking in their native tongue with one another that day. Rose and I spoke briefly in English, my only language. We both received an unusual gift from my future mother-in-law that day. It would be the first of many, I would discover.

We didn't see each other again until eight years later, at Anton's wedding. We then saw each other at his house over the next ten years at barbeques and holidays. It wasn't until a few years ago that Rose and I started our friendship and our families started sharing holidays, alternating between houses. Rose has a doctorate in psychology, and she's insightful about people's thoughts, emotions, and motivations. I am drawn to her intellect, and I find it quite interesting to have a friend who has such a different perspective on life.

Rose is extremely conscientious, strong-willed, and ambitious. She's also a caring woman, and she has one of the biggest, kindest and most loving hearts. She is an amazing cook, and at Rosh Hashanah and Thanksgiving, she and her mother prepare delicious, hearty, American and Russian dishes that my husband loves. She prepares dishes that Len grew up eating, and being at Rose's table takes Len back to his Russian roots, bringing back memories of a land and life so far away. Rose is five-foot-three, slim and has a European flair in her look and style. Her eyes are a greyish blue, and her hair is light brown for now. She changes her hair color, adding dimension to her look from time to time. She is also a cancer survivor.

When Rose was seventeen, just shy of her high-school graduation, a scan was her invitation to the game, the game of cancer. Cancer doesn't discriminate and has no rhyme or reason for picking its innocent victims. Rose was diagnosed with high-risk acute lymphoblastic leukemia and endured over two years of harsh chemo and cranial radiation. Given her age and the severity of her treatment, she lost many of her friends. But Rose is a fighter, and she was determined to overcome the cancer and move on with her life. She is now in her mid-forties, married to her Russian-born but Americanized husband, and has three children. Although she experiences long-term physical side effects from the chemo, including memory impairment and chronic pain, she has made it through a tough cancer journey.

Before we became friendly in early 2016, Rose was faced with another health crisis that included surgery. The details that Len and I heard were sketchy. I asked her to lunch after her recovery, and she shared her incredible story. She felt a sharp pain in her lower right abdomen while stretching at the end of her kickboxing class. She had recently started exercising again after a two-year break due to chronic pain. The pain worsened as the day turned into night, so her husband insisted that she go to the emergency room, both of them thinking that she had appendicitis. A CT scan found a tumor the size of a softball encapsulating her ovary, and the attending physician in the ER told her that she had late-stage ovarian cancer.

Given that she was already a patient at the world-renowned Memorial Sloan Kettering Cancer Center, she was able to obtain an emergency appointment in less than a week from that dire diagnosis. The doctors at MSKCC confirmed the diagnosis, further shattering her world by reporting that the cancer had metastasized to her other organs, including her pancreas, which was supported by cancer markers that were over twenty times higher than normal. She was faced with an uncertain prognosis including a survival rate of two to five years and a future including a colostomy bag.

"It's different when you are seventeen and just lose your friends and social identity for a while," she explained to me. "When you are a wife and mother, it's a completely different ball game. It was the most terrifying experience of my life."

With that dire prognosis, she headed into surgery at 6:30 a.m. on St. Patrick's Day. To the astonishment of the doctors, the tumor was completely contained. Maybe it was the luck of the Irish. Maybe it was a miracle. Maybe it was *b'shert*. Rose made it through her physical recovery and didn't need chemotherapy or a colostomy bag. She is a two-time cancer survivor and considers herself a very lucky woman.

It was *b'shert*. The universe wanted us to meet; two young women dating two Russian men we were destined to marry. We would become close friends and play weekly mah jongg games together on Mondays, but not for at least twenty-five years into the future.

Misha

Len's father, Misha, is like a cat with nine lives. He has had so many health issues. Thankfully, he has survived three cancers and quintuple bypass surgery. His father is a stoic and quiet man. He prefers to speak in Russian, his native language. This creates a communication barrier between us, but we have successfully navigated through our twenty-six-year relationship with smiles, glances, nods and basic conversation. He is the patriarch of the family, the overseer of his sons and grandsons.

Misha had an extremely hard childhood growing up in Russia. His father, Boris, was imprisoned for feeding corn to a horse. His mother did her best to raise two sons and two daughters alone. They were extremely poor, and Misha could only remain in school until the seventh grade because he had to earn money to help his family survive. He worked in an industrial factory and would take breaks napping on heated water pipes to warm up. Food was scarce and very few food stores existed. People grew their own vegetables and pickled them for the winter months. Some people had their own cows and chickens. Life was hard, and survival was a daily chore. I now understand the meaning of a hardened Russian. Misha's childhood and adolescence was the polar opposite of my childhood and my children's upbringing.

Len admires his dad for the hardships he endured as a child, as well as his ability to immigrate and settle in the United States with his wife and two sons. Len knows the sacrifices that his parents made to create a better life for themselves and their sons. Their emigration process was both difficult and drawn-out. People could only leave the country with one thousand rubles, which was a meager sum of money. Their possessions were put in a container and shipped to Israel where they hoped to settle. Their exit interview was harsh, including a humiliating strip down body search. They chose to immigrate to Israel, but when war broke out Misha was told he would have to serve in the army, and they had to decide if they would stay or leave. He already lost his spleen while being injured in the Soviet army and he didn't want to put his family through more worry and angst. They decided to leave Israel and go to Italy. Again, they packed their belongings and shipped them to Italy. Italy revoked their visas, but they were granted access to France. The container filled with all their materialistic possessions was lost on a boat going to a country they could not enter.

They arrived in France without knowing the language. The economy was in a recession. They stayed for two months and applied for American visas. They arrived in the United States with few personal possessions and very little money. The only housing they could afford was a motel in Harlem, New York, which at the time was a dangerous neighborhood. Misha got a job cutting sheepskins for coats, and Len's mother worked in a nursing home as a health aide, although she had a nursing degree in Russia. Six months later they moved to Forest Hills, Queens, to a much safer neighborhood. A wonderful Jewish organization called Hadassah helped them find an apartment and get very basic furniture: a table, chairs, and mattresses, but no bed frames.

The boys were registered in remedial classes at school without a lick of English in their vocabulary. Life was challenging for the two sons, but nowhere as hard as their father's was in the USSR. America offered a future of infinite possibility; a future the Soviet Union did not provide them. They lived in Forest Hills for eight years, and this was when the boys became friends with Sasha, Rose's husband. When Len's parents saved enough money, they moved to the suburban town of Oceanside on Long Island. It was paradise compared to their stay in Harlem. His parents opened a fabric store in Jamaica, Queens, and then moved the business to the Lower East Side of Manhattan a few years later. *B'shert* was spinning a spell.

My Mother-In-Law

Where do I begin? Oh, with the interesting gift she gave both Rose and me all those years ago in Oceanside. We both received packages of panties. Yes, panties. When we each received these unusual gifts, we were polite and thanked her for the gift. We looked at each other and smiled. We would share those smiles in the future as well. My mother-in-law is still a gift giver and still gifting items I find unusual. She sends bags filled with rubber bands, toothbrushes, faded paper napkins, sparkled knee highs, bug spray, toothpicks with umbrellas on them, and sardines. One time she included a douche.

"Really?" I asked Len.

He shrugged his shoulders and said, with a little

embarrassment, "Just throw it out."

I love that Len's mom thinks of me, but some of her presents actually have me stumped. One memorable item was a set of large plastic ants about three inches long attached to a clip. Were they Christmas ornaments? *No, can't be, I don't celebrate Christmas or have a tree. They are too large for earrings, and the clip would hurt my ear.* Len was puzzled also. Hmmm . . . I needed help. I posted a picture of them on Facebook. I asked people to help me figure out what these cute but quizzical items were. A few repeated responses answered my query. They were picnic tablecloth weights! I should have known! Doesn't everyone have a set of these somewhere in his or her closet or drawer?

Len's mother is a very loving and generous woman. She is a dutiful daughter, mother, grandmother, and wife and puts her family first. She is always giving our children money, gifts, and lots of hugs and kisses each time she sees them. She loves to cook and feed her family. I have taken note of this over the years. She takes her roles to heart, and I admire her for that. I will always be grateful that she bore and raised the wonderful man I chose to marry. Len was mothered well, with love and tenderness. But, do read on . . .

Unexpectedness

Life is full of the unexpected. While on my first visit to Len's parents' house, we had slept over. The next morning,

I was in the bathroom on the main floor getting ready to shower. I noticed the door didn't have a lock, but didn't think that was a problem. I hoped a closed door meant, "This room is occupied." Someone would knock before entering, I assumed. I was wrong on both accounts. After I showered, while I was standing in my bra and panties blow-drying my hair, the door suddenly and deliberately swung open. I gasped in shock and embarrassment.

His mother stood there studying me, or more precisely, my body, and said in her thick Russian accent, "Oh, excuse me, dear Ferren." Like she didn't hear the blow dryer and *know* I was in there. "You have lovely large breasts. One day you vill feed babies from them. You also have good hips for childbirth."

"Oh . . . thank you," I replied thinking those must have been compliments.

The door shut as unexpectedly as it had opened, and she left me alone in the bathroom looking into the mirror studying my body in a new and inquisitive way.

Misunderstandings

I have learned Len's mother can also be moody and inconsistent with her behavior. Life can be full of misunderstandings, especially when people don't speak the same native language. A few months into dating, we were back visiting with Len's parents, and his mom asked me an odd question as she and

I were sitting on the couch together in her living room.

"Ferren, vat is your de-fee-ni-shun of cleaning?"

I wasn't expecting a question like this out of the blue. Was this a prerequisite question? Would my answer place me in a category of possible marriage material for her son?

I pondered her odd question and answered it succinctly by saying, "I define cleaning as vacuuming, cleaning toilets, mopping floors, washing windows; it really depends what needs to be cleaned that day. I feel it's important to clean and to keep your house clean."

Had my response been suitable?

I felt cold all of a sudden.

I felt icicles forming inside the living room.

Her posture became erect, her lips pursed. I looked around for Len. I wasn't sure what was happening, but it didn't feel like a good thing. It was getting colder by the second. I called out for Len.

He walked into the living room. "What's up?" he asked casually.

His mother burst out, saying something in Russian. Len raised his voice back in response to what sounded like an incredulous remark she just made. Len's dad appeared on the scene, hearing the commotion. She yelled something in Russian at him. He screamed back at her. I didn't know what to do with myself. This was Russian verbal volleyball, me the American bystander sitting in the bleachers cold and confused.

Len said, "Fern, let's get our things. We're leaving."

I couldn't have been happier to hear those words. We quickly got our bags as loud Russian words were being thrown around us. We thankfully closed the door of the house behind us and opened the door to my safe and quiet car.

"Umm, what exactly happened in there?" I asked indignantly.

"I'm really sorry, Fern. She thought you told her; *her* house wasn't clean," he explained.

Since that day, over twenty years ago, I am cautious with this relationship, and I choose *every word very carefully*. Another soul lesson for me to endure: Karma speaks all languages.

Chapter 6

Shiva

Shiva is the Jewish custom of gathering after a funeral at the home of the mourners. I attended a *shiva* of a temple member in June of 2016 with Sarah and Leigh. This house of mourning was that of a man in his fifties and his two children in their twenties. He was a member of the board of trustees at my temple and had just lost his wife. Although I didn't know him and had only said hello to his wife once briefly while at temple, I felt inclined to go and pay my respects at the shiva. I was the Sisterhood president and would be joining the temple board in just a few weeks. Leigh had been friendly with the woman who passed away. As we entered the house it was full of people, but only a few that I knew. We saw Amanda, a neighbor who lived near me standing in the living room. We walked over and hugged hello. We exchanged the shaking of heads, understanding the immense sadness of this house. Her eyes were filled with tears of her own personal loss. She said she lost one of her best friends, and she wore her sadness openly. I always liked Amanda but never got to know her more than casual hellos exchanged at social gatherings. Have you ever met someone you knew you wanted to get to know better? Sometimes it's their warmth, their style, or something they say in conversation that resonates with you, piquing your interest. She had piqued mine years ago; now here we were standing side by side in this house of mourning.

There is a sense of solidarity during *minyan*. It's a way for Jews to collectively recite the ancient words of Hebrew prayers, chanted at *shiva* houses all over the world. Either a rabbi or *minyan* leader guides the mourners and guests through the prayer book. The *Kaddish* is recited, a specific prayer said to praise God and to honor the memory of the person who has just passed. After the prayer service was over, a few women walked over to speak with Amanda. I kissed her goodbye and told her I would text her to make plans to get together in a few weeks. I knew she had her own mourning to get through. Leigh took me to meet the husband of the woman who had died.

As she walked up to him, she gave her condolences and hugged him. She then introduced us, "David this is my friend, Fern."

I extended my hand to him as I offered my condolences. "Hi, I'm so sorry for your loss."

I remembered seeing him with his wife one time in temple.

He responded in one of the deepest voices I've ever heard, "Thank you for coming. It's nice to meet you. Did you know my wife?"

I responded, "No, I hadn't known her. I'm a temple member and the current president of our Sisterhood. I'm joining the board in a few weeks. I'm sorry we had to meet this way." I continued by asking, "What did your wife pass from?"

"Metastatic breast cancer."

I lowered my eyes, feeling the heaviness of that six-letter word. I was dealing with my own personal challenge with the word *cancer*. It was touching my life too. I told him my husband was diagnosed with non-Hodgkin's lymphoma about a year ago. He was in a "watch and wait" phase as the oncologist called it. The cancer was indolent, slow growing and no treatment was necessary . . . yet. David said he was sorry for what we were going through and called a friend over who was also diagnosed with non-Hodgkin's lymphoma. This man had a port in his head for chemo. I wondered to myself, *Is this what lays in my husband's future? God, I pray it isn't.*

As I drove home that night, I decided I would reach out to David. When I see someone in need, I try to offer my help. It's intrinsic in me; it's how I'm hard wired. A few days after *shiva*, I called the temple office, asked for David's phone number, and then called him.

His sonorous voice answered after a few rings, "Hello?"

"Hi David, this is Fern. We met at your house during *shiva*?" I asked, not knowing if he remembered me.

He sensed the rise of my voice. "Of course; how are you?" he responded.

"I'm fine; how are *you* doing?" I gently asked.

"The best I can," he said.

"I know we don't really know each other, but I'm wondering—would you like to meet for coffee or go for a walk?" I asked.

"Sure, that would be nice. When are you thinking?"

"I'm free any day next week, except for Monday. You pick a day and time, as long as it's before 2:00 p.m.," I said. "I need to be home to get my son off the bus."

"How's Wednesday at 11:00 a.m.? We can walk my dogs if that's okay," he suggested.

"Sounds great. I'll see you then."

When I hung up, I had that familiar feeling of hope fill my body, knowing I could offer help to another human being in need. I hoped to bring a little sunshine into his life, which was clouded over with the darkness and sadness of mourning and loss.

That Wednesday started a special friendship for both of us. We walked his dogs; one a fifteen-year-old husky, and the other a two-year-old Jack Russell terrier that his wife rescued from an abusive home. The dogs were quite different, but they seemed to coexist well enough. After the dog walk, we sat and spoke for about two hours. I learned about his wife, their life, their college-aged children, and their plans of retiring just before she was diagnosed with cancer. Life is so fragile. Tragedy is always so cruel and thoughtless. I told him about my family, my husband, Len, and my three sons Jared, Alex, and Gabriel. We spoke of careers; his coming to a planned end as he reached an early retirement, mine a part-time career offering me the ability to continue to be a full-time mom for my youngest son. We spoke about cancer, life, and death.

My phone call of care and concern started a friendship that evolved into a brother-sister relationship. We spoke often. I sent cards of encouragement and helped David start his life of "new norm" with support and kinship. I helped him pack his 5,000 square foot house to downsize to a condo, which he bought shortly after his wife died. Leigh, her family, and mine helped with packing fervor as his closing date was two days away, and he had half a house left to pack. I reached out to our rabbi and board members to ask for any manpower they could give. We came together as a community to help our brother in need.

When he moved into his new condo, I helped him unpack the kitchen boxes. I bought him disposable sticky blinds so he could have privacy and avoid sunbeams waking him through uncovered bedroom windows. I helped him walk his dogs when he was out for long hours doing errands. When he was ready to date, he joined an online dating service and shared every potential date's profile with me. He named me his dating manager. I got updates after every first date. Len was secure in himself and our marriage not to be jealous of my friendship with David. He knew I was doing a *mitzvah* through being his friend. As David dated, I knew our special friendship would change once he found someone to pursue as a romantic partner. I was right about two things with David. He did need someone to talk to when I made that first phone call to him, and when he did find someone to pursue a love relationship with, our friendship changed both drastically and sadly. He had to make a choice. I knew my job was done. His girlfriend could take over and offer him things our friendship never could. There wasn't room for me in his new relationship, and no girlfriend could easily accept my special place in his heart.

It was *b'shert*. We were meant to meet, to be in each other's lives. Through an act of kindness to a stranger, a special friendship began. We were connected through our temple, cancer that affected both our spouses, and yes, inadvertently mah jongg too. Going to *shiva* at his house and becoming David's friend sparked two relationships in my life that created my mah jongg night games.

Amanda

Mah jongg is a vehicle of connection in my Long Island Jewish world. I texted Amanda a few weeks after *shiva.* She had mentioned she played mah jongg when we spoke.

I texted, asking: Are you available to play mah jongg on Mondays?
She texted back: I would love that, but I work and can only play at night.
I responded: Ok. I'll see who else I can get to play. Would a Monday night work for your schedule around 7:00 p.m.?
She texted back: Yes, that would be great! Thanks for asking me!

Leigh and Rose were also able to play at night, and this is how my night game started. I alternated my day and night games each Monday, referring to this day of the week as Mah Jongg Monday. I was so happy that I would see Amanda twice a month. I knew I was going to love my night games as much as I did my day games. I hosted our first night game. It was so much fun! We were all a great fit. Leigh had known Amanda for over ten years. They both knew David's wife. I got to know a little about his wife from the women sharing stories about her at our mah jongg games. Amanda described his wife's signature look of wearing a colored crochet beret when she lost her hair during chemo.

I'm sorry I only met her once. The encounter was brief. I was in line behind her getting food at an event at temple. We shared a warm smile and a single word, "Hello." I remembered that she wore a berry-colored crochet beret. She did not have hair underneath the beret, I noticed. *Ahhh, chemo,* I thought to myself. I sent her a silent prayer of health and strength standing behind her in line. I did not know her name or who she was. Sitting at the mah jongg table that night hearing about the berets, I connected the dots and realized that must have been David's wife.

It was *b'shert.* The universe wanted us to meet briefly and to be in each other's space for a fleeting few seconds. Who knew her husband would become a close friend of mine? Who knew her death would bring Amanda into the mah jongg fold? I silently thanked her for bringing these two people, David and Amanda, into my life. *I will treat them both well, as I do with all my friendships,* I whispered to her spirit.

Amanda is a natural beauty. She air dries her wavy shoulder-length light brown hair. She doesn't wear very much makeup, sometimes just mascara highlighting her Hershey-kiss-colored eyes that blink with mystery and a spark of intrigue. She always looks pretty in her natural signature way. She has a slim figure and loves to wear dresses. I admire her posts on Facebook; they are inspirational and real. Amanda doesn't hide how she feels. She has a spiritual side and a strong moral compass. She is a doer and a giver. She is a life coach, social worker, and part-time administrator in a local temple. She is witty, confident, smart and has depth. Amanda is someone I'm blessed to now call my friend. She was the former president of a local *Hadassah* chapter, a Jewish woman's organization, and is a devoted member of the tribe. I remember her calling me about fifteen years ago asking if I would be interested in joining her chapter. I told her I would like to, remembering *Hadassah* helped my husband's family when they first immigrated to New York. Days after her call, fire engulfed our house. I forgot about joining *Hadassah* and focused on finding shelter and making sense out of this senseless fire.

It was *b'shert* once again. The universe wanted two neighbors to connect at a *shiva*. Thankfully, some things are just meant to be.

Shiva with Leigh and David

David and I started to go to some *shivas* together for temple members we both knew. One memorable *shiva,* Leigh came along with us. The *shiva* was about thirty minutes away. We met at David's house, and he drove from there. David was a DJ before he retired and had thousands of songs stored on his phone. We decided to make it a fun-filled ride by listening and singing along to some of our favorite songs from the '80s. Madonna's "Like A Virgin," "Sidewalk Talk," and "Borderline" kicked off the music fest. Leigh and I sang along with Madonna. We joined along with Duran Duran, Michael Jackson, Bon Jovi, Journey, U2, Wham!, and A Flock of Seagulls as their music filled the car, blasting out from the speakers as we pulled into a parking spot on the street near the house of mourning.

Anyone hearing as we pulled up must have thought we were teenagers. We most definitely were not. We had to pull ourselves together and shake off the fun feelings we were all experiencing and shift into *shiva* mode. We stepped out of the car smiling and looked at one another knowing we just had the best ride that friends could have going to a *shiva*. Leigh and I linked arms and walked up to the house, David a step behind us. As we entered the house, the atmosphere helped wash away our current feelings, and we were brought into the reality of sadness and loss. I found my friend, hugged her, and said how sorry I was for her loss. David and Leigh took their turns after me. The rabbi was starting *minyan*, and we joined the service in the crowded living room. David and I shared a prayer book, and Leigh was sharing one with someone she knew from temple. The rabbi recited prayers, and we joined in where the italicized words signaled us to recite the words in Hebrew or English. I glanced over at David. He had tears in his eyes. Every *shiva* must remind him of the one he held for his beloved wife, not more than a few months ago. I put my hand on his back trying to give him comfort during his own moment of sadness. He put his arm around me needing a little support. The rabbi led us through the *Kaddish*, the mourner's prayer, and then *minyan* was over. The books were collected. Leigh, David, and I walked up to our friend's mother who just lost her husband.

She was poised, demure, and welcoming as I stepped up to the chair she was sitting in, almost queen-like, I thought to myself. I knelt to be eye level with her beauty as I connected with her by extending my hand and offered her my heartfelt condolences. She struck me as one of the most beautiful older women I had ever seen. She had long and lustrous pure white shoulder-length hair. She had clipped up the sides letting it cascade down to her shoulders. Her face was beautiful and expressive. She had perfectly arched eyebrows, chestnut brown eyes accentuated by eye shadow, liner, and mascara. Her lips were stained red and her cheekbones rouged. Her skin didn't reveal her exact age, but she emitted immense wisdom, beauty, and love, and when I looked into her expressive eyes, I also found sorrow dwelling within them.

She thanked me for coming and told me how pretty I was. I was quite honored and told her how beautiful I thought she was. She said my husband was handsome, pointing to David.

"Oh, he's not my husband—more like my handsome

brother. We're good friends," I explained. "But my husband at home is very handsome." I winked at her as I smiled.

I stepped aside as David and Leigh came to pay their condolences to her. We left the house of mourning and walked back to David's car. Our ride home was nowhere as much fun as our ride there was. We were all humbled by death, but I was glad we could all laugh as Leigh and I sang our hearts out on the ride there, bringing some happiness into David's new world without his wife. None of us had eaten dinner, and we decided to stop at a diner on the way home for a bite to eat. David told us he appreciated the company. He had been eating alone. Leigh and I were happy to keep him company and to help our widower friend.

Leigh

Leigh and I met at our temple about fifteen years ago, first becoming familiar faces to one another, which led to friendly hellos and eventually to a friendship that is strongly embedded in the roots of our religion. We started to attend Shabbat services together and talked afterward, learning about one another, our families, and backgrounds. My husband wasn't connected to Judaism like I was. I was thrilled to have a friend to sit with at Shabbat services, to take classes together with and to grow into my young adult Jewish shoes with. We eventually joined the board of trustees together and became very involved temple members.

Leigh shares with me an appreciation of clothes, fashion, accessories, shoes, and the art of putting it all together. Her long hair is light brown or maybe dark blonde with highlights and lowlights and processes that create her signature look. She is about five-feet-four with the best-shaped arms I've ever seen. Her arms' musculature is naturally chiseled and gives her the appearance of an athlete. Leigh is my friend of depth and wisdom. She is an old soul and is both introspective and emotionally intelligent. I'm like a magnet to people of depth, and that is part of the glue that holds our friendship together along with Judaism, fashion, femininity and mah jongg. It was *b'shert*. The universe wanted us to meet; two Jewish soul sisters destined for friendship and one day in the future to learn and play mah jongg together.

Chapter 7

A Summer Game

Group text: Rose, Leigh, Sarah
Me: Hey ladies! Mah Jongg Monday is at my
house, 12:00 p.m. Who's in this week?
Leigh: Wouldn't miss it!
Sarah: I'm in!
Rose: Me too. See you all then!
Me: Great! See you all on Monday!

June is a beautiful month here on Long Island. Our suburban lawns are lush; the Kelly-green grass is a bold and vibrant backdrop of color enveloping our homes.

Eager gardeners have planted their annual flowers in late May. Dahlias, wave petunias, begonias, gerbera daisies, and impatiens adorn our landscapes. Perennials that have come to life in spring are now ready to add their blooming flowers to the eye candy of floral color tantalizing our eyes. I love this month for that reason alone.

June is also a month that holds a sacred day that is filled with love and remembrance for me. That day is June 10th. That day is the day my mother died . . . in my arms.

I always try to host on the day or anniversary week of my mom's passing. Mah jongg gives me an opportunity to honor my mom and share her memory with the girls through things she gave me or that were once hers. The girls came over around noon. I filled my day with things of Mom. My finger displayed a ring my mom loved to wear. It has a large smoky topaz stone set in a high, delicate gold filigree setting. I wore the only real diamond studs I own, given to me by her when I graduated college. I wore her gold bangle bracelets too. I used beautiful drinking glasses that were hers—no plastic cups today. And of course, we played with her mah jongg set that she gave me over seventeen years ago. The set miraculously made it out of the fire unscathed, despite a smoky smell, and was one of the few things I was able to rescue from the remains of our home. The set had lain dormant in my new home for almost ten years, nestled away in a closet. I had actually forgotten about it until I started playing five years ago. Although I have my peacock set, I leave my mom's set right next to it, so I'll never lose sight of it again, sometimes opting to use it instead of the peacock set. Its place there reminds me of my mom every time I glance at it.

The case is hard, covered in wine-colored snake-skin-like embossing. It opens and closes with a pop latch. There is a keyhole, but the key has been lost. The case has a white plastic handle, and all the metal components of the latch and handle brackets have tarnished, exposing the case's age. The torn and tattered corners of the case also reflect its vintage edge, but those imperfections also add dignity, charm, and history to this beloved case. The tiles are white, solid, and weighted, unlike my new lightweight plastic tiles. There are four plastic racks: baby blue, green, red, and yellow. The miniature dice are white with both red and black numerical dots.

We gathered in the kitchen to play that day. I updated the girls that Robert and Delilah were preparing for hospice. We were all saddened for what their whole family was going through. I checked in every day with Delilah through a text or a phone call. Sometimes I just sent her a text with a heart, so she knew I was thinking of her. She acknowledged this by sending me a heart back.

Everyone took a plate, chose snacks and a drink, and found a seat at the table. Next, mah jongg cards appeared, coming out of purses, and were placed in front of the racks. I took out Mom's special set and spilled the tiles onto the table. I reminded the girls this was the anniversary of her passing. They nodded their heads, understanding the importance of this day to me. Delilah and Leigh knew my mom for many years and were both fond of her. My mother was fond of them as well. She didn't know Sarah or Rose but would have loved them if she did have the chance to meet them. We mixed the tiles, shifting the mood as the click-clacking sound filled the kitchen with Mah Jongg Monday excitement. We started to stack our walls. I was East and dealt after I rolled the dice. We each racked the tiles I had just dealt out. The quiet in the room signified our concentration as we grouped our tiles into suits, pairs, or pungs if we were really lucky, searching the card to find a hand to create. We danced through the Charleston: right, across, first left, second left, across, and final right. I decided on a Winds hand and hoped I'd get lucky as the game progressed.

I thought of my mom as I looked at the tiles, especially the Winds. My mom loved boating, and one of my favorite memories of her is when we were on our boat on the Peconic Bay in Greenport. I'm ten again. Mom was steering, and my twelve-year-old brother and I were sitting at the bow, our legs straddled in safety between the metal rails, the wind whipping into my face and blowing my long brown hair in frantic abandon. As we sped through the water, the wake behind us left an opaque white streak behind the motor, veering out into the expanse of the bay. The smile on my mom's face lets me know she is one with the sea. She has command of the boat. She is in her glory at this very moment.

My mother started learning the beginner skills of

boating from my grandfather before she was five years old. She was connected with the sea at a very young age. That connection grew stronger as she aged, and she developed a love for the sea that lasted for her forever. Mom reveled in the joyous opportunities the water gave her through boating, fishing, clamming, and crabbing along the bog of Pete's Neck in Orient Point. She marveled in the excitement of pulling up lobster pots. Mom taught us how to cut bait; run fishing line with hook, sinker, and bobber; how to cast out for bluefish or sinker-bounce for fluke or flounder. She taught us boating knots, terms, safety precautions, and eventually how to drive the boat when she thought we were ready to take control at the helm. She also taught us respect for the boat, speed, and the sea itself. My mother was a great teacher.

I'm brought back from thoughts of my mother as Leigh called, "Mah jongg!"

Although I didn't win this game, my heart won by remembering loving memories of my mom and summers past as I played the Winds.

Divorce

The lessons my mother taught me about the sea and boating ended abruptly. Our Greenport summer memories came to a halt in 1980 when I was thirteen, the year I became a *bat mitzvah*. The timing of my becoming a Jewish adult freed my mother from a painful and empty marriage with my father. This was the secret time frame she crafted deliberately and with forethought. Mental and emotional endurance helped her to see the finish line. She wanted to get our family through this Jewish milestone intact. I had no idea before, during, or after my *bat mitzvah* that there was anything different between my parents. They were never a demonstrative couple. I can only remember one fight they ever had in front of me. My brother and I spent most of our time with our mom. The pictures I look at from the family *bat mitzvah* album don't give clues of an impending separation and divorce that was to begin just two months later.

My brother and I were sat down one night and told by my mom that she and my dad were separating, making it clear that this had nothing to do with us. Whoosh. Just like that, in an instant of a conversation, my world was about to change. During the divorce, our beloved summer house, which had become a marital asset, had to be sold. At thirteen, I couldn't appreciate the value of waterfront property, but unfortunately neither did the two adults deciding what to do with this precious family asset. I was heartbroken that my parents decided to sell our summer retreat. Unborn generations of both my brother's and mine would never have the summer experiences my grandparents, mother, brother, and I had summering on waterfront property. My grandfather's legacy was cut short by a broken marriage, lawyers, and foolishness.

After my parent's divorce was final, my father bought

a co-op in the East Village section of Manhattan. It was a fun, artsy, and cool neighborhood I loved to visit as a teenager. It was so different from the quiet suburban town of Cresskill and the seaside town of Greenport. Dad and I would go to the Lower East Side of Manhattan together on my visits. There is a famous delicatessen called Katz's where we would eat overstuffed sandwiches of pastrami or corned beef and drink Dr. Brown's black cherry soda. We would go shopping in the local stores. Dad would pay for only half of an item; I would have to bring my babysitting money if I wanted to buy something. At the time, it bothered me that I had to pay half for something I wanted. This was new to me, but divorce brings with it a lot of newnesses. As an adult, I see the value and life lesson in his decision to have me pay half. He taught me the value of working, to save money, and to decide carefully how I wanted to spend my hard-earned money.

On our trips downtown, we would pass a fabric store on the corner of Houston and Delancey Street. This was the very fabric store Len's parents owned and where they worked. It was *b'shert*. The universe was starting to align two paths for convergence: one path, that of a teenage girl of newly divorced parents; the other path, that of an immigrant teenage boy whose parents brought him from the USSR for a better life in America, a life that would include me, but not for almost ten years into the future.

The Promise

June of 2016 was memorable, but in a very sad and unfortunate way. Two spouses died. First was David's wife in mid-June, then on June 28, a little over six months after his diagnosis, Robert passed away. I drove to their house when Delilah's son texted me that he had passed. It was evening. I remember driving there under a darkened night sky. Delilah was on the phone outside when I arrived. I hugged her. This was raw emotion. There was devastation, grief, and darkness surrounding this home and this family.

She held the phone cupped in her hand as she said, "Fern, you can go upstairs if you want to say good-bye to Robert before he is taken away. I'm on the phone, and I'll be right up."

I nodded to her and went upstairs. I did want to see Robert, one last time. I found him lying on their bed. Their daughter was curled up, snuggled right next to her father in a fetal position. This was a surreal moment. I was on autopilot. I held Robert's cooling hand in mine and silently said to him that I would not forget the promise he asked of me. I also will never forget this heart-breaking father-daughter moment that I witnessed.

"My brothers will walk me down the aisle when I get married one day, right, Fern?" she asked with a broken heart.

"Absolutely. Both of them will walk you down the aisle, sweetie," I replied.

"Good, because my daddy won't be there."

"I know, honey. But if this makes sense, know that his spirit will be at your wedding," I tried explaining to my friend's nine-year-old daughter.

Delilah came upstairs. She asked that we all wait together in the basement. She didn't want anyone to see him being taken away or hear the sound of the zipper as it closed shut around him. We all went downstairs and sat together quietly. It was hard to think of anything to say at a moment like this.

Delilah broke the silence by saying, "He died peacefully."

I nodded my head and put my arm around her. It was all I could do at the moment. When the hospice nurse came downstairs to tell us we could come back upstairs, we filed up the stairs one by one; Delilah, her daughter, her older son and her younger son, then me. We ascended into a house that had been forever transformed.

Delilah asked, "Would you mind helping me change the sheets on the bed?"

"Of course I will," I gently responded to my friend.

We climbed the stairs to the second floor of her home. We ceremoniously took off the sheets and pillowcases from their bed. Together we put on new ones. Sleeping in the bed from this night forth would be different for Delilah. This was the bed she and Robert slept on for many years. This was the last place Robert lay before his soul was carried up to heaven. This was a sacred space.

We finished making the bed and then sat on two chairs in their bedroom and talked for a while. We reminisced about memorable times while we were living in Bayside. We talked about how life was so different and so simple then. Then we both moved. More children were born into our families. Then cancer invaded. I never thought all those years ago that we would be sitting together, grieving the loss of her husband in 2016. I was honored to be there that night. I didn't know how much closer a "kitchen friend" could be at that very moment in time.

It was a sad night, and one I will never forget. As I drove home and turned onto the Long Island Expressway, I couldn't miss all the stars twinkling in the darkened night sky above me. *I know you are up there, Robert. Rest in peace, my friend.* I was sad but knew at the same time that I had a mission. *I will remember to keep my promise to you, Robert.*

Delilah had a beautiful celebration of life for Robert along with pictures of him from his birth to a few months before he died. Delilah said he had the chance to speak with everyone he wanted and needed to. He had closure before he died. There were over two hundred people at the celebration of life. They spoke tributes about him; he was a good man, husband, father, and friend. He was loved by many and missed by all. Delilah was proud of her children for being strong when they could, for crying when they needed to, for supporting her and caring for and loving their father so deeply.

Robert asked me to make him a promise before he died. He asked that after he passed away, when the dust settled, not to forget Delilah and his children, to stay connected and continue our friendship. I remembered him asking me this promise days after I found out my own husband had cancer. I was sitting on a bed at the Moon Palace in Mexico. I whole-heartedly gave him my promise that I would uphold that request, and mah jongg has helped me fulfill that promise to Robert. This wonderful game is a way to bring women together, to help a friend slowly heal from the depths of loss and to escape the reality of a sad time, for a few hours, on Mah Jongg Mondays.

Chapter 8

Turning Fifty

It was January 2017, and my fiftieth birthday was coming up in April. Let's face it. It was a biggie. I didn't want to have a party. I wanted to do something different and exciting that included learning or a workshop of interest and stepping outside of my comfort zone. A friend had told me about a women's-only camp experience she recently went to named Campowerment. I Googled it and read: "Campowerment is a sleep-away-inspired experience designed to help women live life better. Infusing the glee of summer camp with wisdom from some of America's celebrated thought leaders, Campowerment provides the time, space and tools for campers to reflect, exercise, socialize, energize, release and reconnect." It's held in the Berkshires in November and Malibu in March. I looked at pictures posted on their website. I was intrigued.

California has always been a favorite getaway, besides Greenport, for me. Hands down, I would prefer Malibu to the Berkshires. I remembered reading about Campowerment in the Oprah magazine a few years ago while I was visiting San Diego and thinking what an amazing experience this camp offers. I called the director-owner to ask a few questions and then decided this is what I wanted to do for my fiftieth birthday. I'd never been to sleep-away camp, but decided that it would meet my criteria of stepping outside of my comfort zone. I asked Leigh if she would be interested in going with me, kind of an early birthday celebration in March. She is into self-exploration like I am, and I knew we would be good traveling companions. She looked at their website and was intrigued too. She discussed details with her hubby and agreed to join me! Len loved the idea also, especially the location, because he knew how much I loved California. We booked our flights, a hotel on the beach in Malibu to stay at a few days before camp, and a convertible to drive around sunny California. I wasn't thrilled about turning fifty, but I was very excited for our trip!

Aging is an inevitable process. The only real choice we have about aging is how we choose to accept the physical changes of time to our face, body, and mind. I am choosing to gracefully accept the subtle lines settling in around my blue eyes and framing my lips when I smile. No thoughts of Botox for me . . . yet. My dark brown, shoulder-length hair is starting to get stray strands of grey, signifying the ensuing shift that is occurring. Middle age had officially begun, and the number fifty welcomed me into the club. Although I still get my period, I'm sure that will be changing soon, too. I wish I could ask my mom when she started menopause, but sadly, I can't ask her anything anymore.

A few weeks before Leigh and I were leaving, David said he was planning a trip to San Diego where he owns an apartment in a high rise, the apartment where he and his wife were supposed to retire. I told him the dates Leigh and I were going to be in Malibu and asked if we could coordinate our trips. We could get together in either San Diego or Malibu, which was such an exciting plan! He agreed and said he would coordinate his travel dates with ours. Since our flights were booked into LAX, we decided we would get our rental car and drive straight down to San Diego. We would spend three days with David and cancel the Malibu hotel. I loved San Diego and was excited to be able to include being there for my fiftieth birthday trip. Leigh hadn't been to San Diego in thirty years and was excited to revisit this beautiful California city. After our stay with David, we would drive back up to Malibu for Campowerment.

Len would be in charge of getting Gabriel up and ready for school and would come home early from work to get him off the bus and be Mr. Mom for a week. He was feeling well and still in a "watch and wait" phase. Our life had barely changed, but I knew this wouldn't last more than another few months to a year. I could see the cancer growing under one of his eyes. Campowerment and all that it offers hopefully would be a birthday gift, that, once unwrapped, would help me to uncover inner strength and other qualities within myself I didn't even know existed.

California Here We Come!

Our departure date arrived. I kissed my boys good-bye and rolled my luggage out to the awaiting car service where Leigh was eagerly waiting for me. We headed to the airport, excited and ready for adventure.

We arrived at LAX, got to the car rental company and were walked over to my birthday splurge, a BMW convertible. The attendant showed us how to make the convertible top open and close. We wanted it open for now and started to load the luggage. We each had a large suitcase, a carry-on, and tote, along with our pocketbooks. Uh-oh, not sure there's enough space for everything. The attendant saw us struggling and came back to assist. "You girls have a lot of luggage for this size car. Good thing it's just you two. How long are you girls on vacation?" he asked.

"Seven days. We don't pack light, but we pack thoroughly with our arsenal of clothes, makeup, accessories, shoes, sneakers, bathing suits, hair dryers, and brushes," I answered.

I had thought about taking my peacock mah jongg set in case we could find two more players at camp, but decided it was too heavy and bulky for travel. I realized what a smart decision that was! The convertible top took up most of the trunk space so we could only fit the small luggage there. The attendant helped secure the large luggage in the back seat. He had to arrange them one horizontal and one vertical, and strapped both in with the seat belts so we wouldn't lose one if we hit a big bump and it popped out of place, or out of the car. We crammed our carry-on totes behind our seats and tucked our purses by Leigh's legs as we drove off into the California sunshine.

I started the drive south as Leigh navigated our ride on Google Maps. I fastened my hair up with a clip and Leigh wore a baseball cap to hold her locks down, the wind whipping around us as we headed south on I-405. Leigh texted with David as we got closer to San Diego and our GPS took us to his high rise without a glitch. He met us in the parking garage, and we all hugged hello excitedly. We took the elevator up to his apartment. The views were beautiful. Walls of windows exposed an expansive view of the harbor and the Coronado Bridge. We put our luggage in the spare bedroom, freshened up and headed out to explore. We walked down by the harbor and then to the Gaslamp district for dinner. David's birthday was in two weeks, and mine was next month, so we ordered drinks to celebrate early. Dinner was delicious, and conversation flowed easily between the three of us. David told us about the new woman he was dating; we saw pictures and learned more about her. We walked around after dinner for a little while, then headed back to his apartment and called it a night. We were tired from traveling.

The next day we drove over to Coronado Island. I had been here a few times before—once with my father, again with Len and the boys, and once with a friend two years ago. It's a beautiful island and home of the famous Coronado Hotel. We parked near the hotel and walked down to the water. The weather was warm and sunny, an idyllic San Diego day. We were wearing shorts and tank tops, clothes we couldn't have worn back in New York in March. I etched our names in the sand, interlocking our names with a common letter each name shared. As I looked at my creation in the sand, I thought how *b'shert* brought our lives together. Destiny and divine intervention crossed our paths and led us all to friendship. David and Leigh came over to see my name-game creation etched in the sand. We took some selfies then David took some fun action shots of Leigh and me holding hands and jumping high into the air at the water's edge. We took our shoes off and let our feet get wet in the sand and stayed to watch the sunset.

There is something so special for me about California. When I was seventeen, my father spent a year in San Diego, and when I went to visit, I fell in love with the weather and the scenic beauty. That visit started my own California dreaming. A seed was planted. When I was twenty-three, I spent a year living in San Francisco. I loved the city by the bay, but it was never a place I wanted to live in permanently. Len and I talk about possibly relocating to San Diego when he retires. I hope we're given the opportunity if only cancer will leave him alone. I sent a prayer out into the universe.

David made plans for us all to have dinner with his brother and family that night. We stopped back in the apartment to freshen up. Just before we were about to leave, David opened a box he had brought with him from New York. Inside lay a *mezuzah*, a Jewish decorative vessel, which holds a prayer called the *Shema* and is nailed or glued onto the doorway entrance of homes and rooms within a house. He opened it up and gasped. The ceramic *mezuzah* had broken in two. He started crying, saying his wife had picked this out and he wanted to hang it up.

"You can glue it back together," I said, giving him a hug.

"Yes, it's a clean break," Leigh said and rubbed David's back reassuringly.

He continued to cry. It was the first time I had seen him really break down. I gave him another hug, and he just cried in my embrace until he was emptied of his sadness. I was on my tippy toes; I'm five-foot-one in a modest heel. David is over six feet, but I stretched, giving him the support he needed through his sadness. I felt so heartbroken for my friend. Then all of a sudden, I felt scared. *Please don't let this be a window into my future of losing my husband. I've seen how hard this has been for Delilah and David.*

They have become walking-wounded spouses, halved

from happy and whole marriages. David's wife died just two weeks before Delilah's husband died. I couldn't miss the obviousness of an unknown lesson shining like a flashlight into my eyes. I thought maybe they would date at some point in the future, but knew they really weren't each other's type. *B'shert* wasn't bringing them together. I trusted time would reveal the lesson, but it unnerved me. I don't want to need their help or experience of losing a spouse. *Please God, let me be the helper. Please, I'm good at this.* Leigh looked into my eyes. She saw my fear. I know it.

David said he needed a few minutes to get himself together before we left to meet his brother. Leigh and I patiently waited in the living room for our friend, both moved and saddened by what had just happened. We drove over to his brother's home, trying to cheer him up. The convertible top was down, and the radio was turned up loud, as the evening sky painted a picture of pinks and oranges as the sun began to set.

David didn't forewarn us of the grandeur of his brother's house. We pulled up, and his brother met us in the driveway. David introduced us, and we all went inside to greet his sister-in-law and nephew. We gladly accepted a tour of this spectacular home, which was spacious and beautifully decorated. We then walked outside where an infinity pool and a large patio were overlooking lush green foliage. I was in awe!

We decided to eat in Old Town for dinner and walked around the shops. David's brother and family were friendly and so easy to talk with. His sister-in-law is from Taiwan, and I asked if she had ever played mah jongg. She did play, but she played the Chinese version where they don't use a card. I invited her to join our game the next time she was in New York to see David. She accepted my invitation months later on a visit to Long Island when she did indeed join our game.

On our last day in San Diego, David and I showed Leigh a lot of the popular San Diego tourist attractions. We visited Balboa Park, the San Diego Zoo, and Seaport Village, and we took a picture at the famous Unconditional Surrender statue, which recreates the famous embrace between a sailor and a nurse, celebrating the end of World War II. We drove to the beautiful seaside town of La Jolla and walked down by the cliffs to watch the sea lions. Leigh loved all the places we showed her. We had dinner in town and headed back to David's apartment to pack our luggage. We needed to leave at 9:00 a.m. the next morning for Malibu and Campowerment. After packing, we sat in the windowed living room, the lights of San Diego illuminating the night as we talked, lounging on the cozy living room furniture as we enjoyed the ease of our friendship.

In the morning, we had a decadent breakfast at a local breakfast spot across the street from where David lived, then strategically loaded the luggage back into the car. Coffee consumed, bellies full, and our hearts filled with friendship and fun San Diego memories, Leigh and I hugged David good-bye and thanked him for his California hospitality. We posed for one last selfie with him, and then he took a picture of us sitting in the BMW convertible, turning back toward him with both of our hands joined, forming a heart. We started our drive back up north with the top down and the radio playing, our hair secured for the windy drive. We were off! Two New Yorkers heading to Malibu to go to camp for the next four days. We were stoked and ready for adventure!

Campowerment

We arrived a few minutes late to check-in. We had turned onto the road leading up the mountain to where the camp was held. As we drove a few miles up the mountain, the double-lane road became a single-lane road. I knew something wasn't right. I was driving no more than twenty miles an hour because there were no side rails on that road! I was terrified of driving off the mountain to our untimely deaths. We apparently missed the turnoff for camp. We decided to turn around, figuring out the camp was definitely not up there. I found a wide enough patch of road to turn around on and asked Leigh if she would mind driving the rest of the way down. We slowly and cautiously headed back down the mountain. This time we had eagle eyes, searching for the sign leading to the camp.

Leigh pointed to the right. "There it is!"

"Thank God!" I exclaimed.

We turned onto the road leading to the camp. Leigh parked the car, we unloaded our luggage, and I pressed the button to bring the top of the car out of its hiding place, fitting snuggly back onto the windshield and windows. We checked in, schmoozed, had a snack then brought our luggage to our bunk. Remember, I have not been to camp as a child. I am familiar with the term "bunk," but I have not ever officially slept in one. Leigh had gone to sleep-away camp for four years as a child and had more of an understanding of camp life. We cheerfully wheeled our luggage over to Bunk 8, our home for the next three nights. We opened the door. I was slightly shocked. Ok, more than slightly. There were six wooden bunk beds filling the room. There was an egg crate, sheets, and blanket on each bed. A pillow and pillowcase were there for us campers, too. I tried to appear enthusiastic, but this was far from my comfort level, although it was clearly written in the camp's lodging description.

The closest I had ever gotten to camp or camping was staying in my mother's trailer with her. I made a deal with myself. This was only three nights, and I would be able to check "sleeping in a bunk" off my bucket list. Actually, "sleeping in a bunk" would never make my bucket list; scratch that. I decided to reframe and began to look at this as part of the Campowerment experience, offering campers the opportunity to challenge themselves. I was ready for the bunk challenge! *I will make the most of it*, I decided. I also decided, from this day forward, I would choose lodging with no more than two queen beds in a room and a private bathroom.

Come to think of it, where was the bathroom? I stepped out from the bunk and saw the sign "bathroom" on the building next door. I didn't know what to expect. I walked in curiously. There was a ten-foot-wide mirror with a counter underneath for putting on makeup, blow drying hair, or any other beautifying technique requiring reflection. There were ten toilet stalls, luckily with doors, so there was some privacy offered. There were four showers and a common area to dry off. *I'll deal with that when I need to,* I assured myself.

I went back to the bunk and made my bed. I could feel the thin mattress under my knees as I opened the egg crate and laid it on top the mattress. Then I put the fitted sheet on. I covered the pillow with the pillowcase and looked at the bed that I would sleep in for the next three nights. I smiled. *I can do this!* Leigh and I met some of our bunkmates who were from all over the country. They all seemed like very nice women, and we were all excited for our Campowerment experience to officially begin.

Campers were asked to meet by the open area near the mess hall at 5:00 p.m. When the time came, all one hundred twenty campers gathered there. There was wine, water, iced tea, and light munchies available, and we started socializing and introducing ourselves to one another. I learned some women were here for their second or third time. After fifteen minutes, we were lined up in two rows, one row facing the other. We were about to do an icebreaker game. *No sweat,* I thought, *I do this in my religious school class. This should be fun!* We were instructed to step forward, facing the stranger in front of us, say our name and then say one thing we are embarrassed about. *Whoa . . . what? I don't do personally-revealing icebreakers like this in my class!*

I stepped forward, looked into this woman's eyes and said, "Hi, I'm Fern. I get gassy sometimes." I stepped back to my space.

The stranger stepped forward and said, "Hi. I'm Cindy, and I pick my nose."

I nodded my head to her, accepting her shame as she did mine. I did not expect this type of icebreaker. Ugh, what would the next question be? We were told to shift one space to the left, so we now faced a new camper. We were instructed to say our name and reveal something that makes us proud of ourselves. Now that's more my speed.

I stepped forward with more confidence this time, smiled, and said, "Hi, my name is Fern. I think I'm a good teacher, and I'm proud to teach yoga and Judaism to children."

I stepped back in place.

The stranger stepped forward. She said, "Hi, I'm Joanna. I'm proud of my parenting." This went on for about fifteen minutes. We stepped to the left each time to meet a new fellow camper and exposed something new about ourselves with each question.

After we finished the icebreaker game, we headed to the mess hall to eat. It was buffet style, and I was impressed that they accommodated all eating styles: vegan, vegetarian, lactose-free, gluten-free—you name it. We met fellow campers at our table as we ate and schmoozed. Dinner was delicious and far better than I thought it would be.

I noticed the sun setting and stepped outside to take in this magnificent mountaintop view. The Pacific Ocean was below us; the greyish blue color of the water was broken at the horizon with shades of fiery orange, yellow and pink. The clouds added texture to the sky art I was viewing. The colors melded and blended as the sun finally slipped below the horizon ushering in the evening sky. I was in awe at this magical view in Malibu.

After dinner, we were instructed to go to the elective of our choice, and I picked an interesting-sounding course with a body language expert. She was phenomenal. She had worked as a federal law enforcement officer in the Justice Department and had conducted hostage negotiations. Wowza! This woman was the real deal and taught us very interesting and informative things about body language. She showed us a few poses and explained what they meant. She went over eye contact, explaining if someone looks away when asked a question what the direction of up, down, left, and right each meant. I picked a great elective, and I would retake classes with this dynamic teacher; I was enthralled with the subject, along with her delivery and vivacious personality.

Bunks and Bedtime

Then it was time to go back to the bunks and get ready for bed. This process was nothing like it is at home in my private bedroom and private bathroom on Long Island. I grabbed my toothbrush, toothpaste, facial cleanser, towel, and pajamas. I went into the bathroom stall and changed into my PJs. I'm just not into communal changing with strangers. That's just strange to me. I washed off my makeup, used a baby wipe to remove the remaining black mascara which refused to wash away, brushed my teeth, and put on my moisturizer. I walked back into the bunk, just as some of my bunkmates were changing into their pajamas as well. I admire women who are comfortable with their bodies and can change in front of other women. I'm not on that list and don't know if I ever will be.

Leigh was in the bunk and came over and asked, "How was your elective class?"

"It was fascinating," I grinned, ready to burst out laughing because I was a little uncomfortable with the women changing around me. "How was yours?"

"Great, I really liked it, too!" She sensed my discomfort. "So, I went to sleep-away camp for four years, and this is just the way it is. You kinda get used to it. Feel free to change in the bathroom if it makes you more comfortable."

I winked at her, signaling that's exactly what I just did. We hugged goodnight and climbed into our separate bunks. I got under the blanket. As the sun sets in Malibu, it gets chilly, about twenty degrees cooler at night. I realized there was no heat in the bunks. I began to shiver. Someone left the small window open near my bunk bed. I got up and closed the window quietly. I put on a sweatshirt and socks. Next, I pondered the question of how the hell do ten women get to sleep in the same room? We're women; women are chatty. This is preposterous! This was neither my norm nor the way I function comfortably. I reminded myself I chose a fiftieth birthday adventure that would have me step outside of my comfort zone. I realized I had accomplished that first with the icebreaker game, then the changing of clothing, and now by trying to get to sleep. Somehow the chatter quieted. I was so thankful. We were all tired and decided it was time to turn the lights off. I discovered there wasn't great phone service on the mountain, and I couldn't connect to the Internet, so I decided to lie there and look at the old and tattered mattress above me. I tried to think happy thoughts and started counting backward from one hundred and finally somewhere around ten I must have fallen asleep despite feeling cold and a little uncomfortable.

At 6:00 a.m. the bunk woke up to someone's phone alarm. The unknown camper turned it off and went back to sleep. I'm a very light sleeper and couldn't get back to sleep. Then the alarm went off a second time a few minutes later. She turned it off again, but stayed in bed. I lay awake in my cold bed, wrapped tightly in my thin blanket, on my thin mattress, on this wooden bunk. Then the alarm went off for the third time.

Someone spoke out, "Please, either get up or turn your damn alarm off. We don't all want to get up at 6:00 a.m!"

I thought, *You go, girl! How inconsiderate of that woman to wake us all up!* Someone from the top bunk on the other side of the room apologized to us all then went back to sleep. Really? I finally got out of bed, found my slippers, and stepped out into the chilly morning. I went to the bathroom and changed into sweats, put on a bra and put my sweatshirt back on, brushed my teeth, and headed to the mess hall for some much-needed coffee. One of the comforts of home that the camp did have for me was French vanilla creamer. I stopped in a store in Malibu to pick up a bottle just in case it wasn't available at camp, but they had their bases covered. I added my bottle to the fridge to share with the other campers. I took my delicious hot cup of coffee and stepped outside to where I watched the sunset last night.

The morning view was breathtaking. The mountain-top was enveloped in a blanket of white mist. I couldn't see the ocean as the mist rose in smoky swirls up the mountain. It was mystical the way the fog slowly glided along with the wind. I felt like I was on a holy mountaintop where an angel was about to present herself to me.

Instead, a camper walked up to me and asked, "Isn't this amazing?"

It was, indeed. We introduced ourselves, shared where we were from and talked about how we found and decided to come to Campowerment. After a few minutes of exchanging pleasantries, she left me to admire the view in solitude. I watched as the mist, oblivious to the rising sun, slowly burned away revealing the world below to us, the women-mountain-campers who were hungry for personal growth, fun, adventure, and the nurturing of their souls. We all have mists that cover our true selves. I was hoping to burn away some of my own and uncover something hidden in myself while here at Campowerment.

Covert Cleanliness

I walked back to the bunk and decided to take a shower. I wondered to myself, *what's the likelihood that four showers would be enough for twenty women sharing them?* First, I had to systematically figure out how to get into my towel wrap, which is just like a sleeveless robe. I decided to take off my sweats and sweatshirt, leaving on my bra and panties and then put on my wrap. It's just like being in a bikini on the beach, except I don't actually wear bikinis. I fastened the Velcro closed. Step one complete. I wiggled out of my undies and put them in my dirty clothes bag. I couldn't figure out how to get out of my bra without taking the wrap off and now that my undies were off that was not happening. I decided to take it off in the shower. Next, I gathered my personal cleaning and beauty supplies: shampoo, conditioner, razor, soap, make-up, hairbrushes, hair dryer, flip-flops, and towel. I couldn't carry all these necessities and decided to put them all in my tote. Better grab my new undies to put on after I shower, too.

It was time to find out how the bathroom functioned with so many women. It was a busy place, indeed! Hair dryers were blowing and makeup was being applied as chatter filled the mirrored area. By good fortune one shower stall was unoccupied. I hung my towel outside the shower stall but wore my wrap inside. Modesty is my motto on this mountaintop. I disrobed in private. As I turned on the shower, I hoped for decent water pressure with so many showers, toilets, and sinks being used simultaneously. Decent it was!

I lathered my head with sudsy shampoo. I finished showering and turned off the water. I opened the shower stall door just enough for my arm to fit out and reach for my prize: the towel. I felt around for it, but my fingers didn't find it. I froze. I needed my towel, but didn't want to step out of the shower stall to search for it. I poked my head out of the stall to look for my missing towel. I glanced down and saw it lying on the wet ground. Thank God! Relief washed over my just-cleaned body. I bent down with the door open just enough for me to grab the towel that had fallen.

Once dry inside the shower stall, I put my bra and undies on, put the wrap back on over them, and joined the women at the mirror. I said good morning to my fellow campers around me and got to work beautifying myself. I wore the towel turban-style, keeping my hair damp while

I applied my makeup. After applying foundation, powder, and blush to my fair skin, I put on mascara and a little liner to bring out my baby blues. I dabbed some shiny clear lip gloss on my lips. I blow-dried my hair and headed back to the bunk to get dressed. The bunk was busy with activity. I picked out my clothes for the day and slid my leggings on under my wrap, then took off the wrap and put on my shirt. I slipped my feet into a pair of flip-flops, then hung the wrap in my cubby and thought to myself, *That was a challenge, but also a success!*

Leigh came into the bunk, and we said good morning. She asked, "Did you see the mist? Oh my God, it was amazing! I took some great pictures."

"Yes, it was amazing! How'd you sleep? I was really cold," I whined. Then I whispered, "What's with the alarm going off at 6:00 a.m. three times in a row this morning?"

"I know, that was rude and inconsiderate, but somebody said something, so hopefully she won't do it tomorrow. Let's go eat breakfast and look at our workshop options," Leigh said.

The Sisterhood of Campowerment

We had breakfast, chatted with our bunkmates, and picked our workshops. There was a breakout session by alphabetical groupings that we went to first. We learned about the history of Campowerment then went around the room to introduce ourselves and said why we chose to come here.

When it was my turn, I said, "Hi, I'm Fern, and I'm from Long Island. I'm turning fifty next month, and Campowerment is my birthday present to myself. I have three sons, ages twenty, nineteen, and twelve. My husband has been diagnosed with non-Hodgkin's lymphoma. He has nine cancerous lesions throughout his body. His cancer is treatable but not necessarily curable, and I'm hoping to dig deep while I'm here and face some fears, including the possibility that cancer may . . . change my life permanently." There, I said it out loud for the first time. Funny though, I said it to a group of strangers, women I didn't even know.

Over the next few days, I took courses in nutrition, body language (I loved this class and took it three times), yoga, spirituality, mindfulness and meditation, and journaling with Grandy, the camp founder's adorable mom. She is a powerhouse of wisdom and cuteness wrapped up in one. There were so many memorable and fun activities besides the courses. There was a dress-up dance night where each bunk picked a song and created a skit or choreographed dance moves to go along with it. Some of the costumes were hilarious and over-the-top, and there was a chest filled with neon-colored wigs, feather boas, sunglasses, and Mardi Gras beads to accessorize any costume. I dressed as Snow White and Leigh dressed as a penguin. Our bunk chose "Love Shack" by the B-52's. We had so much fun singing and being silly!

There was also a color war, which had guest appearances

from Jenna Bush Hager and Natalie Morales from NBC's the *Today* show. They were doing a segment on Campowerment and came by to film. We dressed up in orange or green, depending on our team color. We added war paint on our faces, wore bandanas, and added colored ribbon delineating our warrior color. We practiced growling techniques and looking warrior-like to stand off against the opposing team. Then we played silly games: a mummy toilet paper wrap, tug of war, a whipped cream pie-eating contest with gummy worms mixed in for an added gross effect, and a stuffed animal relay game where we were lined up in two rows descending about thirty stairs. We raced the stuffed animals from the first person standing at the top stair to the last person at the bottom stair. It was all a lot of fun, and the games created camaraderie between the women on each team.

My favorite activity was the evening drumming circle. This was a very moving and spiritual experience for me. We all sat around a huge campfire. Each chair had a drum under it. The phenomenal percussionist started drumming as her accompanying musicians played a rhythmic beat. She had us drum along with her and then had us begin to chant. It was so amazing! We did this for about an hour, and I didn't want it to end. Some of the campers started dancing by the fire as the music played, the drummer drummed, and we chanted to the rhythmic beat they created. It was totally tribal. We were women-warriors, chanting around a campfire, drumming in unison, searching for self-discovery on a mountaintop in Malibu.

On the day we were leaving camp, we had break-fast and then joined in an emotional closing ceremony. We then all hugged good-bye, exchanged phone numbers and connected on social media with those we wanted to keep in touch with. Leigh and I were now part of another sisterhood, the sisterhood of Campowerment. I chose a fabulous fiftieth birthday gift. I did grow. I did dig deep. I faced my fear and needed to fly my resolve back to New York with me. And . . . I made it through three nights in the bunk! Campowerment was a wonderful gift I gave to myself. I was armed, ready, and excited to be my best version of "fabulous fifty."

Chapter 9

Phyllis

My friendship with David led to yet another meaningful relationship and mah jongg connection. On a summer day in July of 2017, I was driving in his townhouse community to discuss business; that is, his dating business on Match .com. As I was driving away from the guardhouse, I thought I saw my first cousin crossing the street. Instinctually, I waved hello but didn't stop to talk, not being 100 percent sure that it was her since I hadn't seen her in many years.

I parked at David's house, and the first thing I said was, "Oh my God, you won't believe who I just saw!"

He looked excited for me, but was clueless as to whom I was referring.

"My cousin, Phyllis! David, she lives *here* in your townhouse community!"

He asked, "Did you two speak when you saw her?"

"No," I answered with immense regret. I felt like I had been given a free raffle ticket and just threw it away not knowing if I had won something special. This was *special* to me. My immediate family is extremely small, which makes me extremely sad. My extended family isn't much bigger. My mother was an only child, and my father had one sister, who was Phyllis's mother. We hardly ever saw my aunt, uncle, and cousins as children growing up, and the last time I saw her was about fifteen years ago. I barely remember much about her as a child. We were in just a few pictures together as children, and I have only one where I was maybe eight years old, she about eleven or twelve, and we were on the beach in Greenport. What was the likelihood that my cousin lived in the same development as David and walked by my car at that *exact* moment in time? This was *b'shert.*

We decided I should call her. David looked up her phone number online, and I wrote it down on a piece of paper and decided I would call her later in the day. In the meantime, David proceeded to show me his new love interests on Match.com. It was a good diversion to help me reel my mind back in after this chance encounter.

I did call my cousin later that night. I was a little nervous as the phone rang. On her end, my cell number would show up and be meaningless to her. After four rings an answering machine picked up.

I left a message, "Hi, Phyllis, this is your cousin, Fern. I think I saw you earlier today in your development, and I waved hello. I know it's been a while since we have spoken or saw each other, but I would love to talk or get together for coffee or lunch."

I left my phone number and hung up the phone, wondering if I would hear back from her.

The following day, she did indeed call back, and we made plans to meet for lunch a few days later. We met at my favorite diner and spoke for over two hours. Phyllis has short ash blond hair and our family's signature blue eyes and petite stature. My grandmother was at least a few inches less than five feet tall. She showed me pictures of her husband and two children. Phyllis's dad still worked part-time teaching at a local university. I saw pictures of him, her brother and his family as well. She told me about her work and hobbies, and where her kids attended college. I knew her mom had died about five years earlier. I tried to recall the last time I saw my aunt, and I realized that it was at my grandmother's funeral twenty years earlier. Phyllis also asked about my parents. I thought I might have seen a hint of a twinkle in her eye when she asked about my dad. I told her my mom had died about nine years ago and filled her in on my father and his colorful life.

I shared my life with her next. I told her about my part-time work teaching fourth graders in my temple's religious school and yoga to preschoolers. I shared pictures, too, and told her about my husband and three children; my two oldest children are almost the same ages as her two children. I felt sad knowing our children had passed each other in the halls of the same school yet never knew each other or even what their cousins looked like. I knew they were in the same school because of a crazy twist of fate: Leigh's daughter dated Phyllis's son for over a year! When Leigh told me this a few years ago when the two started dating, I was surprised and asked what he looked like and what type of personality he had. I felt sad knowing about him only through my friend. But here we were, having lunch and reconnecting.

As our fifteen-year catch-up lunch came to a close, she said, "Let's move on from whatever has happened in the past." I processed her words and nodded my agreement, although I wasn't aware of anything that had happened between us. I thought her parents' disdain for my father had just kept the families apart. Perhaps, since our parents didn't foster a bond, we as children weren't offered an opportunity to foster a cousin bond either. As adults, we had a very limited history and sense of family connection. I was hopeful that we would stay in touch and change the negativity that plagued our families in the past. I'm glad that I took a chance and called her, and it seemed like we were both interested in building a relationship without letting the past get in the way.

B'shert created our chance encounter. My wave hello and phone call started a new family relationship for both of us. Before we left the diner, I asked Phyllis, "Do you play mah jongg?"

"I've been playing for about ten years," she replied. "With my work schedule, I can only play at night."

No problem, I've got that option covered, I thought to myself.

"I play too. Maybe we will play together one night," I said as I smiled.

B'shert and mah jongg. Those two words were creating another beautiful spark in my life. As I drove home with a smile on my face, warmth and connection filled my heart. I silently thanked David and his wife for their involvement, unbeknownst to either of them here on earth or up in heaven, for helping me reconnect with my cousin. I decided as I pulled into my driveway that I would call Phyllis and ask her to join my night game. *Wait till I tell my father this story!*

Night Games and DJ Len

Group text: Leigh, Amanda, Rose, and Phyllis
Me: Hey ladies! Monday is a night game. I'll host 7:00 p.m. Who's in?
Amanda: I'll be there!
Leigh: Me too!
Rose: Me three!
Phyllis: See you all then, looking forward!
Me: Awesome, see everyone then!

It was late August and the nights were finally cooling down as the humidity and temperatures were starting to give way to the cooler, crisper weather that September ushers in. Tonight, we were playing in the mah jongg/meditation room. This room is on the main floor. It is the lower level of a turret, which is circular. It was initially intended to be Len's office, so we decorated it with some Russian flair. The blue and gold wallpaper we chose was inspired from visits to Russian restaurants where we've dined in Brooklyn with his parents. The window treatments covering the four windows of the turret are blue linen, fabric from one of Len's linen lines, and trimmed with golden tassels and beads. I've read that the Chinese word "mah" in mah jongg means flax plant. I love this connection, as the linen fabric Len sells is made from the flax plant.

The office was rarely used, and once I started to play mah jongg, I thought it would be a great space to play, especially for night games. I decided to rearrange the desk and bookcase and created a beautiful Zen-infused room. I added Buddha statues on the floor, scattered battery-powered faux candles around the perimeter of the room, along with a Himalayan salt lamp. I arranged four yellow velveteen floor pillows around a small golden metal table topped with a candle and gemstones in the center of the room for the times I meditate here. A two-foot-tall chubby Buddha with his hands up in the air, palms open to the sky, and wearing an infectious smile welcomes guests as they pass through the French doors.

It was time to start my mah jongg hosting ritual. I slid the pillows and golden table to the side and set up the round mah jongg table and chairs. I placed four racks around the table and spilled out the tiles. The sound of mah jongg, an echo from a distant Chinese past, was alive again, here at my mah jongg table in Long Island. I turned the tiles face down, mixed them, and stacked a double-tiered wall along each awaiting rack. I brought in my iPad and a Bluetooth speaker and put on the Chill station from Sirius XM. I turned on the Himalayan salt lamp hoping it would clear away any negative energy. I added a few drops of lavender oil to a diffuser adding its calming effect into the air. I turned on the battery-powered candles creating a Zen-infused atmosphere for my ladies. I set up snacks and drinks on the kitchen table. It was mah jongg time!

I was excited for my first night game with my cousin. I filled in Leigh, Rose, and Amanda about my reconnection with Phyllis and conferred with them about her joining our night games. Leigh, of course, remembered Phyllis from when their kids dated in high school. Jewish geography linked Amanda and Phyllis, as they were both members of the same Hadassah chapter and have known each other for years. Rose hadn't met her, but everyone was agreeable to the new addition and playing with five was always safer in case someone couldn't make it. By now, Sarah had started working full-time and occasionally played if she had a Monday off. Delilah didn't play in our night games as she had mothering and driving obligations due to her daughter's extracurricular activities.

The four girls arrived around 7:00 p.m. We greeted each other, and I introduced Rose to Phyllis. We each chose a chair, placed our cards in front of our racks, and settled in. I was East for the first game. Rose offered to sit out the first game and chose not to be the bettor but instead sat with me since we had five players. I rolled the dice, broke the wall, and started to deal. We racked our tiles and started to group suits and numbers together. We chatted as we passed our tiles through the Charleston. Phyllis and Leigh caught each other up on their kids. As I listened to them speak, I still felt their children dating for over a year back in high school was a coincidental and mystical connection.

Back at my rack, I was hoping for a connection between my tiles and a hand. The tiles were pointing me toward Lucky 13. As I've played over the past five years, certain mah jongg tiles and hands have a deeper meaning for me. I see not only with my eyesight but also with my insight. This particular hand, Lucky 13, although a paradox, shows how an unlucky number like thirteen can create a winning hand.

At around 8:30 p.m., Len and Alex arrived home from a long day of work. I was excited to reintroduce Len and the boys to my cousin since they had met only once. Len came in to greet the ladies and kissed me hello. I'd left the guys dinner in the kitchen; playing in this room gives them some privacy to eat and unwind.

Shortly after, our background music mysteriously changed, and "Unexpected Lovers" by Lime started playing from the speaker. We all looked around the room, wondering what had happened. Unbeknownst to me, Len synced his iPhone to the speaker I had in the mah jongg/meditation room. Then "Babe We're Gonna Love Tonight" by Lime came on. We liked his choices and cheered from our room. Next was "Turn Me Loose," and we sang the chorus along with Lover Boy. Then Len appeared in the hallway moonwalking to "Dirty Diana" by Michael Jackson. He can be such a character! "Party Train" came on next as Len passed the French doors, pulling an imaginary train whistle bobbing his head like a chicken.

DJ Len was in the house, ladies! We laughed at his antics. He kept such a positive attitude despite the fact that by then he had twelve cancerous lesions slowly growing within his body. I wanted to believe in luck, not only in my mah jongg games but also for my husband whose battle with cancer was about to take a new turn.

Options

We did a great deal of research while the cancer was indolent and decided to hold off starting chemotherapy as long as possible. We watched cancer documentaries, learning about the history of cancer, Big Pharma, and the destruction chemo can do to the body despite its ability to kill cancer cells. I found two naturopathic clinics, one in Florida and the other in Arizona, and Len decided to visit both in person. This was such an important decision, both because his life depended on it and the fact that it would be an out-of-pocket expense.

After much consideration, Len decided on the clinic in Arizona. I found him lodging in Scottsdale, and he was set for what we hoped would be a non-toxic treatment plan to help his body fight the cancer naturally and bring him to remission. He was scheduled to begin ten weeks of treatment in December 2017, two months after Gabriel's *bar mitzvah*.

Bar Mitzvah

Becoming a *bar* or *bat mitzvah* is a milestone in a Jewish child's upbringing. Long Island has its own high standard for some over-the-top parties after a meaningful and dignified temple service, ushering young Jewish boys and girls into adulthood. (Of course, no twelve- or thirteen-year-old is technically an adult by today's standards, but it must have been the case thousands of years ago when life spans were about forty.) Many Long Islanders like to choose elaborate venues. DJs are hired, along with a florist or decorating company, photographer, photo booth, video gaming area, and perhaps temporary tattoo artists to add extra fun for the guests. I've been to *mitzvah* parties with elaborate ice sculptures, stilt walkers, electric violinists, and artists with the amazing ability to contort their bodies. The list is endless. Photo montages are put together, beautiful dresses and expensive suits are purchased, nails and hair are professionally done, and speeches are prepared. My childhood *bat mitzvah* party was simple and nice, nothing elaborate or extravagant. How times have changed!

For my older boys, Len and I had modest parties to celebrate each boy becoming a *bar mitzvah*. For Gabriel, we took it up a few notches. Len felt the cost of the typical *bar* or *bat mitzvah* party was like taking a new Mercedes and driving it off a cliff. We decided instead to drive a Mazda off a cliff when on October 17, 2017, Gabriel became a *bar mitzvah*.

There is a lot of preparation for a *bar mitzvah* student to lead the Saturday morning service. He prepared for his special day with our beloved Cantor Sarene for six months. He practiced Hebrew prayers, songs, and his *Torah* portion dutifully for those six months. The cantor audiotaped everything he needed to practice. Just about every day for those six months Gabriel and I practiced together until he could practice alone and stand on his own two Jewish feet in confidence.

He was ready when the big day came. He led the service like a pro. He has no stage fright, which amazes me. He is a natural up on the *bimah* (a raised platform in the synagogue from which the Torah is read), making eye contact with friends and family as he led us through the service and into his Jewish manhood. I sat in the front row beaming. This is my youngest son, my last child, and my final display of physical love, which created this amazing human being. Gabriel and I are extremely close. We have our own rhythm and unspoken language.

It was almost time for the speeches, everyone's favorite part of the service. Many guests and family members are brought to tears by the heartfelt sentiments of mothers, fathers, and grandparents spoken to their child or grand-child. I was hoping my voice wouldn't shake as I spoke. Public speaking unnerves me to my core.

The rabbi called Len and me up to the *bimah* to pass the *Torah* to Gabriel and to say our speeches and bless-ings to him. Len went first. We decided not to share our speeches until we read them that day. As I listened to Len saying loving words to our son, my mind wandered for a few moments. I feel very close to God on the *bimah*. I am so close to the ark and the *Torahs* that rest in that holy space. Gabriel was holding a small *Torah* that Len had just passed to him. This small *Torah* was saved from destruction during the Holocaust. I thought of what would be happening in six weeks. Len would be leaving our family and moving to Arizona for almost three months to start naturopathic treatment for the cancer that is living like a parasite within his handsome body. I looked at them both, my loves, my family, my everything.

The rabbi turned to me and handed me the *Torah*. She knew how nervous I was speaking in public. She smiled reassuringly at me. I knew all eyes were on us. I was wearing a French couture dress in my favorite color of royal purple with navy blue tulle swirling from the sides and back of the dress, cascading to the floor. The dress was on sale, but still more than I have ever spent on any article of clothing in my life. It cost more than my wedding dress! I was wearing high-heeled shoes dyed to match the dress. They were uncomfortable but looked good with the dress, and I also needed the added height. I decided my feet could suffer for a few hours in honor of fashion. As I stood in front of Gabriel, I noticed we were the same height. I knew this would change in a matter of time as he lives in the last few months of boyhood. I was nervous speaking in public, but I knew I could do this. I lovingly handed the *Torah* to Gabriel. I took a deep breath and began. I prayed I would speak calmly so he could hear the words that I so deeply felt and was about to express openly to him.

I started speaking while looking into his eyes as I gazed up at him from the sheets of my speech, "Gabriel, I'm starting before my blessing to you with a question. What does your name mean? Gabriel in Hebrew means: God is my strength. It is the name of the Archangel Gabriel who sits at the front of God's throne. Your name is both heavenly and earthly. I would like to talk to you about your name's earthly and personal meaning to me. Gabriel, you are my son, my love, and my angel. I believe you possess some angelic characteristics that I want to share with you. Like an angel, you look past the surface and see the potential and goodness within each person. You let your inner light shine, and you bring that light to the darkness in a situation, always finding something positive to focus on. You often say to me if you sense I'm upset or stressed, 'Well at least we have each other Mom, always you and me.' The essence of an angel is love, and you, my son, emanate love through your eyes, your heart, your words, and your deeds.

"Now I want to share with you some things I want you to remember in life. I am both your mother and your friend. I am here for you when you are happy or sad, good or not so good, joyful or sad. I'll always share your joys and sorrows, encourage and guide you and care enough to always tell you the truth. I am your helping hand. I helped you learn how to use a cup, fork, and spoon as a toddler and helped guide you up the slide, waiting with open arms at the bottom, seeing your smiling face filled with wonder and excitement. I have helped you in school with projects and studying for tests, and I have helped you prepare for this special day, as you become a *bar mitzvah*. Remember, my hands are always here for you, and that you can always count on me to help you, with open arms.

"I am your protector. I'm always in your corner, ready to help you to take on the world. Sometimes, I need to take out my motherly boxing gloves. I'll swing gently or use my one-two punch technique when needed. I'll teach you how to use your own pair of boxing gloves with consciousness and righteousness.

"I am your safe place. When you fall or fail, or are

hurting, come to me. I'll always have my arms open for you. I hope to help you turn your wounds into wisdom and to see the lesson in difficult experiences. I want you to always remember to let your faith be stronger than your fear.

"I am your confidant. Whether you are proud of yourself and want to boast or feel ashamed and need to confess a mistake, I'm here to listen, not to judge, but to understand with an open heart and an open mind.

"I am your cheerleader. When you try, I'll root you on. When you succeed, I'll cheer until my voice is hoarse. When you fail or falter, I'll hug you close and whisper in your ear, 'One more time, Gabriel—never give up.'

"I am your example. I'll respect you, so you will learn to respect. I'll listen to you, so you learn to listen. I'll forgive, so you learn to forgive. I'll show compassion, so you'll learn to be kind. I'll be honest, so you'll learn to tell the truth. I'll love you with all my heart, so you will know how to love someone deeply. I'm your parent, but know I'm far from perfect. When I'm wrong, I'll admit it. When I'm hurting, I'll let you help. When I'm struggling, I won't pretend everything is okay. I'll be real, so I can teach you to be real, and we can have a real relationship.

"As long as I'm alive, you'll always have arms ready to hug you, ears ready to listen to you, and a heart that will never stop loving you. You are a gift that forever changed my life, and I am forever grateful to have been chosen to give you the gift of life. Gabriel, my angel, I am so proud of you today and every day."

I finished. I made it all the way through without gulping for air or freezing mid-sentence. I looked out into the sanctuary. I saw tissues blotting carefully made-up eyes and fingers wiping away tears, but the biggest emotional response came from Gabriel. As I looked away from the congregation and back into my son's eyes, I was reminded he has the same greenish-brown eye color as his father. Len's DNA shines out into the world through Gabriel's beautiful eyes. Then Gabriel stepped up to me and hugged and squeezed me tighter than he has ever hugged me before. He didn't let go. He heard every word and took each one in, first into his mind and then letting them settle into his heart. As he hugged me, he whispered in my ear how much he loved me. I was overwhelmed by this holy moment on the *bimah*. This was what a *bar mitzvah* is all about to me—my son leading us in prayer, and loving words expressed in front of family, friends, clergy, and God. Maybe Gabriel just did become a Jewish adult. He has never hugged me like this before. *Todah rabah*, thank you, God, for this beautiful and splendid moment in time.

After the service, we drove five minutes to Jewel where we had our party and luncheon. It is one of the most beautiful restaurants on Long Island. The glass-enclosed entrance has huge vases filled with silk flowers next to lighted fountains of water. All the trees in front of the restaurant are decorated with thousands of white mini lights, which at night look like a winter wonderland even in summer. The entrance walls are floor to ceiling glass windows. A blue tile waterfall-wall backs the expansive bar. Lamps bolted to the ceiling unexpectedly hang upside down to the left of the bar over tables and chairs. Multi-sized bulbous glass light fixtures hang from different lengths looking like glass balloons suspended above the tables. Heavy multi-layered carved wood wraps around the perimeter of the back of the restaurant where it meets up with the waterfall-wall. We decorated all the tables with large table lamps with personalized lampshades displaying Gabriel's initials. The clear glass lamps were filled with colored water, and strands of clear glass beads hung from the rim of the glass. Votive candles and pictures of Gabriel were placed on each table.

We sectioned off a portion of the restaurant for the kids. There was a gaming station and photo booth area for their enjoyment. There were two temporary tattoo artists adorning the arms of the kids. We had a DJ and MC, but our intention was more for background music and a few dance floor games for the children to interact in. We don't like loud music at parties. We wanted our guests to be able to have conversations with each other and not have sore throats from having to talk over the music. People schmoozed, ate, and drank. Both grandfathers cut the *challah* and said the *motzi* just like my grandfather did at my *bat mitzvah*. Gabriel and his friends had fun. Len and I celebrated with our family and friends. It was perfect for us. After the party ended, we were happy we only drove a Mazda off a cliff for four hours of celebrating our son becoming a *bar mitzvah*.

Greenport with Grandma Esther and my brother.

Me driving the boat with my brother water skiing.

Me fishing in Greenport on my mother's boat.

My mom in her glory, fishing.

Len and I dating. Picture taken on a trip to Boston.

Our wedding day.

My father and I on my wedding day.

Jared's first birthday with Delilah and Robert
at the Plaza in New York City.

Len kissing his mom.

Jared and Alex fishing with mom and Len in Greenport.

Three generations: Misha, Len, and Gabriel.

Gabriel on the carousel in Greenport.

A selection of items in a care package from Len's mom, including the gloves and Russian hat.

Mah Jongg Mondays.

Sarah (left), me and Leigh,
my 'Big Idea' original Mah Jongg players.

Leigh and I at Coronado Island.
You can see David's shadow as he took the picture.

Driving with Leigh to Campowerment in Malibu.

Leigh and me hugging in the bunks at Campowerment.

*Dancing with Gabriel at the party
after his bar mitzvah service.*

*Mah jongg on the beach during our Greenport getaway.
Me (left), Delilah, Leigh and Rose.*

Paja-mah-jongg Monday. Rose (left), me, Amanda and Leigh.

Mah Jongg with Hope (left), Amanda, me and Leigh in the formal living room, a.k.a., the museum room.

My father and me. Dad is fully accessorized of course!

My writing desk and decorated cork board.

Len, Gabriel and me walking on the beach.

Chapter 10

A Holiday Game

Group text: Leigh, Rose, Delilah
Me: Hey ladies! Who's in for tomorrow's game and who's hosting?
Leigh: I'm in, and I'll host. 11:30 a.m., girls!
Delilah: Count me in!
Rose: Add me to the fun!
Me: Great! See you all tomorrow. Thanks for hosting, Leigh!

It was December and getting cold on Long Island. I settled in as I do every early winter for months and months of colorless New York days. The sun tries to burn through the thick grey clouds to reveal the true-blue that is hidden behind the murky winter sky. It appears as a dull bulbous orb, trying to break through the cloudy barrier to warm and illuminate the earth below. There are no pops of color from vibrant flowers adorning our manicured lawns. The warm colors of autumn are long lost. Any remaining leaves on the trees are brown, crisp, and lifeless. The color of evergreen shrubs and trees, as well as dormant lawns prepared for the harshness of this season in the Northeast, are the only green left. My winter eyes search for color on my drives through suburbia. I rely on the colors of man-made things: houses, cars, and the coats of those walking their dogs in the neighborhood. Nature has gone to sleep, creating a blanket of bleakness for my outside world.

Mah Jongg Mondays are a way for me to light up my inside world. Tiles etched with the colors of blue, red, green, and black excite my eyes. The bright red and green Dragons look like they are dancing on the tiles. The Flower tiles keep me in anticipation of the coming spring, and the blue Dots remind me of the never-ending cycle of seasons we experience here in New York.

We all gathered at Leigh's house on that chilly Monday morning with a wrapped gift. We exchange holiday gifts each December. As I entered her home, I could smell the scent of pine. I took a deep breath in and closed my eyes. Smell has the power like no other sense to activate our memory. For a moment I'm a young child, back in Cress-kill. For some reason never explained to me, we celebrated

Christmas even though we are Jewish. As a child receiving extra gifts after Hanukkah, I wasn't about to ask why! We had a small tree my mom called a Hanukkah bush. Each year, we would decorate it with lights, tinsel, and ornaments. We left cookies for Santa on Christmas Eve and awoke early on Christmas day excited to unwrap gifts. My favorite childhood gift was the Easy Bake Oven that I received when I was six years old, which is funny because I don't like to cook as an adult!

I smiled and opened my eyes. I was back at Leigh's house excited to play mah jongg and do our gift grab-bag. Leigh's mah jongg table and chairs were set up in the living room near the beautiful and fragrant Christmas tree. We all commented on how pretty the tree was and how good it smelled. She showed us certain ornaments and explained their significance, like the ones from the year she was married and when her children were born.

Leigh's husband is Catholic, and they decided to raise their children Jewish and have them attend religious school, but they would also observe and honor all of her husband's holidays as well. I was happy to be in someone's house that celebrated Christmas and be able to enjoy the tree and holiday decorations. December is a month of holidays and a time to reflect on religion and ritual. Hanukkah and Christmas add sparkle, light, and cheer to this month. It is also the month Alex was born, adding an extra special meaning for me personally.

We decided to do the gift grab-bag before we started

to play. We wrote our names on a piece of paper and put them in a bag. Leigh picked and called out the person's name, and she got to pick a gift on the table. This ritual added extra fun and excitement to this Mah Jongg Monday. When my name was picked, I chose a blue bag with silver tissue paper peeking out of the top. When I opened it, I was thrilled to see a gold and glass jewelry box.

Delilah said, "I brought that. I hope you like it."

I responded with a smile, "I love it! It's beautiful."

This was the second Christmas for Delilah and the children without Robert. I remember fondly Robert dressing up as Santa Claus when the kids were babies and toddlers. Delilah wasn't much in the holiday spirit, and I could see she was pushing herself to get through this season. There was a huge hole in Delilah's life and heart, and it was taking time for her to move on. I was thankful mah jongg was helping Delilah to connect, to be part of our sisterhood and to bring a little light to the darkness of mourning and bereavement. I prayed she and her children would find light, hope and healing in 2018.

We gathered in the kitchen to get our snacks and drinks. Leigh had wooden snack tables set up by two corners of the mah jongg table. We placed our plates filled with munchies, water-filled glasses, and phones on the snack tables, and took our seats. Her set was out, and the racks created a square on the table. Her mom passed her mah jongg set on to Leigh. Sometimes, Leigh texts her mom to help us answer a mah jongg question we can't figure out in our games.

As I sat opposite Leigh, I decided I wanted to try a hand I'd never played before. In this game, a lot depends on luck—the tiles you are dealt, and what gets passed around in the Charleston. I've learned that when the tiles speak to you, it's best to listen. I was hopeful I would get tiles that would allow me to be adventurous. Leigh rolled the dice, counted out the tiles for the last wall, and started to deal. I looked down at the group of thirteen neatly stacked tiles that had been dealt to me. As I turned each tile over and placed it in my rack, anticipation stirred within me with the reveal of each tile. Each new game offers a fresh start, another opportunity to create order out of mayhem.

We racked our tiles and started the search for a hand to play. We scanned our cards, grouped our tiles, picked three unwanted tiles, and started the Charleston. Conversation flowed as our hands evolved and our minds could relax after the Charleston was complete. I decided to try and fill in a Like Numbers hand with the suits of Craks, Dots, and Green Dragons. The hand wasn't as adventurous as I had hoped to play, but when a hand presents itself, it's wise to build on it and let go of any preconceived plans.

As I have played mah jongg over the past few years, I have also studied the tiles, their Chinese meaning, and value. There is a rich history to this game. Paper tiles first used hundreds of years ago evolved into bamboo tiles, wood tiles, bone tiles, and finally into Bakelite and other plastic-based tiles, which my peacock set is made from. On my next turn, I picked up a 1 Crak. As I held the tile in my hand, my thumb ran over the etched markings. I felt the number one in the left corner of the tile, then my finger found the Chinese line depicting the number in the center, and at the base of the tile, I felt the Chinese character *Wan* representing the value of 10,000. The tactile action brings me a deeper connection to the tile and the game. There is meaning in everything, even the simple tile of this game. This tile's name, Crak, has another significance in my life. Although the mah jongg tile name Crak is missing a 'c' in its spelling, it sounds the same as the English word crack.

Two years ago, Len was diagnosed with non-Hodgkin's lymphoma. Our lives were cracked open by cancer. Cracks create openings. Fear tries to creep through the cracks, bringing along its companions worry, anxiety and insecurity. Uncertainty is my new "it" word. Len's health and our hopes of a long future together rest in the hands of destiny.

I racked the 1 Crak and discarded a West. As the game continued, we picked, racked, and discarded tiles. Jokers were exchanged, and we were down to the last wall.

Rose called, "Mah jongg!" She surprised us all, with a concealed hand in 2 4 6 8.

Prayers and Blessings

I pray a lot. Prayer has quietly entered my life on a daily basis. I can't recall when this started. It must have been when I was about ten years old before I attended religious school. I've always had an awareness of being thankful for the people in my life, for health, and for the things around me, both the wants and the needs. I didn't take things for granted. I couldn't explain or articulate this as a young girl. It was just an intrinsic knowing. As a mature woman, I have become mindful of this, and I am grateful for everyday things as well as things of grandeur. Lately, I'm focusing on this prayer: *May we be blessed with health and strength, especially for Len.* I pray this a lot either silently or out loud. I pray that 2018 will be a year filled with health, remission, and the promise of time, *more* time precisely.

Prayer is my personal conversation with God. When I pray to God about cancer or Len, it is almost always a prayer of petition. I'm usually asking for something; health, strength, time, remission. I find balance by saying prayers of thanksgiving for my basic needs of food, shelter, and health being fulfilled. I am thankful for family, friends, and the ability to be a woman living in a country where I have choices and endless possibilities. I can vote, wear clothing of my choice, drive a car, and obtain an education. I am able to choose and practice my religion freely. I am very blessed and thankful to be an American woman. In addition to praying alone, I love communal prayer. Friday night prayer services are an opportunity to pray collectively. Our voices in unison fill the sanctuary with energy, volume, and holiness.

Life Coaching

I've been seeing Holly, my life coach, for about six years. We met when she did a coaching presentation at the temple that both Leigh and I attended together. I liked what we heard about coaching, and I liked her energy too. I had a private consultation and started working with her one-on-one. One of my goals when I initially started working with her was to finish writing a book I had started. Along the way, I learned a lot about myself. I learned about positive and negative energy levels in my coaching sessions. Although I decided to abandon that book, I'm thinking *Mah Jongg Mondays,* which I'm working on right now, will be the one to make it to publication. Once we completed my private sessions, I asked Holly if she would consider a group session if I got a few more participants. She loved the idea and was in agreement. Our group included Leigh, Sarah, and two other women. We saw her once a month for almost two years. We each had personal goals we were working on and used the tools of this coaching method to help us navigate toward them. We were a small sisterhood of women with the common goal of becoming the best version of ourselves as women, wives, mothers, daughters, sisters, friends, and professionals.

I went back to private sessions to help support myself through this time of uncertainty as I navigated through this cancer journey with Len. I needed Holly and coaching to help me make it through Len's Arizona treatment. I scheduled weekly visits with her—ten, to be precise. We focused on my strengths of independence, fortitude, and my tenacious nature to persevere despite the outcome from the treatment plan. We would keep my goals short-term, sometimes one or two days ahead if Len was having a scan. Waiting for results is challenging to say the least. Some goals were weekly. I still had daily house chores, my part-time work, and managing Gabriel's schedule and activities. Keeping busy was helpful. I even cleaned out and organized drawers, my walk-in closet, and Gabriel's closet, removing clothes he had outgrown. Organizing helped me stay somewhat in control of small areas of my life while I felt out of control with the outcome of my husband's health crisis.

Holly is also a social worker, which adds another layer to her background, and this is appealing to me. Although I've been to traditional therapy before, I feel that coaching is a better fit for my personality. I'm very interactive, and I enjoy learning about the "whys" that hold me back from reaching some goals. Holly has helped me understand my limiting thoughts, assumptions, and self-created gremlins shouting their negative criticisms: "You can't do this! You aren't smart enough, creative enough, or witty enough." Once we know what to look for, we can stop and reflect, then take action to squelch these negative energies.

Another great tool I learned from Holly is reframing. Here's an example: I'm sitting in traffic. Instead of getting angry or frustrated, I'll turn the radio on and listen to music or Dr. Laura Schlessinger on Sirius XM radio. I can't stop or change the traffic, but I can redirect my energy and thought process to help me get through the situation as best as possible. It's a skill I use daily. I have taught it to my three sons, too. Holly checks in to make sure I've completed my coaching homework, or a goal I have for the week, or to check on test results Len has received. Life coaching has been a great source of support for me.

It was *b'shert*. The universe wanted us to meet and knew I needed a skilled helper to teach me tools to navigate through midlife and through my husband's battle with cancer. Our temple was the chosen place where our lives intersected. It is where I decided *yes* to learn new methods and tools for the mind to broaden my scope in life. Holly and life coaching have become important and fortuitous blessings in my life.

Arizona

I am an independent woman, and I did not think twice about Len leaving our family for ten weeks to live in Arizona to get treatment. Len's travel for business for twenty years in our marriage had helped shape me. We decided

Alex would fly out with Len the first week in December to help him get set up in the condo he was renting and to be with him for the first few infusions at the center.

Alex flew back home a week later. He is a great son! He is a kind and compassionate young man, and I am so proud of his strong commitment to his family. Back in New York, Alex was Len's connection to work, and he was indispensable in streamlining Len's ability to continue to manage his business from his makeshift office in the rented condo in Arizona. Naturopathic cancer treatment didn't stop Len from being dedicated to his business and work obligations.

Gabriel and I visited Len during winter break two weeks after Alex returned home. Just six weeks earlier we were celebrating Gabriel becoming a *bar mitzvah* as an intact family. These experiences remind me that time ushers in change, sometimes positive, sometimes negative. It slips through our fingers no matter how hard we try to stop it. I remember marking time most distinctly when I would gaze at my sleeping children when they were younger and see how their bodies had grown, or when I looked at old pictures and saw how time had aged faces of friends, family, Len, and me. Time shifts and shifts us along with it. Our family was shifting too. We were shifting into treatment and uncertainty. I wondered what 2018 would be like for our family.

My older son, Jared, was living in Florida at that time with his grandparents, away from the epicenter of cancer.

He was pursuing real estate and planned to move back to New York in six months and join in the family textile business. He checked in on Len and was supportive in his own way. I noticed how each of my sons dealt differently with their father's diagnosis.

Gabriel and I visited Len again during another short school break. We went to the clinic with Len where he was getting his infusions. We met people from all over the country with all different types of cancer: lung, prostate, breast, bladder, vulva (yes, vulva). He introduced us to Jim, who was a fellow patient at the center. They became fast friends and spent many hours sitting next to each other in their recliners as the IV dripped hope along with high doses of Vitamin C and other vitamins and minerals into their veins. They went hiking together, shared meals, and supported each other through their different cancer journeys. They created a special bond; they believed in their treatment choices and were 100 percent invested, each believing wholeheartedly this treatment would bring them both into remission. Len felt lonely and isolated when a family member wasn't there visiting with him. Jim filled that void and helped him get through ten weeks being so far away from home. They became kindred souls as *b'shert* and cancer crossed their paths in Arizona.

Each infusion took about an hour. Recliner chairs were lined along the perimeter of the room, occupied by patients and their caregivers. I was overwhelmed and saddened by this sight, and it tugged at my heartstrings.

Gabriel was a strong boy and was able to look beyond the sadness and found the hope in the room, coming from the patients, their family, and caregivers, as well as the nurses and doctors. Let a thirteen-year-old teach us a great lesson here. Let's look for hope in obscure places and faces. Hope hides, waiting to be discovered, like a diamond in the rough. I started looking for hope when we went with Len for his treatments. I saw it; it was there in a smile or a knowing look between a nurse and patient. I saw it as an invisible lifeline between Len and Jim. I found it when I held Len's free hand. I saw hope dripping through the IV line into his arm.

We made the most of our Arizona visits. We went hiking most days, enjoying family time and the physical challenge. Jim and his wife came on a few hikes with us, and I saw the special bond these two men shared. I saw the hope that existed between them and the hope they created for one another. I noticed how the climate in Arizona was so different from Long Island. It was arid, a stark contrast to Long Island's often humid summer heat, and of course, its cold and dreary winters. The cacti presented an interesting contrast to the foliage we have on the East Coast. Gabriel loved the change of landscape.

We went horseback riding along a winding and dusty trail one day, learning the different varieties of cacti from the guide. One day we drove to Sedona, which I thought was one of the most beautiful places I had ever seen. The striated red rock was truly breathtaking. The town had great shops and fun restaurants with delicacies such as snake and cactus on the menu. I decided I needed to come back to Sedona and stay a few days sometime in the future. Spending five hours here was a tease to my senses and my soul. Gabriel and I flew home on January 1, 2018, bringing back to New York the hope we found at the clinic. It lived in our hearts and our minds, and I tucked some extra hope in our luggage, which would fill the house when we opened them at home. I needed to be mindful of hope and to search for it when I felt its presence starting to fade.

Len had another six weeks of treatment. His mother flew from Florida and spent a week with him in Arizona, alternating with his father when she left. Len's brother, Anton, and his friend, Sasha, joined them for four days. It was four Russian men bonding on a guys' getaway. All these visits were reassuring and helpful to Len through those ten weeks. They were positive and helpful distractions from the treatment and its outcome. Back in New York, the boys and I missed Len, and I needed some distractions, too. Mah jongg was the perfect distraction for me.

Reunited

Len returned home from Arizona in February after his ten-week treatment, and we left for a family vacation in Mexico with his brother, Anton, and his family. Len looked amazing. He followed the clinic's low carb-no sugar diet and lost twenty pounds. He already had a naturally athletic build, but as he aged, some weight crept on. Now his naturally cut abs were chiseled, and he looked great and felt fit. After our vacation, we flew home with an appointment set up to see the oncologist and to schedule a PET scan. We were excited to prove chemo isn't the only way to battle cancer.

"See," we would tell the doctor. "It worked!"

Sadly, the PET scan results proved the vitamin and mineral infusions didn't work and were not effective in killing cancer cells. We felt disappointed, confused, and abandoned by the clinic and its treatment plan.

Len's cancer was in twelve spots, the only noticeable one being under his right eye. It was puffy, looking like it was filled with fluid in two separate areas under his lower lashes. Then there was unseen cancer threatening the optic nerve on the left eye. I thought on a spiritual level that the cancer was near his eyes, giving him a strong sign that he needs to see something in his life. We are often blind to the very things we need to see. Cancer gave him the opportunity to reflect, to search, to see. I reframed (as Holly taught me) and I thought that maybe the universe was giving him a message, although it was unclear what that message was. The cancer was also in his thigh muscle, chest wall, shoulder muscle, and armpit. Who knew where else this sinister systemic disease would appear? Following his doctor's recommendation, we followed up with an eye specialist in New York City, who confirmed that the cancer was extremely close to the optic nerve in his left eye. He strongly recommended systemic chemotherapy ASAP. Oh boy, here we go . . .

I hated the thought of chemo and what could potentially happen to my handsome and strong husband. I joined three Facebook cancer support groups. The agony many patients were going through was overwhelming. One site was specifically for wives whose husbands had cancer. It was heartbreaking more than heartwarming. I had to unfollow the groups, but sometimes random posts still popped up on my news feed. These comments drained my always half-full cup. Cancer is an epidemic. Humanity is in trouble. Big Pharma cashes in along the way, but really, what other option is left? The naturopathic treatment didn't work. We met with the oncologist to hear his treatment plan, then saw two other lymphoma specialists, one from Memorial Sloan Kettering Cancer Center and one from Hackensack Medical Center.

Len was an engineer before he went into the textile business. He is a black-and-white thinker. I was surprised he even considered, let alone tried, the naturopathic treatment plan. There isn't a lot of data or statistics available at these centers, but there is a lot of hope. The problem is that quantified hope doesn't cure cancer. We finally decided to proceed with chemo, choosing to stay with the oncologist from the Monter Cancer Center and get treatment here on Long Island.

Chemo would start in April. Len called Jim and told him about his PET scan results and his decision to start chemo. Jim supported Len's decision, although he was strongly against using it to fight his own cancer. Jim left Arizona after the naturopathic treatment didn't slow down his cancer. He bought a FAR sweat machine which brought his body temperature to one hundred two degrees and was on a juicing protocol. He found another clinic in Florida and hoped that it would succeed where the Arizona one failed. He texted Len: "We are still fighting the good fight!" Both men were on to the next attempt to save their lives.

Chapter 11

Birthday Mah Jongg

Group text: Leigh, Amanda, Phyllis
Me: Hi ladies! It's Mah Jongg Monday, and it's a night game. I'll host, 7:00 p.m. Who's in?
Leigh: Me!
Phyllis: Looking forward to it.
Amanda: Count me in too!
Me: Great! See you all tonight.

It was April 2018, and I was turning another year older on the twenty-second. I would be fifty-one years old on this birthday. It had been over a year since my gift to myself of growth, adventure, and self-exploration at Campowerment. It was time to bring forth the resolve I found when I was there. Chemo was starting in three days. I would dig deep and find the strength I needed to help Len through his treatments. I prayed he wouldn't become feverish, achy, nauseous and weak. I was so thankful to have mah jongg to help take my mind off this worry, even if only for a few hours each week. Mah jongg reinvigorates me. I love spending time with the women I play with. The mental stimulation challenges me. It also occupies my mind and doesn't allow space for worry to sneak in.

I prepared the mah jongg table in the mah jongg/meditation room, set up the racks, and spilled the mah jongg tiles out. The noise of the tiles brought a smile to my face. It stirred up mah jongg excitement as I turned them all face down and mixed the tiles, stacking them two by two down the four racks. I turned on the electric candles, added a few drops of lavender oil to the diffuser and turned it on, inhaling the soothing scent. I put out snacks on the kitchen table, along with drinks, plates, and utensils. There was a knock on the door. I saw through the glass panes that Phyllis was here. I welcomed her in, and we kissed hello.

"Hi, it's so good to see you!" she said in her upbeat manner.

"You too, cuz," I replied with a smile.

"Hello, hello, ladies!" Amanda said as she came in, wearing her big smile.

We both greeted Amanda warmly.

Leigh came in next holding a cake she made for my birthday.

"Happy Birthday, Fern!" she said as she hugged me with her one free arm.

"Oh, thank you!" I replied.

Leigh brought the cake into the kitchen and placed it on the table, put a candle in it, and took out a pack of matches. She lit the candle, and the ladies started to sing "Happy Birthday..." to me. I smiled, thanked them all, and as I blew out my candle, I wished for the chemo to work and to help bring the cancer into remission for Len. I cut the cake, and we each prepared our plates of goodies, glasses of water, and got down to business at the mah jongg table.

We all had our new 2018 cards. We were excited to see the new hands and to see which hands were repeated. I find when the new card first comes out, it levels the playing field because we are all seeing the card for the first time together. Since I started playing mah jongg five years ago, I recognize I now celebrate three New Years: the secular New Year in January, the mah jongg New Year in April, and the Jewish New Year, which generally falls between September and October. Life is full of celebrations! We took a few minutes to look at the new card, commenting on interesting new hands.

"Ok," I said, raising my plastic cup filled with water. "Let's welcome in the mah jongg New Year. Cheers!"

We all clinked our cups together and took a sip to

commemorate the new card and the mah jongg New Year.

I rolled the dice. Snake eyes. That's a really small wall to be left with. Four tiles are all we'll have if we get down to the last wall. I thought how each mah jongg game is different just like each cancer experience is different. Different variables, luck, and skill are needed to win both. Although they are both games of chance, one is full of pleasure, fun, and excitement; the other game is a fight for someone's life.

I dealt out the tiles. We racked them, sorting them into matching suits or pairs. I had a lot of singles and searched for a hand to try to build. I had a Flower, a White Dragon or Soap, and to my surprise, a 2, 1, and an 8 Dot! I searched in the 2018 section and decided on the second hand listed. Not being familiar with the new card yet, I double-checked my tiles and the hand listed under the 2018 heading. It looked good. We started the tile dance of the Charleston; first right, across, first left, second left, across, and final right. We optioned across. I filled in three tiles through the Charleston. I love this game and the fun and excitement it creates! I still needed six tiles to call mah jongg, but I thought I had a solid hand and was off to a good start.

I started the game by placing a 5 Crak on the table. Amanda picked, racked, and discarded a tile. Leigh picked next, racked, and discarded. Then it was Phyllis's turn. I notice when we play that Phyllis stands her tiles in different places—some on the rack, some on the table. Each of us has a unique way of playing. I try to keep all my tiles touching, so my opponents can't see if I'm breaking tiles into pairs, pungs (three tiles), or kongs (four tiles). As Phyllis picked a tile from the wall, she racked it, rearranged things, and discarded. I picked next. Yes! It was a Joker. I racked it and discarded a tile. The game and conversation flowed. I needed five tiles to call mah jongg. No one had exposed any tiles yet. Maybe someone was playing a concealed hand. I shy away from them, personally, and rarely win when playing a concealed hand. I find it too challenging!

Leigh pushed out her wall. She picked and discarded. I called for the discarded tile and made an exposure with the Joker I had. I was getting closer. I discarded, and Phyllis called for the tile and made an exposure. I got to pick again. Yes! It was a Flower, which I needed. I racked it and placed down a South. Leigh called it and exposed two Jokers, a South, and the South tile I just discarded. Now it was getting dicey. Two other players were getting closer to mah jongg beside me. Phyllis picked and discarded. We were almost down to the last wall. I picked a South and replaced one of Leigh's Jokers. I was getting so close. Anticipation was building. I was getting antsy. My stomach had butterflies as I discarded. Amanda picked, racked, and discarded, then Leigh, and then Phyllis. It was my turn again. I picked and froze. *Oh no, it's a Flower. It's not the tile to throw at the end of a game. I'm one tile away! I need a 1 Bam or a Joker. Do I throw my hand? We're down to the final wall. There are only a few tiles left.* I made my decision. *I wouldn't throw my game!*

I placed the tile down pursing my lips and almost whispered, "Flower?"

"Mah jongg!" Amanda called slyly, exposing a concealed Singles and Pairs hand nonetheless!

Amanda is a very good player. Her hand was worth fifty cents, but because I threw it, I owed her double, one-dollar.

"Nice win!" Phyllis said as she exposed her hand.

"Wow, that's a hard hand to win, Amanda!" Leigh exclaimed, exposing her Winds hand.

"Watch out for those quiet players," Amanda smiled at us, feeling satisfaction and contentment.

Len and Alex came home from work and stopped in to say hi to us. The girls all wished Len well. Chemo was scheduled to start in just a few days.

Chemo Chronicles

D-Day finally arrived. We had tried to avoid it. Len had changed his diet, he had taken supplements, and he had moved to Arizona for ten weeks, taking intravenous vitamin and mineral infusions. He was devoted to a naturopathic treatment plan. "Let's do this!" we had said with conviction as he left for Arizona. We were all in. We believed. Unfortunately, life had a different plan.

Reality set in when his first scan following naturopathic treatment revealed that the cancer had spread. What frightened me the most was the possibility that it could travel from the optic nerve to his brain. David told me what happened to his wife when her breast cancer metastasized to her brain. I couldn't think about that; it was too scary. Len chose to undergo chemo, and we needed to trust the doctors and drugs to work together to put this disease into remission. We needed to have faith in this process. *B'shert* worried me for the first time. Possibilities worried me. Remission worried me. If he was lucky enough for the cancer to go into remission, how long would it last? I was unsettled and unnerved!

Round One

Round one. Day one. We were ready to start the fight. Our teammates were the drugs Treanda and Rituxan, nurses, and the oncologist. They weren't who we had hoped for, but now I prayed they would be the teammates that helped Len reach a lengthy remission. We arrived at the Monter Cancer Center at 10:30 a.m. We pulled up to the valet service and stepped into the new multi-million-dollar center. A smiling, enthusiastic attendant greeted us. "Checking in?" he asked cheerily.

"Yes, my husband is starting chemo today," I responded, preferring to be checking into a hotel or spa.

"Right this way please," he responded with a smile.

Len went to the lab to get blood work to determine

red, white, and platelet counts along with his potassium level. We would come to know these terms well. Afterward, we were walked to a private room in the chemo area. There was a comfortable recliner, a television, and sitting chair for the caregiver—in this case, me. The nurse came in. She wore a blue disposable gown and gloves, which nurses wear for protection. Chemotherapy is toxic. This toxic substance was going to be administered into my handsome husband's body. I felt like I was watching a movie, like this was someone else's life and her husband was getting chemo. This couple could be any couple, except it was us, Len and Fern, starring in our own movie; the genre, drama. We were not paid actors; just regular people, a textile business owner, and a religious school and yoga instructor. We were parents, like so many other people. Len was someone's son and brother. I was someone's daughter and sister.

These rooms and cubicles were filled with lawyers, plumbers, professors, garbage collectors, masons, nurses, librarians, poor people, rich people, Trump supporters, Trump haters, people without insurance, people with insurance, and people just like you and me. This disease doesn't discriminate.

Len was given Benadryl to help avoid an allergic reaction, along with anti-nausea medicine and a steroid. A second nurse came in with a disposable blue robe and gloves on her hands.

"Name and date of birth?" she asked flatly.

"Len Bernstein. 1/8/68," he replied.

"Check," one nurse said to the other nurse. Two nurses always do the chemo check; it's their buddy system to make sure the right patient is getting the right chemo and dosage. The first nurse had drawn the IV line and started running the saline solution. She added the second bag, which contained the Rituxan, after the buddy check. Ready, set, go. By now, the Benadryl was having an effect, and Len was getting drowsy.

His parents would be arriving shortly. They were his rock, besides me. I knew he had mixed feelings about them being here. He wanted their love and support, but he didn't want to worry them at the same time. He couldn't have stopped them from flying up from Florida if he tried. His mother has the will of a Spanish bull. They arrived around noon. I received a text from her saying they were in the hallway. I told Len I was going to meet them and bring them inside. I walked out into the brightly lit hallway lined with pictures of flowers on the wall. We spotted each other. Two worried parents walked toward a worried wife. There was too much worry in this space, and I knew it was not good for Len. I could hide it; they couldn't.

"Hello, Ferren. Vhere is my Lyonchick?" she asked, concerned.

Misha trailed behind her, stoic as usual. We kissed hello.

"Hi. He is doing really well so far. He is just sleepy. Let's all stay positive for him. Please don't let him see you are worried, ok?" I asked, hoping I hadn't offended her.

"Oy, I just vant this chemo to vork and not destroy

my handsome and beautiful son," she said.

"Come," I said taking her hand, Misha in tow.

We entered the room and closed the door. Len made a joke to lighten the mood for his parents. He knew the sight of him with tubes of chemo in his arm tortured them, and that tortured him. We sat down in the room with only one chair for the caregiver. Now there were three caregivers. We got creative. I was respectful. I offered his mom my chair. I offered Misha the spinning stool, but he opted for the garbage can. I took the stool. We crowded the room. Then the nurse came in to check Len's blood pressure and temperature. We were busted. "Um, there is only supposed to be one guest at a time," she said.

"Dear nurse, vee have flown all zee vay up from Florida and vant to comfort our dear son. Please, maybe an exception can be made?" she asked—no, she pleaded.

"Ok, but you have to be quiet," she said as relief washed over my mother-in-law's face.

I thought about how hard this must be for her. Cancer wasn't a stranger to her. Her husband had kidney, bladder, and prostate cancer. Both her mother and father had colon cancer. Her brother-in-law had lung and bone cancer. Now her beloved son had non-Hodgkin's lymphoma. It softened my heart when I thought of how she must be feeling at this moment. I saw the pain in her eyes as we sat in the treatment room. The pain crept up from her heart, too big to be contained there, and found expression in her watery eyes and pursed lips. Emotion can't always be contained. It needs to be expressed, released, and liberated. Len looked down at the floor in defeat, knowing he was causing her sadness and pain. I tried to change the mood in the room and asked about Florida weather and their house overlooking the harbor.

"Any good fishing?" I asked my father-in-law. I would say anything to alter this looming feeling in the room.

Four and a half hours after the Rituxan was started, it was finally finished. I needed to leave to meet Gabriel when his bus dropped him off back home. We planned that Len's parents would drive him home after the Treanda was finished. I kissed him goodbye on the cheek, both of us knowing that we couldn't kiss on the lips due to the treatment. I walked to the valet to get the car. Outside it was a beautiful April day. The car pulled up, a new Mercedes SUV Len leased weeks before the treatment started. He wanted to make sure bases were covered with certain things, like the car, investments, and other financial matters. He told me he was worried about his future and my future with the children if the cancer became aggressive and . . . you know the sad ending he was talking about. He was a doting and hardworking family man and wanted to make sure his family was well taken care of now and in the future.

As I drove home from the cancer center, I reflected on feeling like I was in a movie earlier. I felt like an actress, but one who wasn't prepared for the role. But this wasn't a movie. It was reality. It was *my* reality. It was *my* husband battling cancer. It was *my* role to be his strong and supportive wife and caregiver. I knew I would do this to the best of *my* ability. Whatever came tomorrow or the next day or week or month, I would give *my* all to help my husband through this horrible journey. I thought of Delilah and Fran. They were strong. I am strong too. I continued driving on the Long Island Expressway and prayed to God that this treatment would work and would send the cancer into remission. I didn't feel so alone all of a sudden. I had welcomed passengers with me. God was riding next to me and Faith was in the back seat. I was comforted and was in good company. I pulled into the driveway and waited for Gabriel's bus to pull up.

Len finished the Treanda around 4:00 p.m. and his parents drove him home from the cancer center. Gabriel and I greeted them at the door at about 5:00 p.m. Len looked tired; it was a long day, and toxic chemicals were flowing through his body. I ordered dinner from our favorite diner. We all ate together, and then his parents drove to their apartment in Brighton Beach, Brooklyn. Len lay down in the spare bedroom upstairs and played his favorite video game. He sometimes goes into this room when he can't fall asleep. There is a forty-two-inch television, a PlayStation, and a laptop handy; it's an electronic oasis. I'm a very light sleeper, and I didn't want a television in our bedroom when we moved in thirteen years ago, knowing he would keep me up almost every night, so he made this room his late-night man cave. I left a bell next to the bed in the room in case he fell asleep there and needed help. I reminded him of the bell as I hit the dinger on top, kissed him on the forehead, and left him playing his game as I went to sleep in my princess bed in my princess bedroom. I turned on relaxing music and drifted off to sleep. Day one, round one is complete. Check.

Almost.

At 3:00 a.m., Len woke me. Shit. I thought this was going too smoothly.

"I can't stop the hiccups. They are every seven seconds, and I'm having trouble catching my breath," he said while hiccupping.

"Ok." I jumped out of bed, processed what he was saying, and decided we needed to call the emergency line on the discharge papers. Hiccups? I've read about lots of chemo side effects but not the hiccups. No one discussed this on the Facebook cancer sites either. I called the number on the discharge sheet and was connected to the doctor on call. The groggy-sounding doctor said we could go to the ER and have a drug administered, which would stop the diaphragm from spazzing. I relayed this to Len. He said he didn't want any more drugs in his body. I thanked the doctor and hung up. Len told me he had tried home remedies while I was still asleep.

I said, "Let me try one thing, and if it doesn't work, I think we'll need to go to the ER."

I walked into the bathroom, grabbed a tissue, put six drops of lavender oil on it, and placed it on Len's upper chest. I told him to take a deep breath in and count to three then exhale to the count of three. In less than a minute the hiccups stopped, and he was asleep. Lavender and *pranayama* (yogic breathing techniques) training came in handy. *Namaste* and good night.

Day two started with me waking Len at 8:00 a.m. I was thankful he had five hours of sleep. I had been up since the hiccup incident and knew I would need a nap later in the day. I got Gabriel ready for school and watched him step onto the bus. Then I dressed, put on my makeup, and we left for the cancer center at 8:45 a.m. We were in a cubicle this time, since he was receiving just the Treanda, and we hoped to be done in an hour. The cubicle fit a recliner chair for the patient, an armchair to the left of the recliner, and a television. Tidy and efficient. The nurse was different from yesterday. She was all business—terse, economical with her smile, and she seemed rushed. We didn't like her edginess. The IV was put in the other hand today. She connected the saline into the line. Her buddy-check partner came in with the Treanda bag. Same drill as yesterday—name and birthdate. Check. The Treanda was added to the line, and after a minute Len started feeling a burning sensation as the poison entered his arm.

"It feels like fire running into my vein," Len said to me through clenched teeth.

I ran for the nurse. She came in and stopped the drip. Len took a breath of relief. Then she pressed some buttons on the machine and said it would be a slower drip and would hopefully be less painful. It was tolerable. I was relieved. I reflected on Len's analogy of the chemo burning like fire going into his vein, and I was brought back to our house fire in my mind. Fire burns, scars, and is destructive. A fire displaced our family. Scarring memories are imprinted permanently in my mind. What will the fire Len feels in his vein do to him? To our family? Will this fire help him?

I was snapped out of my thoughts as the bag was emptied and the machine beeped. The nurse came in and started to remove the IV in a fast and detached manner. I screamed and jumped out of my chair. In her hastiness and due to the unfortunate placement of my chair, fluid from the line she just removed from Len's hand sprayed across the room and right onto my forehead and shirt.

"Holy shit!" I yelled, "I'm wet! This toxic shit is on my face!"

She panicked. "I'm so sorry! Quick, go to the ladies' room and wash your face immediately!"

I literally ran into the bathroom, waiting for a burning sensation to start or my skin to begin to redden and peel away. Moments like these aren't where I shine in life. Panic sets in. I quickly took soap and water and washed my forehead fiercely and ferociously. Three separate times. Do I wash it all off my face or just my forehead? If I wash off all the makeup, I will have raccoon eyes because I need a baby wipe to get off the black remains of mascara that pool under my lower lashes. Soap and water alone can't do the job. Raccoon eyes would make it look like I had been crying, and with everything Len was dealing with, I didn't want to upset him by making him think that. *Screw it; I'll just wash my forehead.* I toweled off and anxiously looked in the mirror at the area that got splashed. It was okay! No redness, no irritation, no peeling! I was just a little two-toned now, seeing where I washed off the makeup. I was so relieved. I quietly thanked God. I took a deep breath in, then exhaled the remainder of stress filling my body. Now, back to Len and the nurse.

"Are you okay?" asked the nurse. "I'm very sorry about that. It was just saline. I retraced my steps and saw the line that got you wet was attached to the saline bag. I know that was scary for you," she said with a change in her voice.

"I'm fine now, thank you," I responded coldly, turning the tables on her. "I think you need to slow down and be more careful." Then I turned to Len and asked in my cheerful and loving manner, "How are you feeling, sweetie?"

We received the discharge instructions and headed to the valet.

"Should I complain to her supervisor?" I asked as we walked down the hallway with the flower pictures on the wall.

"No, let it be. Thankfully it was saline, and you are okay. Maybe the nurse is having a bad day; you never know what someone is going through at home," he replied.

"Okay, I'll let it be."

I thought to myself he must just want to get home. Situations like these become so inconsequential when you are battling cancer. I needed to remember this. David said something similar, too. Don't sweat the small stuff. This was small stuff, I decided.

I gave my ticket to the valet. Len sat down on the bench. I sat next to him and held his hand. It was April 27. My birthday was five days ago. Birthdays are always a time of reflection and renewal for me. I squeezed his hand and wondered what this year of life had in store for me. Obviously, lessons, but which ones? Five days in and I was learning about cancer, hiccups, patience with a terse nurse, and getting through round one of chemo with Len. What does *b'shert* have in store for me this year? I was hoping for good things. *Please God, only good things,* I prayed.

The car arrived, I helped Len into his seat, reclined the chair for him, and I got into the driver's seat. I put relaxing music on the radio and started the drive home. His phone sounded, alerting him he had a text. It was Jim checking in on him. He texted Jim back that he had finished round one and was doing well, besides some crazy hiccups. Jim texted back, hoping the chemo would rid Len's body of cancer. He and his wife were heading to San Diego to another clinic for treatment including a special tonic, supplements, and a recommended diet. Len felt good texting with Jim. They had a special bond and checked in on each other. Len drifted off to sleep as the music filled the car. God and Faith, my constant companions, were sitting together in the back seat today. I had a buddy check, too.

I decided that after each round I would post about Len's accomplishment on Facebook. He didn't have a

Facebook account, and I thought it would be a good way to let everyone in our lives know when the rounds were finished. This would be part of my strategy to help get me through the chemo rounds with Len. Each post would mark a goal achieved on the way to the finish line.

For my first post, I chose a picture of a boxing ring against a bright yellow backdrop. This wording accompanied the picture:

> Round 1 of chemo: ✓
> Len and Fern: Hey cancer!
> Cancer: Hey what?
> Len and Fern: Here's a chemo punch [picture of boxing glove]
> And 'F' you! We're ready to knock you out!"

I hit post, and round one was now officially complete.

Strategy Class

Fran was running a strategy class for intermediate players. I decided to go to sharpen my mah jongg skills. At the class, I learned new ways to look for hands, and I became bolder, trying for more challenging hands such as concealed hands or hands with multiple pairs. I learned how to better optimize the hand I had after the Charleston. Fran's trained and experienced eye saw possibilities I didn't see. Mah jongg is a mind sport. It's a game of mental gymnastics, including strategy, memory, tactics, observation, and a poker face. This skill is important and useful in not letting your opponents know what tiles you need or if you just picked up a Joker. I'm working on all of these skills at each game I play in, but I find keeping a poker face to be the most challenging at times. I'm so honest, and I wear my feelings on my sleeve so openly that when I need a tile, and it gets discarded, and I can't call it, I either make a quiet noise of frustration, purse my lips, or shift in my chair unconsciously.

Seriously? I ask myself when I know my cover is blown. I might need an acting coach in addition to a life coach. The women I play with definitely have better poker faces and body control than I do. It's a personal goal I'm working on in my games.

At the class, Fran strategically placed me at a table with women I'd never met. The three women were all friendly and at the same skill level as I am. Fran came over and whispered in my ear that the woman sitting across from me had a husband who also had non-Hodgkin's lymphoma and had successfully finished chemo. I appreciated her seating arrangement. Debbie, who was sitting across from me, was in her fifties with two children in their twenties. As games, strategy, and learning continued, so did the conversation. Eventually, the topic of cancer came up. After the class was over, we exchanged numbers. We connected our husbands on the phone, and Len had the opportunity to speak with a fellow lymphoma patient. Every conversation Len had with another patient, doctor, or caregiver was helpful. Information was exchanged, and the new-found knowledge helped him navigate this cancer journey with greater hope and strategy. The added bonus was Debbie has since joined as a fourth in a game or two with me.

Fran is a more private person than I am, and she never reveals to her students that her son is battling cancer. She finds her teaching to be a time to escape from the reality of what her son is going through. I watch her when I take her classes, and I marvel at her resolve and ability to separate the two worlds. No one would know what she is dealing with.

I understand the separating of the two worlds. I do it too when I teach yoga or religion. My mind is occupied with my students and doing my job to the best of my ability and with total focus. The only time I share that my husband has cancer is when I do a healing circle with my students at the end of class in religious school. I learned this technique from Rabbi Susie, where she often does this at Torah yoga. I have the children sit in a circle on the floor. I put on the song *Mi Shebeirach*, which is a Jewish prayer for healing. I instruct the children to rub their hands together, creating friction. Then we slowly separate our hands, and many of the children can feel the energy between their palms. We do it a second time. More students open their eyes wide, sensing the mysterious energy between their hands. I instruct the children to hold hands and create a link of energy between us. As the music plays softly, I ask the children to say the name of a loved one, friend, family member, or pet who is in need of healing, either of body, mind, or spirit. The children say the name of someone and often why they are saying their name. When it's my turn, I say Len's name and tell them he has cancer. I want to be real at this moment. I want to teach the children that disease and hardship touch us all. This is the only time I discuss cancer in my classroom, because it is an opportunity to teach the children about faith, prayer, hope, and strength.

Chapter 12

Round Two

Chemotherapy rounds were scheduled every twenty-eight days. It was May and time for round two. We were assigned a private room again for this treatment. The nurse came in. *Oh no. It's her again.* Len and I locked eyes. She was nicer this time. She was more talkative and showed a more caring side. Maybe Len was right, and she was having a bad day last month. She handed Len a mini cup with a few pills of Benadryl, a steroid, and anti-nausea medicine. She carefully inserted the IV into Len's arm and started the saline. Nurse number two came in with the Rituxan. Buddy-check time. Name. Birthdate. Check. The Rituxan was added to the line.

Len's parents came in around 11:00 a.m. They brought

snacks and drinks for Len. They were more at ease this time, thankfully. We talked about the children, current events, and the weather. Len was feeling well, and his energy had rebounded from the first round. He took the IV pole and went for a walk in the hallway trying to get the Rituxan running through his body. He was able to fight off sleep today, and the drip was finished in just over two hours. The Treanda was infused next. Again, it burned his arm after about two minutes. He was clenching his teeth in pain.

His mother sat up straight, her blue eyes wide with fear. "Lyonchik, vat is going on?"

Misha asked, in his broken English, "Vat problem, Son?"

I ran for the nurse who came right in and shut the drip off. Len was relieved from the burning pain. His parents were clearly distraught seeing their son suffer. They felt so helpless. I felt so sad watching this whole scene. But I noticed she had relinquished her caregiving title to me, for now. I was content with that role, relieved she wasn't vying for the caregiver's hat, which would only cause tension. The nurse pressed some buttons on the dispenser and turned it back on. I ran my fingers up and down Len's arm. I remember reading you can't feel two sensations at once. I hoped to prove that true. Len said it was a helpful distraction, and fifteen minutes later the bag was empty. I was cautious to move my seat when the IV was removed from his arm this time. As I watched the nurse, I could tell she was being extra careful. We received the discharge instructions, and we all headed to the valet.

Len suggested it would be nice to have lunch with his parents on the way home. We decided to eat in Roslyn at the Persian Grill. I was on a vegan diet and ordered grilled vegetable skewers. Len and his parents ordered branzino. The whole fish, you know, served with the head on, eyes looking forward in a frozen stare. I had to look away from their plates. Everyone started eating.

The conversation started to disintegrate for me as they slipped into Russian. Being with my mother-in-law for four hours was tiring; being on guard isn't an easy job. I didn't need to talk anymore; my mouth was busy chewing anyway. Len reminded them to speak in English. She processed his request and started speaking in English then slipped back into Russian. It was futile. I looked at Len, and my eyes told him not to worry. Lunch finally ended. I had disengaged about twenty minutes before, so I was ready to head home. Len got his parents' car that was parked across the street and drove it back to the restaurant. He is always a doting son, and as I learned that day, he still doted, even after a chemotherapy treatment. They got into their rental car and drove away. We got into ours and headed home too. With Len's belly full and Benadryl in his body, he started to get very sleepy. Five minutes later, he was fast asleep and snoring.

I decided to listen to the Dr. Laura show on the radio during our ride home. She is one perky and straight-shooting talk show host. She answers callers' questions, displaying a high standard of morals, values, ethics, and principles. Her bar is very high. She teaches women the proper care and feeding of husbands to have fulfilling and successful marriages. One of her mottos is Choose Wisely, Treat Kindly. She provides shock value to listeners and brave callers. She puts men in their places in the blink of an eye, tells a parent if she thinks they are raising a snowflake and isn't worried about hurting someone's feelings. She is brutally honest. I've learned a lot listening to her, and yes, I admit it's a form of entertainment listening to other people call in with their problems as I listen to her offer her help and advice.

I was listening to a caller ask her a question that made me uneasy. Her husband died three years ago, and she thought she was ready to get back into the dating game but didn't know where or how to start. Dr. Laura gave her suggestions of joining meet-up groups, taking adult classes, and said introductions through friends and family were other good opportunities to meet men. (Dr. Laura is not a fan of dating web sites.) The caller was in her late fifties. She said it had been thirty years since she had dated, and she was hesitant.

Dr. Laura wasn't hesitant and asked her bluntly, "What do you want to do between now and dead?"

The caller paused. Dr. Laura waited. More silence filled the airwaves.

Then the caller responded, "I want to move on and find love again."

Dr. Laura worked her magic unapologetically. The call hit a nerve in me. I'm scared of cancer and its brutal consequences. My eyes started to fill with tears. I couldn't let my mind go there. *Shoo, bad thought, go away. There's no room for you here in my car. Look in the back seat. God and Faith took the only two seats left. Get out of my head and out of my car!* I pulled into the driveway and gently woke Len. I helped him out of the car, into the house, and tucked him in bed. He went back to sleep.

Gabe's bus pulled up thirty minutes later, and I met him at the door. I always feel good when he comes home from a happy and successful day at school. He was home safely. In these turbulent times sending our children to school is often unnerving. Not only do I have to worry about cancer daily but also the safety of my son at school. Gabe and I spent time talking as he had a snack. He asked how Dad felt and how chemo went that day. Gabriel is a kind-hearted child and is very sensitive. I was thankful that Len hadn't lost his hair or started to look ill from chemo. That would have been hard for Gabriel to see, and to understand how something that can make someone look sick actually was helping him fight a disease. Len slept until 7:00 p.m. when I woke him for dinner. We can say round two, day one went very smoothly until the hiccups started at about 10:00 p.m. again. I tried the lavender oil, but it didn't work this time. I Googled all sorts of things to try to help reset his diaphragm. This time, pulling on the edges of his tongue worked. I know this sounds crazy, but it really works. It stimulates the vagus nerve and eases diaphragm spasms that cause hiccups. The hiccups were a side effect of the anti-nausea medicine, and we made a mental note to tell the oncologist to lower the dosage next round.

The next morning at treatment, Len only received the Treanda. We had a new nurse today. She was Filipina. She had a kind and gentle disposition. All nurses should possess these qualities, but sadly they don't. She put in the IV line as kindly and gently as she spoke and acted. I often think that how someone does one thing is how they do everything. She was a perfect example. A second nurse came in for the buddy-check system. The Treanda was started with a slower drip rate to avoid the terrible burning sensation. Twenty-five minutes later the bag was empty, the nurse kindly and gently removed the IV, and we were free to enjoy the rest of the day. We went for lunch afterward, and Len felt well enough to do some work from home. This was bearable. He was tolerating the chemo and immunotherapy, and his appetite was relatively good. The two bumps under his right eye looked about eighty percent gone. *Holy shit—I think this stuff is working!* Len texted with Jim to give him his update and find out how things were going for him. It was time to post on Facebook that round two was complete. I decided on a colorful picture with the words round two and a picture of Superman punching outward as he is flying, his cape billowing behind him. Above the pictures I wrote:

Round 2 of chemo: ✓
Len is fighting cancer. What's your superpower, Facebook peeps?

We received so many likes, comments, and prayers from our family and friends. It was helpful and heartwarming.

A Deadly Game of Mah Jongg

My next-door neighbor, Marissa, learned how to play mah jongg recently. Of course, Fran taught her. She invited Leigh and me over to play with her. It was the last Wednesday in May. Leigh and I didn't play on Monday because the kids were home from school for Memorial Day. Marissa set up a table and chairs outside so we could enjoy the beautiful late May weather as we played mah jongg. The fourth player cancelled last minute, but we decided to play the three of us and make the most of the moment, the company, and the weather. Marissa and Leigh went to the same college, and both women reconnected through me when Marissa moved in. Marissa was East and started to deal. We altered the Charleston since there were three of us. Game one began as Marissa threw out the first tile. As we were playing, we heard some low flying planes overhead. It spooked me just how low they sounded. Leigh stood up to look skyward, trying to figure out what was happening. She saw four vintage planes flying overhead, probably heading back to Farmingdale Airport which is a few miles away. They were recently in an air show for Memorial Day. She sat back down, and we continued to play until I jumped out of my seat and ran for the back door to Marissa's house. It sounded like a plane was right behind us.

Then I heard a crash and screamed, "Oh my God! Did you hear that?"

"Hear what?" they asked.

"That sound!" I said, knowing something terrible had just happened.

"No, come back and sit down," Marissa said. "All's good."

"I didn't hear anything either," Leigh said.

I came back to the table with butterflies in my stomach and a sense of unease. We continued the game as I tried to calm down. Then the sirens started. Then more sirens joined in. I couldn't concentrate, and I couldn't play.

"Girls, give me a minute to go to the corner and see if I can figure out what's going on. The sirens are close by."

I walked to the corner where a few neighbors were standing, and I asked if they knew what had happened. They told me a small plane just crashed around the corner, and the pilot had died. The plane exploded upon contact, nose first into the wooded area facing the street lined with houses. I was speechless. I was sad that someone had just died. I said a silent prayer for the pilot. I knew I'd heard something terrible. I found it strange Marissa and Leigh didn't hear it too. I walked back to Marissa's and told the girls the tragic news. I did my best to get through the next few games. Afterward, Leigh and I drove around the corner to see if we could get a closer look. The street was blocked off with a police car and an officer redirecting traffic. It would remain closed for the next two days. Neighbors on the block who were home when it happened posted a video of the fiery remains of the plane on Facebook. The tragedy made the five o'clock news. As I watched the footage, flames engulfed the forest as the firemen fought to put the fire out. There was almost nothing left of the plane and sadly nothing but a memory left of the brave pilot who must have tried so hard under immense stress not to crash into a house. It was a deadly game of mah jongg that day and one that I will never forget. Rest in peace, dear pilot.

Marissa is the best neighbor anyone could ask for, and I'm lucky to have her in my life. The day of my house fire, she was one of the friends who walked through Target with me, helping me find the essentials we needed: clothing, footwear, toothbrushes, deodorant, and a comb to bring order to our hair, if not our lives. We had no personal possessions but those on our backs. She helped us find a hotel to live in temporarily and let us do our laundry, washing our new but few items of clothing in her washer and dryer until we moved into a rental house. Once we decided to rebuild, she let us meet with contractors in the warmth of her home. It was December and bitterly cold outside. The temperature in my unlivable house was the same temperature as it was outside. She let us run over to use the bathroom when we were returning to the remains of our home after the fire to go through papers or to see if anything was salvageable. She was so kind and generous to us. It's times like these when people show their true colors, and Marissa's was pure gold. She is an amazing neighbor and friend, and now a sub for my mah jongg games too.

Chapter 13

Round Three

It was June and round three of chemo. Len's parents flew back to Florida a few days before, feeling comfortable with how this process was working and seeing that Len was tolerating it well. Gabriel had finished school days earlier, and we had just celebrated his graduating from middle school. We were left with lingering feelings of happiness from the graduation as we pulled up to the cancer center. We dropped the car with the valet service at 10:30 a.m. and entered the building. We knew the routine by now. We checked in, Len went for a blood test, and we were taken to the private room assigned to him. We had another new nurse. She was efficient and no-nonsense and reminded me of the terse nurse. I hoped she was skilled at removing IVs. Len took the Benadryl, steroid, and we made sure the doctor had reduced the dosage on the anti-nausea medicine. No more hiccups, thank you! The new nurse put in the IV line and started the saline solution. Buddy-check occurred, and then the Rituxan was administered. Len became groggy and was soon asleep in the recliner. The only time he woke up over the next two and a half hours was for blood pressure and temperature checks. I never saw him this sleepy before.

I kept busy by reading an Oprah magazine and texting with friends. When the Rituxan was finished, the nurse added the Treanda bag to the hook and connected it to the line. The burning sensation woke Len, and the nurse slowed the drip down until it was tolerable for him. I ran my fingers up and down his arm as I had done before. About twenty minutes later, the bag was empty, and to my relief, the nurse successfully removed the IV without spraying me. We retrieved the car from the valet, Len settled in, and I started the familiar trip home. Within minutes, Len was back asleep.

I had started listening to the audiobook of *Eat, Pray, Love* by Elizabeth Gilbert, and as I drove home, I decided to play it quietly as Len slept. I escaped into the story with the author. I was in Italy eating delicious Italian food in my mind as I drove east on the Long Island Expressway. It was good to fill my mind with a diversion. I was happy and relieved to escape the constant fear lurking in dark places in my mind, ready to unfurl itself into my thoughts at any moment. Instead, I went on a mental vacation with the author. Italy is a better, safer location than the cancer center. I learned that Elizabeth, like me, had invisible companions who drove in the car with her. When I drive in my car, God is always with me. I have a myriad of other ethereal passengers with me at different times.

As we pulled into the driveway, I left Italy in my imagination and reality brought me back to Long Island. Len was still asleep. I gently woke him and helped him into the house.

Gabriel met us at the door. "Hi, Dad. How do you feel?" he asked while giving Len a hug.

"Hi, Goobie. I feel really tired, but the treatment went well. How was your day so far?"

"Good. I played piano and then video games," he responded. "Go rest, Dad. I'll play some video games with you later if you want."

"Sounds good to me," Len tried to sound enthusiastic, but he was too tired to make it sound authentic.

I brought him up to Jared's room, tucked him into bed, and rubbed his back. He fell back asleep until 8:00 p.m. When he awoke, I gave him some dinner I had delivered earlier and then he joined Gabriel for some father-son video bonding time. I took note that he was groggier than in previous rounds. He had been asleep since almost 11:00 a.m. This would prove to be a problem. At 10:00 p.m., I said goodnight as the boys finished a few more minutes of gaming and suggested Len stay in Jared's room so he could watch a movie, catch up on emails, or play the video game he loves, *Civilization Revolution*. I needed some uninterrupted sleep. I reminded him to ring the bell next to the bed if he needed me. Little did I know, his day was just starting.

I awoke at 7:00 a.m. the next morning and checked in on him. Good. He was asleep. I decided to let him sleep until 9:00 a.m. since his treatment appointment was at 10:30 a.m. When I woke him, he was groggy. He told me he was up all night until 6:00 a.m. when he finally fell asleep. His sleep schedule was upside down. He pushed himself to get out of bed and took a shower. He put on sweats and a T-shirt and wearily walked down the stairs. I helped him lace his sneakers, and we drove to the cancer center. Like a baby in a car seat, the movement of the car rocked him back to sleep. We arrived back at the cancer center for a quick and uneventful infusion. We asked the nurse to please keep the drip slow to avoid the burning sensation in his arm. He thankfully stayed awake through it. Twenty minutes later we were back in the car, and Len fell asleep again on the drive home.

I decided to travel back to Italy with Elizabeth again today. I turned on the audiobook and listened as her calm voice took me back on her journey. The drive home was relaxing and imaginative. I would love to go to Italy on vacation. Maybe one day. As I pulled into the driveway, I sat and contemplated that thought as I gazed at Len asleep next to me. Then I thought, *Elizabeth Gilbert was on a personal quest, and so am I.* We all are on different quests at different times in our lives. My quest right now was to help Len eat, pray, and love his way through these treatments. I thanked her for bringing that awareness to me. Len eats and loves just fine, but his biggest challenge will be praying his way through all this. He isn't a spiritual man, but more a scientifically minded individual. Praying isn't something he does. Religion isn't something he connects with. Who knows—maybe these treatments and this cancer experience will open a portal for the potential of praying.

I helped Len upstairs and settled him back into bed. He was still so sleepy. Time for my Facebook post:

Round 3 of chemo: ✓
Len is halfway through treatment, upcoming scan in a week to check progress. We appreciate all the love, calls, texts, and prayers!

I chose a smiley face blowing a kiss and green hearts. Below I put a picture that read:

"We don't know how strong we are until being strong is the only choice we have. (National non-Hodgkin's Lymphoma Awareness.)"

The lettering was in black and the same green as the hearts. It coordinated nicely, I thought. Round three was officially complete.

Greenport Getaway

In June, I asked the girls if they would be interested in taking a day trip to Greenport in early July. I suggested we could have lunch, shop in town, kayak, and play mah jongg at the beach. With schedules coordinated, Delilah, Leigh, and Rose were able to come, making four the perfect number for mah jongg! The day of our trip, Rose and Leigh met me at my house, and we headed east to pick up Delilah. I packed my old square bridge table and my mom's mah jongg set. Delilah had four folding chairs. We were prepared for mah jongg! We had our bathing suits, towels, and a cooler filled with snacks and drinks. On our scenic drive to the North Fork, we passed vineyards and farm stands. We parked in town by the old Arcade where I used to shop as a kid. It was Greenport's version of a five-and-dime store. We walked to the pier and had lunch overlooking the Peconic River and Shelter Island. After our yummy lunch, we sat on lounge furniture on the open deck near the bar basking in the sun and friendship. We talked and laughed and just enjoyed being four women with no familial responsibilities for ten glorious hours.

We walked in town and passed the famous Claudio's Restaurant that was built in the 1800s and is an anchor of Greenport's history and charm. We shopped in a clothing store on Main Street, where Delilah and I got a few new fun things to wear. The store was crowded, and there was a line for the two dressing rooms. When a dressing room became available, Delilah and I decided to go in together to save time. We giggled as we wiggled into jumpers, tops, and leggings side by side in this tiny dressing room. After shopping, I showed the girls the carousel in town, and we walked by the water looking at the huge yachts that were docked as their owners enjoyed this old port town. On our drive to Orient State Park, we stopped at Lavender By the Bay to take in the serene beauty and the calming smell of what seemed like endless fields of fragrant lavender.

We arrived at the park around 3:30 p.m. ready for kayaking. Rose and I changed into our bathing suits. Delilah and Leigh had their bathing suits under their clothes already. Rose and Delilah hadn't kayaked before, so Leigh and I decided that we would each take a newbie. The attendant suited us up with life preservers and oars, and he dragged two double kayaks to the water's edge. Rose and I were together in one kayak, and Leigh and Delilah were together in another. The wind was calm and the water placid, so kayaking was easy and relaxing. Rose and I started to paddle in tandem, creating a rhythm that glided us through the water. We talked about our families, work, and cancer. The sounds of nature filled the quiet moments between conversations. Leigh and Delilah were doing great in their kayak and were busy in discussions of their own. Our hour flew by on the water. I was so happy to share this beautiful, scenic, and nostalgic place with my friends. We marked the occasion with a photo after we paddled back to shore.

After tipping the attendant, we walked back to the car to get our mah jongg gear: table, chairs, mah jongg set, cards, munchies, and drinks. We picked a shady spot under some trees on the beach near the picnic area to set up shop. Once we got settled, we mixed the tiles and stacked our walls. I was East and rolled the dice. *Funny,* I thought. *I guess this is closest to being my home, or at least it used to be so many years ago.* I felt happy being on the east end of Long Island sharing friendship, celebrating Delilah's birthday, and playing mah jongg. I smiled as I dealt the tiles. We all began to rack them, gathering like suits and like numbers. I had an East tile in my rack. As I glanced at it, I thought of the compass direction east and the significance this has in my life. It is the direction that will lead Len and me to our future summer home. It is the same direction my grandfather followed almost seventy-five years earlier from Yonkers, leading him to the seaport town of Greenport. If we take the time to look and to ponder, we can notice significance in something as common as a mah jongg tile. There is often a connection or hidden meaning in the things we are surrounded by. We can discover these hidden connections if we just take the time to search them out. I look through the eyes of wonder, and it enables me to find little treasures of meaning, little nuggets of gold that make me smile, nod my head in understanding, and say, "ah-hah."

As the sun began to set, it grew chilly, so we moved the table and chairs into what rays of sunshine were left and grabbed sweaters and shawls from the car. On the third game, I was playing a hand of Like Numbers, and I picked up a 2 Dot when it was my turn. I held the tile in my hand. My finger traced the circle round and round. Dots represent the circle of life. I thought of the generations of family who have passed on—my mother, grandparents, and great-grandparents. I am the third generation enjoying this beautiful town. I knew my mother and her mother and father were looking down and smiling on us playing mah jongg on the beach. I knew the seeds my mom planted in my heart so many years ago are still rooted there as I continued to visit the memories of my past with visits to this beautiful and quaint town.

As it got chillier, I looked down at my watch and couldn't believe two hours had flown by as we played on the beach. Mah jongg is a healthy distraction to keep my mind away from the fear cancer tries to impose on me along with the unpleasant company it keeps: sadness, worry, anxiety, and darkness. Mah jongg and my ladies bring me happiness, comfort, laughter, light, and delight when we play. This game and these ladies always refill my cup, keeping it never less than half-filled, just the way I like it.

It was almost 7:00 p.m., and we planned on having dinner at Hellenic Snack Bar in East Marion before heading home. We finished our last game, put away the mah jongg tiles, dice, and racks, packed the car, and went to the women's locker room at the beach to change into our clothes. We drove west a little until we saw the restaurant. We parked in the gravel parking lot. Rose saw a fawn nibbling on the grass about a hundred yards away from us. This was a Kodak moment, or more modernly known by Rose's phone as an Android moment. The way the rays of sunshine were shining through the trees was enchanting. We all took a few moments to watch the fawn and the God-like golden rays of sunshine coming toward us through the trees, like beams of holy light coming from the heavens. It was a breathtaking view.

We walked into Hellenic to be seated. We decided to sit inside as it was getting chilly, and we watched the sunset through the clear glass-enclosed dining room. The Greek salads here are probably the best I've ever eaten. Of course, the secret is all in the dressing. They use local produce in the summer months, but their dressing is the secret key ingredient to create a salad of pure yumminess. Delilah's birthday had been a few days ago, so I planned to celebrate with a piece of cake and a fun candle I had bought at Party City for the occasion, which played music and opened like a flower. I told the girls and the waitress beforehand what I had planned, hoping to keep it a secret from Delilah. I slipped the waitress the boxed candle while Delilah went to the ladies' room, and I hoped she would figure out how to use it. She thankfully did. After dinner, our waitress and her crew walked over with a piece of Oreo cake and this crazy candle that opened like a flower blooming while playing a warped rendition of "Happy Birthday to You." I also brought a foil happy birthday tiara, which I placed on Delilah's head as Leigh, Rose, and I joined in together singing "Happy Birthday to You." We brought a smile to Delilah's face, my friend whose husband's anniversary of passing was just a few days ago, two days before her birthday. I hoped Robert was smiling along with Delilah as I remembered to keep the promise he asked of me.

Chapter 14

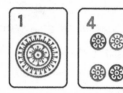

Mid-Treatment Scan

Halfway through treatment, Len was to be scheduled for a scan to see how the treatment was working. He was apprehensive, but I had deep-seated faith. The oncologist recommended a PET scan, but Len had doubts after learning it could be toxic for his body, and he would only agree to one after the sixth treatment was completed. He requested to have an MRI instead, and the doctor acquiesced. The MRI would scan and focus on both eyes and the chest area. The doctor instructed us to call and make an appointment with the radiology department. Len decided that before we scheduled the MRI, he wanted to plan a vacation.

Interesting, I thought to myself and said, "Fine, where to?"

I decided if this was what he needed to help him get through the scan, so be it.

"I've been reading about Halifax. It's a fishing seaport, and I'd like to go. Let's shoot for August in between treatments," he suggested.

"Ok, let's explore Halifax," I responded in agreement.

We looked at dates for me to schedule the scan for him. I found it curious that he wouldn't let me book the scan until he booked our trip. I respected his feelings. I knew it gave him a sense of control, something he got to make a decision about. So much was dictated by tests, medical procedures, and doctor visits. He made plane and hotel reservations for Halifax. Then I made a scan appointment in the radiology department for him for the end of July, a few days after the next chemo treatment. I knew the hotel bed would be one of comfort, relaxation, and rest. The MRI bed is one of discomfort, anxiety, and fear.

The day of the scan, Len decided to go alone, leaving work early that day. He had two separate MRIs in one session. He explained the procedure to me that night when he came home. An IV was placed in his arm for when the contrast was to be administered. First was a brain and orbital scan. This was necessary because he had cancer under one eye and by the optic nerve in the other. The second scan was of the upper chest. He lay down on the narrow bed and was slowly brought into the tubular machine. For the facial MRI, Len had to wear a mask that helped the test to pinpoint cancer cells. He said he had to wear the mask for the whole test, which was forty-five very long minutes. He described feeling like a sardine in a can.

He told me about the flashback he had while lying in the MRI machine. He was ten years old again, at camp in Forest Hills. He and a group of boys were in the locker room doing silly boy things, and they each put themselves into their locker and closed the doors shut. Just so happened Len's locker jammed, and he couldn't get it open. The other boys tried but couldn't open it either. Len started screaming for help. He panicked, feeling the smallness of this space while being in near darkness. The only light was coming from the slats in the locker door. He was using up the stagnant air in the locker while screaming and breathing heavily. One of the boys was smart and ran for help. A counselor rushed into the locker room and, after fiddling with the latch, finally got it unstuck and opened the door, giving Len air, light, and freedom.

That same feeling of panic started to creep down his spine during the scan. The staccato noise drumming into his ears from the machine was unnerving for him. The earplugs they gave him were useless. After thirty-two minutes, he finally came out. He thought he was finished.

The tech said, "Now we need to give you contrast."

Len said, "Guys, there's no way I can do more of this. I'm having trouble."

"It's only seven to eight minutes for this one, sir. It's important to complete the test with contrast for the most accurate results," he was told.

"Okay. I think I can get through just a few more minutes. This sucks, you know."

"I've heard that from many patients, Sir. I've never had one personally, but I do them all day, and honestly, some patients can't finish the test. You are doing great."

Len went back in; he felt the contrast going into his vein. He explained to me it was like a mild burning sensation in his arm, but nothing like the chemo burn.

The repetitive noises of the machine sounded again and, after about eight minutes, the tech's voice filled the tube, and he said, "We are done. You will be coming out of the machine now."

Len heard a click, and the table slid out of the tubular chamber back out into the spacious room, giving Len air, light, and freedom. He was out of the locker in his memory and was of the MRI tube. The mask was taken off, the IV removed, and Len was more than relieved. He faced his fear. He used his cancer patient artillery; courage, strength, and fortitude. I was proud of him as I sat and listened to him talk about the scan.

Waiting for scan results is a time of worry and hope mixed up together. To help me through the waiting, I relied on faith. We received the results the next day. The treatment was working! The eight-centimeter legion in his chest, being the largest, was almost resolved. The two areas of the eye had gone down about 20 percent. This was good news, but Len was hoping for it to have shrunk more. This test didn't give us results on the iliacus muscle legion and a few other areas where there was cancer, but the eyes and chest areas were of major concern and were focused on for this test. The PET scan in three months would give us a whole-body image and show if and where any cancer remained. We were happy with the results and felt confident that the chemo was working. The test results were a relief to our worried minds.

Faith helped me through. Faith has always been an integral part of who I am. It's ethereal and intangible like emotions and time are, but I clearly feel its effects within me. Faith fills me with hope; it's a warm and expanding feeling. Hope fills me with peace, bringing me a sense of calm and repose. Peace leads me to grace, where I bask in its golden glory. Maybe faith, hope, peace, and grace keep company with *b'shert*. I will have faith in the doctors caring for my husband and faith that chemotherapy and immunotherapy will help put Len's cancer into remission for as long as possible. I have faith that each day will be manageable for my husband physically and mentally. Faith will carry me through this journey as Len's partner, wife, and caregiver. I have faith in *b'shert*, but still, I know *b'shert* has the final say in the outcome.

Poolside Mah Jongg

Group text: Delilah, Rose, Amanda, Leigh
Me: Hi girls! Who can play and who can host on Monday?
Rose: I'll host, 11:30 a.m. We'll play poolside, weather depending.
Amanda: Sounds enticing! I'm in!
Delilah: See you ladies then!
Leigh: I'll be there too!
Me: Awesome! Have a great weekend, and I'll see everyone on Monday at Rose's.

It was late July, and summer was in its full glory here on Long Island. Gabriel was at camp enjoying studying art and piano at Usdan. I drove him to camp, came home, practiced yoga, meditated, showered, and got ready for mah jongg. Monday was my favorite day of the week! I dressed in shorts, a floral top, and wedges. I accessorized with a floral costume jewelry necklace, CZ studs, my mom's sterling silver bangle bracelets, and a few rings. I do like my bling! I blew my hair out straight, despite knowing the summer humidity would change my straightened locks into waves within two hours. I grabbed a hair clip for a twisted updo, if necessary, later.

I drove to Rose's, looking forward to seeing my friends and playing mah jongg. I was eager to share the good news about Len's scan with them too. We all arrived at Rose's house and decided to play outside since it was a lovely summer day. We put suntan lotion on, poured glasses with ice and water, filled our snack plates, and sat at the mah jongg table set up next to the picturesque pool. Rose had six planters filled with colorful and blooming annual flowers. Purple wave petunias draped down from the tall planters. White and pink impatiens added color and beauty to the mix. The flower bed next to the house had pops of red color from geraniums. These are Delilah's favorite flower. Rose turned on '80s music.

"Ladies, I feel like I'm at a hotel," I said, feeling relaxed. "I feel as though I am on vacation here at Rose's Mah Jongg Resort."

"Me too!" Leigh agreed.

If there are five of us playing, we usually take a turn rotating out or play two together at one rack. Fran taught us to have a bettor when we have five players. It's a good learning opportunity for the bettor. She can watch how other players rack their tiles, form hands, and strategize as the game progresses. It's fun to decide who you think has the greatest chance to win after the Charleston is complete. I decided to be the bettor for the first game. Rose had set the mah jongg racks and walls of tiles up for the players. She was East and rolled the dice, each displaying a six.

"Love a last wall of twelve tiles, *and* the winner gets paid double!" Delilah said.

Rose dealt, giving herself fourteen tiles and the other girls thirteen tiles. Everyone got to work. This is where you bring your skill into play, grouping suits and searching for possible hands to develop. It's a quiet time of the game, as concentration is needed for the search. They started the Charleston. I had been walking around the table, watching each woman create a sense of order out of the random tiles on her rack. I decided the person with the strongest chance of winning would have the fewest pairs to fill in, be playing an exposed hand, and have the most tiles in her hand after the Charleston. I bet on Rose, who was playing a Quints hand. She had six tiles, and a Joker filled in. She needed seven more tiles to win. She had the strongest hand, in my opinion. As the game progressed, I walked around and checked on how each player's hand was developing or not. A lot of this game is luck.

Amanda was working on a hand in Consecutive Run, Delilah was filling in a 1 3 5 7 9 hand, and Leigh was playing an Any Like Numbers hand. Tiles got picked, racked, and thrown. I liked to see how the women played, what chances they individually took, what strategies they used, and what luck came their way. Jokers are picked in a clandestine manner. No smiling—you don't want to give any sign of excitement. You can only smile when replacing a Joker from an exposure and of course when you call mah jongg, which Amanda does on her next pick. I bet wrong.

Her Consecutive Run hand came in beautifully, and she was lucky to get two Jokers. She exposed her winning hand as the other players exposed their losing hands.

"Which hand is that?" asked Rose.

"The second line under Consecutive Run," Amanda replied.

The girls started looking confused. Apparently, Amanda's tiles didn't match correctly. Amanda picked up her card and turned it over.

"Oops. It's the 2017 card!" she said. "I crack myself up!" Everyone started laughing along with her. As bettor, I didn't notice the hand was off. Just two tiles were different and, since I don't memorize the card, I didn't catch it. Amanda fished around in her purse for her mah jongg cardholder, took out the 2018 card, and put away the 2017 card. Rose as East, rotated out and was now the bettor. I took her seat to play in the next game.

I was waiting for the right moment to share the news with the girls about Len's scan results. As we mixed the tiles, I said, "Ladies, I have really exciting and promising news. Len got his scan results back, and the cancer is shrinking! The treatment is working!"

Everyone stopped mixing the tiles and started clapping and gave me comments of support and love. Rose came over and gave me a hug. I knew how lucky I was to be among these women, my friends, my confidantes, my supporters, and my cheerleaders. If the results weren't good, I knew they would be there to help me through that scenario too. Our mah jongg sisterhood is so special and important in my life. Mondays have become a day I cherish every week because of this game and these wonderful women.

I'm part of the Facebook group: Mah Jongg, That's It! I posted this question: What do you love most about your mah jongg game?

I received two hundred comments from mah jongg-loving players. They welcomed the opportunity to answer my question. At that time, this Facebook group was a sisterhood of 17,000 mah jongg players! We are a fun-loving group of women, and even some men, who share the love and camaraderie mah jongg creates. Comments included how the game keeps our minds alert, sharp, attuned, and uses the critical thinking part of our brain. Women feel mah jongg is like therapy. I agree! My group agrees too! One woman responded that she is a therapist, and playing mah jongg, being with friends, and laughing is therapy to her! We love the food, the socialization, and a break from careers, household chores, parenting, responsibilities, and obligations to others.

It was clear we all feel the same—game time is our time! We're one strong sisterhood of players. I loved reading all of their responses. Their answers were spontaneous, heartfelt, and real.

Round Four

I took Len for his chemo appointments, but it was July and Gabriel was in camp. He is still the center of my life, my schedule revolving around his. I was in a scheduling dilemma. The camp bus picked him up at 9:30 a.m. Len's appointment at the cancer center was at the same time. Alex thankfully was able to help out and dropped Len off at the cancer center. He is a dutiful, responsible, and family-oriented young man. After Gabriel left for camp, I left to meet Len.

I pulled up to the valet service and dropped off the car. As I entered the sliding doors and got my bearings, I figured out I was in the radiology department and would have to walk through the waiting room to get to the treatment center. I took in so much on that short walk. I saw patients who were going through chemo treatment, leaving some of them bald, looking tired and fatigued from their battle. The men were less self-conscious of their hairless heads, while women donned baseball hats, scarves, or bandanas. I thought of David's wife and the berets that were her signature head-covering. Some women wore make-up, some didn't. Some smiled as I passed by, our eyes meeting for a fleeting moment; some stared out, their gaze lost in thought. I felt self-conscious, almost guilty for my hair and my vitality. I saw couples sitting and holding hands, an invisible bond of love and strength between them. Some patients were with friends, some with family. I hardly saw anyone sitting alone in the radiology waiting room or the chemo treatment rooms. Maybe there's a silver lining to cancer. Maybe it brings people together. It reveals the fragility of life, love, and time. What are the lessons one learns from cancer? I guess the answer is different for everyone you ask.

Rose answers, "Cancer taught me not to take life for granted, to live for today, and be mindful of enjoying as much of life as possible."

Delilah answers, "Cancer has taught me two things. First, it is possible to experience intense pain and still have the capacity to experience great joy at the same time, and that is okay. The second is living your life the way you want. Put it all out there because you only get one chance."

David answers, "Life is too short. Cherish the time you have and don't sweat the small stuff. You learn what big stuff versus the little stuff in life is."

Fran answers, "I've certainly learned a lot. I observed my husband form a friendship in the waiting room of the cancer center with a man who did not speak English. Words need not be spoken. Compassion and understanding transcend all languages. I learned, after spending days and nights in a frantic race to research any available treatments that could save my son, that honesty exists through uncertainty. I spoke with doctors at leading hospitals around the country about clinical trials, a Chinese herbalist, a marijuana dealer in Oregon, and naturopathic clinics offering alternatives to chemo.

"All of the people I spoke with I found to be honest and compassionate. No one could promise us anything and felt Sam was at the best place receiving the best care. The only problem was . . . it wasn't working.

"My world changed immediately to a parallel universe, with one foot in my original world and the other foot in the New York City cancer world filled with doctors, chemo, scans, surgeries, meetings, days, nights, and holidays spent at my son's side in the hospital.

"I quickly realized who would be there for me, offering continued support through this long ordeal. Surprisingly, it is not always who you think it will be. Some are there, but then it's those who surprise you with their strength, compassion, and wisdom who make you cherish your friendship and moments together more than you ever thought possible.

"I noticed the transition to the new me and saw changes in my family. Banding together and being there for Sam changed us. We discovered strength and resilience that I can assure you none of us knew we had hidden within us. These are the gifts that, despite everything, I will always be appreciative of. Sam leads the way . . . with his determined attitude to beat this, with an amazing ability to stay strong and resilient. He rarely complains and never asks, 'why me?' He makes the most of each and every day. I know everyone thinks they have the best kids, but I really do. Even cancer can't change that."

Len answers, "There are so many things in life that are precious but are often taken for granted. We hear this a lot and often simply nod our heads and concur. I, for one, have been guilty of this. I believe this is due, in part, to never being faced with a painful, debilitating disease that can quickly rob you of your precious future years of life. A cancer diagnosis dramatically changes your perspective on life. Suddenly, one needs to plan for an untimely death and make sure that all pieces are put together for the long-term survival of the rest of the family. It is truly overwhelming and very sad for the entire family. After I discovered I had cancer, I deliberated with alternative treatment options for over one year before I started with traditional chemo and immunotherapy treatments, which lasted for six months. During that time, I came to realize how lucky I have been and how precious the most basic human conditions are in one's life. Allow me to explain.

"Your memory is precious. Through my treatment, my short-term memory has become severely affected. Common words to finish sentences sometimes escape me. Remembering things I did the day before is cloudy and troublesome. The abilities to taste, chew, and swallow are precious. During treatment, my ability to taste became compromised. Most foods became bland and tasteless. Brushing teeth is precious. It is normally a painless and mindless experience until you get mouth sores. Chewing and swallowing are precious until gum sores hurt so much that you lose your appetite. Your sense of touch is precious. Through treatment, I developed neuropathy in my left arm. I am a righty, so I was partially spared. But basic things like taking a shower or wearing a coat as it brushed up against my left arm hurt.

"Through all this, I remembered what one of my oncologists said about my cancer. There would be good and bad days. The six months of treatments I experienced, I suppose, were the bad days. I was hoping for better days to come. And they will. I have completed half my treatments to date, and the MRI shows the treatment is working. Hurray! But not so fast . . . my cancer diagnosis does not have a textbook cure. I am hopeful, but no matter what happens, I now sincerely understand how precious life can be and how amazing it is to go through each day, with our mundane tasks, and do it all pain-free. I've been blessed to be comforted before, during, and after treatment by my loved ones, family, and dear friends. I feel that everyone should go through six months of cancer treatment and then be cured. Each of us would then appreciate life in a new way, and the world would truly be a better place to live in."

Here's what I have learned so far: cancer can start as a quiet tempest, growing in intensity and scope. It creates reflection not only for its host, but also for those who love its host. Reflections about mortality, life, love, relationships, feelings of fear and uncertainty have risen to the surface of my consciousness. When I reframe, I can say cancer creates an opportunity for education, understanding, acceptance, and growth. It strengthens bonds and opens hearts. It opens new relationships and may close others. It's an opportunity for people in your life to show up and show you who they are . . . or not. I know who my people are through this life challenge.

It's a journey no person wants to take. It offers round-trip tickets to some and one-way tickets to others. It creates the opportunity to become a warrior and to dig down deep and pull every ounce of resolve your cells own to fight this bitch of a disease. I also learned Len is lucky so far, in cancer terms. Len's cancer is slow growing for now. His treatment plan of chemo and immunotherapy is tolerable. There are much harsher cocktails used for more aggressive lymphomas. I pray he won't need one in the future. I have learned cancer doesn't discriminate about age or gender, but I question its goal as I do with all disease. If it kills the host, it dies too. It doesn't discriminate about longevity either. It can only focus on the here and now, multiplying and mutating to preserve its existence. But there's a lesson in its survival mechanism—for each of us to live in the here and now too. I've learned writing about it helps me understand myself on this journey with Len and how I deal with the fear and uncertainty that cancer brings along with its diagnosis.

I walked through the exit door of the radiology department, entered the treatment center, and found Len in a private room. Today's treatment was going to take about two and a half hours. He was seated in a recliner. The IV was in his hand, I noticed. I asked why? They need to let the veins in his arms heal I was told. I sadly realized that the chemo has started damaging more than the cancer. The Benadryl made him sleepy. I brought my laptop to keep busy while he slept. I put on relaxing music to keep him in a restful and peaceful space. I wonder what he dreams about. *Maybe, being in a healthier place, a place without cancer, without chemo and its side effects. Sleep and dream of pleasant things, my love; dream of Halifax.*

Day two of round four went well. We knew to tell the nurse to keep the drip at a slower rate so that the Treanda wouldn't burn so badly. We sat, hopeful, through July's treatment knowing the results from the MRI showed that the Rituxan and Treanda were working. This round was thankfully uneventful. Len updated me about details for the trip to Halifax. I was glad he chose the destination and planned this trip. I knew it helped him get through the scan and gave him something special to look forward to. The scan results promised us hope and time—hope for health and remission; time to create moments of togetherness as a couple and as a family. Moments that will become cherished memories until we create more moments and more memories and perpetuate this cycle as long as we can. Please, God. Grant us longevity.

When the Treanda was finished, we headed outside into the hot July day. I gave the valet my ticket, and we sat together on the bench. A car pulled up, and the driver went to get a wheelchair. He arrived with it and opened the back door of the car. Inside sat a frail elderly woman coming to get chemotherapy. I assumed it was the driver's mother. I stood up and walked over to the car as her son tried to help her out safely. Len got up and held the wheelchair after locking the wheels in place. I helped the man get his mother into the wheelchair, offering her my hand and guiding her steps up the curb and then getting her seated comfortably into the wheelchair. She and her son thanked Len and me as the valet drove off with their car. We sat back down on the bench, holding hands as we waited for our car to arrive. This is one of the values we both share in our marriage—helping others, even strangers. This is not only a Jewish value but also a human value. We are *mitzvah* people, driven by the intrinsic desire to help others. Now only if this treatment will help my husband, we will both be eternally grateful. Our car pulled up, and I got Len into his seat.

The valet walked over to the passenger side of the car and said, "That was really nice of you guys to help that old lady and her son."

"Cancer won't stop me from helping others," Len said with determination.

I smiled at the valet. "Have a good day and stay cool; it's going to be a hot one."

When I got home, I made my Facebook post. I chose a picture of two boxing gloves. I wrote above the picture:

Round 4 of chemo: ✓
Len is more than halfway through treatment! A recent scan shows the cancer is getting smaller. We're feeling thankful and blessed!

Chapter 15

Halifax

Len started a bucket list. He was putting together a list of places he wanted to visit and things he wanted to do. I thought this was a great idea, and I planned to start my own. No one needs to wait for a life-threatening illness or circumstance to think about his or her bucket list. Italy and India are two destinations that will be on my list. Len recently went to North Dakota with his dad and Alex. They went fishing and hiking and had some male bonding time together. North Dakota was checked off his list. Len also wanted to go to Halifax. He booked our trip, then I booked his scan in June. I agreed to wait like he requested, mostly because I wanted to be amenable and say yes to nearly anything he asked since he started chemo. He excitedly planned the trip in between treatment sessions. The Halifax trip provided a token for accomplishing three rounds of treatment and making it to the halfway point. We all do things like this, don't we? Sometimes it's a treat in the form of a celebratory dinner, a piece of jewelry, an article of clothing, a massage, or some other special something that resonates with us.

In early August, we embarked on a family journey to Nova Scotia with Alex and Gabriel. I dropped our dog, Coco, at the pet sitter's. We arrived with plenty of time at LaGuardia Airport. Our flight was scheduled for 8:02 p.m. We checked in, deposited our luggage, and to our surprise, there was no wait going through security. I was hopeful this was a mystical sign that our trip was off to a smooth start. I was wrong.

We got our first delay notice by text around 6:00 p.m. The flight was delayed twenty-five minutes. This was only a slight inconvenience. It gave us some added time for a leisurely dinner in the airport. The second text came in around 7:00 p.m. The delay was now an additional hour. We had finished dinner and decided to proceed to the gate to wait there. We had electronics to help pass the time with ample charging stations to help keep our devices charged while we were waiting. The third text came in saying an additional thirty-five-minute delay was now being added to the departure time, along with a gate change, which we discovered was on the lower level of the airport. When we arrived downstairs, all the seats were taken, and we had to sit on the floor. As we sat there, I realized I had never taken a flight from this level before. Len asked the attendant at the new gate what was going on. She said the pilot who was supposed to fly the plane was over his fly limit for the day. The airline was searching for a relief pilot. Anxiety started to set in. The change of the pilot just altered this flight. That unsettled me. Was this bad juju? Flying isn't something I'm comfortable with. I usually take Xanax with me when I fly, but I had run out.

Finally, at 10:00 p.m. we were notified a pilot had been assigned to our flight. We were asked to start to board at the gate. We lined up, gave our tickets to the attendant, and instead of walking through a boarding bridge to a plane, we stepped onto a platform where a bus was waiting for us. Anxiety started creeping up from my stomach into my chest now. I was getting a little short of breath. I know what this bus means and where it was taking us. I've heard about these flights. Yes, the ones with a small passenger plane that boards out on the tarmac. I wasn't feeling positive at that moment of discovery.

Oh no! I thought. *It is pouring rain outside. When did this happen?* The last time I saw daylight, it wasn't raining. We boarded the bus. Wind and rain were whipping against the windows as we were driven to the plane. Anxiety was reaching my eyes. They are too expressive. I barely have a poker face for my mah jongg games, let alone in times of stress. Len sensed my unease. The bus came to a stop. I held my purse tightly and braced myself as I entered the threatening storm between the bus and the plane. As I stepped down off the bus, strong gusts of wind whipped my hair around. The rain felt like pellets stinging my skin. I ran up the wet stairs hoping not to slip. A smiling and dry flight attendant greeted me. I tried to smile back, but it wasn't real. I was drenched from the rain, and my nerves nearing meltdown status overtook my command station. I couldn't force a smile on my lips. I wanted to stay on the ground, here in New York. *The skies aren't safe tonight.* I think she saw my eyes filled with fear and anxiety.

I walked farther into the plane. Our seats were rows twelve and thirteen. Good. I assumed that was the middle of the plane. I was wrong. Bad. It wasn't a very long walk to get to our seats. Shit, we're the last two rows in this small plane. Thirteen is the last seat number. That's kind of ominous, don't you agree? Who decided this was acceptable? Elevators don't have a thirteenth-floor button, what's wrong with the airline industry? Don't the people deciding these small details know some travelers have anxiety and believe in superstition? My anxiety reached my imagination. Wild and scary thoughts tried to surface. My will tried to squelch them, but it was losing.

We sat down. The seats were small and cramped. Although I'm petite, I felt claustrophobic. The flight attendant came over to tell us that we are delayed yet again. Apparently lightning struck on the tarmac, and all ground personnel were directed to safe shelter inside the airport.

Our luggage was abandoned along with my sense of calm. I was breathing heavily. Len joked with the flight attendant that I needed a double vodka with cranberry juice. She smiled at him. I glared back at him between the crack of space between my seat and Gabriel's.

"Look, Mom," Gabriel said, showing me his phone with excitement. "There's a tornado watch right now, here in Queens, New York!"

My heart raced. That was why it was so windy when we got off the bus. This wasn't going well. Then the flight attendant came back with a drink in her hand.

"Ma'am, your double vodka with cranberry," she said with a smile.

I thought she understood Len was joking, but she took him seriously.

"Thank you," I said, as calmly as I could.

I took the drink in hopes it would calm my nerves. I rarely drink. A tornado watch as I was about to take off in a plane was also a rare occurrence. I started sipping. I needed to relax. I had no Xanax to ease my anxiety. Gabriel was holding my empty hand reassuringly. The rain stopped. This was good. But I kept sipping anyway. Who knew what was next tonight? As the vodka burned my throat, it created a warm sensation in me, and I was beginning to feel less anxious.

Then the pilot came on the loudspeaker. "Ladies and gentlemen, I'm very sorry, but I was just informed that our flight to Halifax has been cancelled. Please gather your belongings, exit the plane to the awaiting bus, and see the attendant back in the terminal to make alternate flight arrangements. We are very sorry for any inconvenience."

I took another sip of the vodka. My anxiety lifted completely. I was calm again. I knew what just happened. *B'shert.* Our flight was cancelled, but I thought to myself something terrible that was going to happen was also cancelled, averted by destiny. I was content with this thought as I departed the thirteen-row aircraft.

It took another hour and a half to retrieve our luggage. We used the Uber app and were driven back to Melville. We finally arrived at 1:45 a.m. Home sweet home.

Vacation Plan B

We decided to go to Greenport for a few days since our Halifax trip was cancelled. Delta had rerouted the flight two days later with two connecting flights. It would turn a two-hour flight to Halifax into twelve hours. No thanks! After last night's fiasco at the airport, I preferred a getaway that included a car, not a plane. I was able to book a last-minute reservation at a condo called Cliffside Resort in Greenport for two nights. It has water views, a beach, and a pool. It was the height of the summer season, and unlike the sleepy town Greenport was when I was a young girl, it has now become a popular spot for tourists and people wanting a quick getaway from Manhattan and western

Long Island. We unpacked our large suitcases from the cancelled Halifax trip and packed smaller suitcases and totes for Greenport. Len wanted to take our bicycles and skillfully got the four of them on the bike rack of Alex's car. In the meantime, I dropped our dog back at the dog sitter's house. When I returned home, the suitcases were packed in the car, and the bicycles were secured on the bike rack. We were ready for family fun and adventure.

Len loved the scenic drive once we exited the Long Island Expressway. Fields of green replace the mega malls and urban sites we were accustomed to seeing in western Long Island. There are no tall buildings here. Macy's and Bed Bath & Beyond aren't doing business here, even in 2018. Nature provides generations of families their business out east. Vineyards as well as sod, fruit, and vegetable farms are the common commerce in this area of Long Island. The scenery was soothing, relaxing, and inviting. Len has mentioned on these drives how he has always wanted to get a summerhouse out in the Greenport area. I agree it would be a nice dream. Maybe one day . . .

We arrived an hour and twenty minutes later in town and decided to eat lunch and walk around, as check-in time at the condo was at 3:00 p.m. We ate lunch at the same restaurant where I took the girls a few weeks ago on the pier, overlooking Shelter Island. We had locally-caught fish and crab. The salads were made from fresh locally-grown produce. The tomatoes were sweet and delicious. I made sure Len had a seat overlooking the water and Shelter Island. He was relaxed. I was thankful. He needed to slow down from the intensity of his job and his very long commute, as well as take a break from the constant worry of cancer. After we finished lunch, we sat on the outdoor couches and lounge furniture on the pier. There were multimillion-dollar yachts and a replica of a British sailing vessel docked nearby. We gazed out at Shelter Island, breathing in the salty air as the four of us nestled together on the couch. We were happy and relaxed, soaking in the summer sun. Len's phone rang. He looked down and saw it was Jim calling.

"I want to catch up with Jim. I'll be back in about fifteen minutes."

"Sure, say hi for me, please."

I sat with the boys like a momma bird does with her hatchlings in her nest. I felt happy and relaxed at that very moment. When Len came back, he told me Jim was holding his own, but in pain from the cancer in his bones. He was deciding whether or not to try traditional radiation and hormone therapy next week. The alternative treatments weren't stopping the growth of his cancer. Len said Jim sounded upbeat and positive. Little did we know this would be the last time the two men would ever speak.

Later we stopped in the local food market to get food to prepare for breakfast: fruits, vegetables, coffee, and milk, then headed over to the condo and checked in. We were directed to our second-floor unit on the left side of the development. We discovered there were no elevators. We'd have to carry the luggage up the stairs. When I checked us in, I saw there was a bike rack next to the pool where we could leave and lock up our bikes. Our unit was around the corner from the pool and a short distance from the steps leading down the cliff to the beach. Len untethered the four bikes and put them to the side of the car. He fiddled with the bike rack and was then able to open the hatchback so we could unload the luggage. We started the procession of parading the luggage from the parking lot up the flights of stairs.

The unit was the perfect size for us. There were two bedrooms—the master with a king size bed, and the second bedroom with two twin beds. There were two bathrooms, a small living room, and a functional kitchenette. There was a balcony as well. I opened the sliding doors that led to the balcony. We overlooked the pool. No, more precisely, the pool was directly below us. It was so close I could throw a stone into it. I saw the bike rack and suggested we take the bikes there now.

"Um, we have a problem. I left the bike locks in the garage," Len confessed.

Years ago, I would have been very frustrated by this mistake. Cancer changes things, though. I let so many things roll off my back nowadays, and this was one of them. I'm trying not to sweat the small stuff.

"I'm sure if we just leave the bikes there unlocked, they will be fine," I calmly responded.

"No way, those bikes are worth over $2,000," Len said with responsibility and authority.

"Do you want to strap them back onto the bike rack then?" I said, raising my eyebrows inquisitively.

"No, we'll have to bring them up here."

Alex and I looked at each other incredulously.

"Are you kidding?" I asked.

"No. Let's go—they will be stolen if we leave them unlocked," he said with conviction.

So the four of us went down the stairs to retrieve our bikes. We wheeled them over to the stairway and assessed the situation. The stairway was narrow with a bend up to the next level of stairs. So that would be two bends and two flights of stairs. It was easy to navigate luggage, but a bicycle? This could be a little tricky. Len went first, taking his bike up five stairs to the first level, around the first bend, up ten stairs to the in-between floor balcony, around that bend, and up the stairs to our unit. He placed his bike in the living room. I followed next. I grabbed the handlebars and proceeded up the first five stairs. The weight of the bicycle seemed to increase as I climbed the stairs, making it more difficult than I expected. I slowly and methodically made it up to the first landing. I took a break for a few seconds. This wasn't an easy task, but I like challenges and was determined to do this.

Noticing the time lapse, Len asked, "Need help?"

"I've got this, thanks," I responded with determination.

I pushed the handlebars up the incline. Damn! This was difficult. I stopped and tried to pull instead of push. That didn't work. The weight of the bike from that angle was impossible for me to wheel upwards. I went back to pushing. I made it to the second landing that overlooked the stairs. The boys were watching me. I waved and said, "Dad will be down to help with Gabe's bike in a minute or two."

Ten more stairs and I've got this, I thought. I was sweating but still determined. Len opened the door and met me on the stairs to grab the bike. He wheeled it into the cozy living room, housing one bike already. He kicked the kickstand open and rested my bike there. He wheeled his bike into the master bedroom. He came back for my bike and wheeled it out onto the small balcony. He went to help the boys with their bikes up the stairs. Alex was able to maneuver his bike up the stairs, but Gabriel needed help. Len put one bike in the boys' room and the last one out on the balcony with the other bike. Our perfectly-sized condo now had four unexpected residents on wheels, making it a little overcrowded.

We decided to take a walk down to the beach together. We walked back down the stairs, passed the pool and the useless bike rack, and crossed the expansive lawn heading to the beach. We found the stairs and walked down to the beach below the cliff. The music of the beach welcomed me back. I could hear the waves gently crashing on the shore. It melodically soothed my soul. We walked along the rocky water's edge, taking the salty air into our lungs, and letting any stress from work or cancer or bikes be carried away by the sea breeze. There has always been something about the beach that attracts me to it. It is calming, serene and therapeutic. It's as though the mermaid's call lures me here.

It was getting late, and we decided to eat dinner at Hellenic Snack Bar and started to walk back up the stairs from the beach to our condo. We freshened up, then drove a few minutes east. Dinner was delicious as it always was at Hellenic. Of course, I had the Greek salad. After dinner, we decided to drive into town and walk around. We stopped at the carousel and watched the colorful wooden horses filled with smiling children and adults go round and round as carnival music added to the festive ambience. This carousel is almost one hundred years old, and it adds to the charm and grandeur of Greenport. Gabriel used to love going on the carousel on our visits here when he was younger. We all decided to connect with our inner child and take a ride that night. We bought tickets; each chose a horse and climbed up. Time was marking itself. I thought of Gabriel being thirteen years old, enjoying thirteen years riding on this carousel and visiting Greenport, just as I enjoyed thirteen years of my life in my summerhouse, this beautiful town and all it had to offer to me as a young girl. As the carousel started moving forward, for a brief moment, I was taken back in time and surrendered to the innocence of my childhood, my adult worries of cancer and uncertainty gone, if only for a few minutes, as I was lost in this feeling of resplendent bliss.

After the carousel, we stopped for some ice cream and sat by the pier overlooking Shelter Island. I was happy and content, and so was my family. The following day we chartered a boat and captain to take us fishing, a sport we all enjoy. We took the ferry from Greenport over to Shelter Island and then drove to the pier where the captain was waiting for us. The sky was sunny and clear. We fished for three hours. Thoughts of my mom filled my mind as they do any time I'm on a boat or fishing. I felt connected to her as I dropped my line into the water.

The captain instructed us how to release our line and feel when the sinker hits the bottom of the sea floor. No need captain, my mom taught me well. We caught porgies, a few sea robins, and black striped bass. We kept five porgies that the captain filleted for us. Len was eager to cook the fish for our dinner. As we headed back to Greenport, we were all a little tired. I was so happy to spend time together with Len and the boys. I missed Jared not being with us, but he was living in Florida with my in-laws, and I was content that he was happy and exploring a career in real estate. Family time is precious. Life is so busy, and I see now more than ever how precious time is, and the importance of creating time together as a family when we can.

When we arrived at the condo, we rested up for a little while. Later Len got busy preparing the fish, and I started making the salad. We had forgotten to buy olive oil spray, but we did have olive oil. The pans in the kitchenette weren't nonstick. Len used so much oil to prevent the fish from sticking; I couldn't begin to figure out the fat and calorie content. The condo filled with the smell of cooking fish. I had to open up the patio door to diffuse it. Kids were swimming in the pool below the balcony, their voices loud and . . . well, kind of annoying. At that moment, I had to choose between smelly fish or noise. Smelly fish won out, and I kept the door open. I turned on some music to drown out the swimmers' voices.

When Len finished cooking the fish, we decided to eat on the balcony despite the noise and the bikes crowding us. We moved the table and four chairs over so we could fit along with the bikes. As the sun was setting, the air grew cooler outside. The fish was fresh, breaded, and dripping with oil, although we patted the pieces with a paper towel. We ate our catch, salad, and potatoes. Len felt very proud and accomplished catching and cooking the fish. I secretly prefer going out or buying prepared food. I really don't like to cook. I made some tea for us, and we sat outside a while longer enjoying the view and the family time. If only the kids in the pool were a little quieter, this would be a near perfect moment. We put the leftover fish in the fridge and cleaned up. I texted my childhood friend, Soula, who still summers in Greenport, to see if we could get together while I was in town. We set up a time to meet later that night around 8:15 p.m. at her house.

We arrived at her home that she had recently rebuilt. It was a beautiful, modern home with large windows to take in the beautiful scenery of the property and the view of the harbor. We had only seen each other three times in the last twenty years. I recalled her mother's memorial service, which was about eight years ago. It was an informal, touching service where we all shared memories of her mother. It was a nostalgic and emotional day for me. Our mothers were very close friends. The service was held in the original house, in the sun parlor, a room where we hung out as kids.

We reconnected last year when I was visiting Greenport. After driving through my old neighborhood and passing my house on Inlet Lane, I passed Soula's house. I saw two cars were in the driveway and decided to knock on the door and see if she was home. I walked up the stairs and knocked tentatively on the door. Her daughter answered. I introduced myself, and then my old friend appeared at the door. Soula and I hugged hello and were excited to see one another. So many years had passed between us. Our moms were the best of friends, and we spent many summer days on the beach together swimming, digging in the sand, boating, and water skiing. We hung out at night with some other local kids and were part of each other's Greenport memories for many years. She welcomed Len, Gabriel, and me into her home, introduced us to her husband, and gave us a tour. Afterward, we sat, spoke, and reminisced for an hour. Before I left, we exchanged phone numbers and connected on Facebook. It was *b'shert* that I was visiting Greenport that day and passed her house, seeing the cars in the driveway. We were meant to reconnect.

On this current visit, Soula showed us old pictures she had found with my family in them. Our mothers looked about thirty years old in some of the photos. She and I must have been children of about eight and twelve years old in others. There was a picture of my mom at the wedding of one of Soula's brothers. As I studied the picture closely, I saw that my mom was wearing the smoky topaz ring I have and adore, the very ring I was wearing. Time is forever frozen in a snapshot capturing youth and innocence, creating a memory for a lifetime. My heart ached for my mom. This is where she most loved to be, in this small and quiet fishing village on the east end of Long Island. She sacrificed her Greenport home to raise my brother and me in New Jersey, knowing we would have a better education and upbringing there. This visit took me back to my past, to happy childhood memories, flooding my heart with joy.

We were leaving the next day and heading back to Melville. We hadn't used our bikes yet, and after the ordeal of getting them upstairs, I wasn't going to let the trip end without them being ridden. We decided that the following morning before check-out we would ride on the North Road and explore. We called it a night and headed to sleep. It was a great day of fishing, family time, and a nostalgic night with Soula. I decided to sleep on the other side of the bed tonight as my foot kept hitting the bicycle leaning on the wall next to the bed disturbing my sleep. I don't fall back to sleep so easily. Tonight, Len could play footsie with the bike.

The next morning, I awoke at 7:30 a.m. It wasn't my phone alarm waking me but the voice of a child calling out the name Juliana. Over and over. I looked over at Len; he was fast asleep and snoring. I got out of bed and followed the calling voice. I opened the balcony door. In the pool at this very early hour was a child calling out to Juliana to join him in the pool. What pool opens at 7:30 a.m.? What parent lets a child yell out to someone when you are living in a common area? I was annoyed.

I bent over the balcony and asked, "Did you find Juliana yet? We're sleeping up here and would appreciate it if you used your inside voice even though you are outside. It's just a time thing; it's kind of early," I reasoned.

"Oh. Sorry," a child's voice responded from the pool.

I went back inside and made a pot of coffee. Around 8:30 a.m. everyone started to get up. We had a fast breakfast and got dressed to go biking. We took the bikes out of both bedrooms and wheeled them back down the stairs and around the bends. Then we took the bikes from the balcony and got them downstairs, too. We put our helmets on and started our ride. We explored streets off of North Road and found a trailer park we decided to ride through. I noticed there was a section that had old unused trailers. I could have sworn I saw the trailer my mom owned. She would summer out here in another campground after my brother and I each were married and started our own families. It was the only way she could afford to spend three months here. I rode over to the trailer and remembered staying in it once with my mom. It slept two and had a small kitchen and sitting area. I barely slept that night, hearing animal noises and activity, people partying nearby and feeling completely out of my element. I gazed at the old worn trailer, feeling sorry for the financial hardships my mother had been left with after divorcing my father. But she was freed and happier after they divorced. My brother and I helped out in small financial ways once we started working as teenagers. She never appeared mad or regretful because of the financial consequences of the divorce. I always admired that about her, and hoped that I would possess those qualities if I were faced with loss financially. My stomach tightened at the thought of Len's cancer.

I turned from the trailer as I got back on the bike and peddled over to my family. We rode back to the condo parking lot and circled around a few times, coasting down a sloped section of the parking lot, the air refreshing and cool against our faces. Bike ride—check. Time to pack up and check out. As we were driving out of the parking lot, Len realized he left the fish in the refrigerator and headed back to get it. He was proud of our catch and his cooking abilities, and wouldn't let it be thrown out. He parked the car, ran up to the condo unit and returned with the breaded fish. It was another great Greenport getaway and a perfect substitute for Halifax.

Chapter 16

Round Five

It was a hot and humid mid-August day on Long Island. I didn't bother with too much makeup and hair prep; the weather would fight my futile attempts. I decided on just some mascara, and I twisted my hair into an informal updo and used a large clip to hold it in place. Alex drove Len to the cancer center. I needed to get Gabriel set up with breakfast and activities to do until Len and I returned in a few hours. Len had been lucky that he hadn't lost his hair, eyebrows, and eyelashes. His coloring hadn't changed; his olive complexion was untouched by the chemo, too. I think Len's appearance staying the same had made a huge difference in how Gabriel was responding to his father's treatment. I was thankful for that.

Len's tolerance for the treatment also made his chemo treatments easier for his mother to deal with. She loves him fiercely. He is a lucky son indeed. She texted me before each treatment, her broken English bringing a smile to my lips. For example, the night before round five, she texted, "Tomorrow is Lenchikel procedure. Shall be eazy and ok. Please make sure that he eat and feel strong. Watch if no ik ups. And thank U for everything. Please let us know. Baba."

I responded back, texting, "Hi. Yes, please God, it will be easy for him. So far, the side effects are fatigue and hiccups. I will make sure he eats well and rests. I will do my very best. I promise." I added a heart to the end of my text.

I met Len around 11:00 a.m. at the cancer center. An IV line had been run and attached to the saline bag. The nurse was perky. She was in her late fifties, short in height, with long blonde hair and big blue eyes. They were accentuated with eyeliner and mascara, making them her dynamic facial feature. Her personality was fun and electric. As I walked into the treatment room, the two of them were chatting away. I noticed where she placed the IV into Len's arm. Hmmm, this was different; it was placed in a large vein on his forearm. No other nurse had placed it there before. Len saw me noticing the IV.

"This lovely nurse says that using a larger vein will help with sensitivity during chemo," he said.

"Thirty plus years doing this gig has taught me tricks

of the trade, darling," she responded to him.

It was buddy-check time. The second nurse came into the room carrying the bags of immunotherapy and chemo. Name? Check. Date of birth? Check. The bag of Treanda was placed in a drawer for later, and the Rituxan was hung onto the IV pole. The nurse attached tubes, twisted and tapped them, pressed some buttons on the machine, and *voila*, round five had begun. The perky nurse left the room. Len had already taken Benadryl and the anti-nausea medicine. He was starting to get sleepy. I closed the door and put relaxing music on his phone to help him drift off to sleep. I turned off the ceiling lights and put on the side light near the sink and took out the current book I was reading to keep busy while he rested.

I don't like my mind to wander too much. I find reading keeps it safely on track in someone else's story as my eyes are focused on words, my mind takes me to another place and time while my hands are busy holding the book and turning pages. Otherwise, this is what I can think when my mind is left to wander for too long as I sit and watch him sleep: *He is sleeping. I see that clearly. Why does a sleeping person also have to look like they could be dead?* I've seen three dead people: my grandfather, my mother, and Robert. They looked like they were sleeping. They were just paler. I don't ever want to see Len . . . not alive. I can't even write the other word here. My stomach tightens as I think, *what if this cancer turns aggressive? What if remission doesn't last long? What if . . .*

People die from non-Hodgkin's lymphoma. I've seen

those Facebook posts on the cancer groups I joined. All of a sudden, the room had uninvited guests. Fear, anxiety, and sadness sauntered in. There were no seats left in the room, so they stood around me as sadness tried to sit on my lap. My mind pushed it off, willing it to leave the room this instant! *There is no space for you here,* I yelled in my mind. Next, anxiety tried to creep up my back to peer over my shoulder and whisper anxious words into my ear. I reminded myself that I am strong, just like my friend Delilah. I am stronger than this feeling trying to threaten me. I shrugged my shoulders, whisking off anxiety and I shooed it out of the room. Then I was faced with fear, the mother of all negative and dark emotions. Fear is faceless and fierce, but I am fierce too, like my friend Fran. I closed my eyes and thought of a bright white light. It filled my mind and rushed down my shoulders, filling my chest and shot to my legs and down to my feet. Every fiber of my being was filled with this emanating, bright white, purifying light, and I opened my eyes back up and looked Fear right in its face and said, "Fuck you—get out of this room!" I stood up, feeling electrified, opened the door, and threw Fear out of this space.

The nurse looked up at me from her desk in the hallway as I opened the door.

"All good in there, honey?" she asked.

"Oh . . . yes. All good, thanks. I just . . . need to go to the bathroom," I responded, not knowing what else to say at the moment.

I gently closed the door behind me and walked to

the bathroom. When I returned a few minutes later, the nurse and I smiled at one another as I passed her desk. I opened the door quietly and picked up my book. This is why I keep my mind busy.

Len woke a little while later as the machine beeped. I put the book down and smiled at him. The Rituxan was finished. He smiled groggily back at me as the perky nurse came into the room.

"How's that arm feeling?" she asked.

"Your plan is working like a charm. The Treanda is what usually burns when it goes in, so let's see when you start it," he responded.

She worked on the tubing and attached the Treanda.

"Three, two, one . . . give me some feedback," the nurse said.

After a pause to ascertain, Len said with relief, "You win nurse of the year! This is the first time I haven't felt a burning. Thank you!"

Fifteen minutes later, he was finished. We walked out into the ninety-four-degree day. I was relieved not to be wearing a face full of makeup today. Some days a girl just has to go with the bare beautifying basics of mascara and lip-gloss. We got our car from the valet and drove home in air-conditioned bliss. Len reclined the seat and closed his eyes. I turned on the spa channel on Sirius XM. Angelic music filled the car. I noticed a bumper sticker on the car ahead of me. It read Peace, Love and had a mah jongg tile. Love it! I needed to buy one online. I don't see too many mah jongg bumper stickers. I pondered the succinct message and images on this one.

I'm trying to hold on to peace through this cancer journey. I'm filled with love, and I consciously share it every day. The mah jongg tile on the bumper sticker just made me smile. This game has changed my life. So much goodness has come from my Monday games. I reflected on the friendships it has created and the closeness we ladies share. I think of the skills I have learned and use at each game. Mah jongg has created a weekly opportunity for relaxation, fun, and letting go of stress and worry. I'm able to forget for a little while about cancer, worry, and fear.

Today was good. Len didn't have any pain except for the insertion of the IV needle. I had wrestled with some unwanted emotions and dealt with them successfully. Although it was a hot day, nearly ninety-five degrees outside, it was still a good day. The bumper sticker reminded me of that fact. I glanced at myself in the rearview mirror.

"I've got this," I said to my reflection. My invisible back seat companions gave me added hope and support.

I turned to Len and said, "I love you. You are doing a great job getting through this." I squeezed his hand, and he squeezed mine back as he drifted off to sleep.

Day one of round five went so smoothly that Len decided to drive himself to chemo and go to work afterward for day two tomorrow. He has never felt strong enough to go to work after the other treatments. I was supportive yet cautious. I wanted to sit with him while he got the infusion then drive him into work, but Len vetoed that suggestion. I acquiesced and let him go. He was a big boy and at the moment feeling bigger than the cancer. The following day I checked in on him as he was getting the infusion. He assured me it was going smoothly, and he was feeling strong, ready, and eager to get to work.

Later that day, I posted on Facebook. My post read:

Round 5 of chemo: ✓

Len has finished Round 5! Thursday went smoothly and no pain, thankfully. He felt strong enough to go to work after today's treatment, which he hasn't done before. He is a fighter and a strong-willed man. One more round to go—we see the finish line!

Now round five was complete.

Lunch with Fran

It was August, and Fran and I were overdue to see each other. We made plans to have lunch together and catch up at the diner in Woodbury. We gave each other a huge hello hug. She had just come from a yoga class and was literally glowing, radiating light, love, and positivity. She looked beautiful as always, her dark shoulder-length hair framing her face and bringing out her hazel eyes. Her smile, always warming my heart, didn't let me down. Feelings of happiness filled every fiber of my body, and as smiles always seem to do, hers brought forth my own.

We were seated and started perusing the menu. The waiter came over and took our orders. Now we could get down to business and catch up. Fran had started teaching other women mah jongg soon after teaching my friends and me five years ago. It went so well with us that she and Susan decided to offer lessons at her temple. It was a huge success, and their new business as master mah jongg teachers was started. She and Susan now teach all over Long Island, and they have taught over a thousand women. I was honored to be in her first class five years ago in my kitchen.

I asked, "So how is teaching going?"

"You first. Tell me about Len and the kids and all that you have been busy doing." She sat back in the booth ready to listen.

I told her Len had one treatment left and then he would have a PET scan. She and I spoke the same cancer language and knew not only what certain words meant, but also the emotions that came along with them. I explained to her that I felt like I was always looking over my shoulder; I didn't feel safe or secure. She nodded her head, understanding only too well. I filled her in on the kids, my writing, and my upcoming teaching at the temple.

She asked, "Are you taking care of yourself through Len's chemo?"

I nodded my head. "Yes, I am. I nurture my soul

every day, and I'm mindful of what I need to refill my cup if it loses its level of hope and happiness. Of course, that includes Mah Jongg Mondays." I smiled. "So that's my update. What's been going on with you?" I asked, taking my turn to sit back and listen.

Fran's eyes filled with tears. *Oh no.* I reached out and held her hand in mine.

"Sam had a setback. He had pain in his hip, and the oncologist recommended a scan. The sarcoma had moved to the other side of his body and was in his hipbone. He had surgery to remove the cancerous bone and then rehab to help him regain strength to walk. This all happened in July," she said softly.

We had texted over the summer, but I didn't know this was happening. She told me that his wife had been by his side, and only left the hospital to shower. He wasn't considering chemo. He wanted to go away with his wife on vacation and deal with the cancer when they returned.

I was honored that she shared this with me. I know I'm a kitchen friend to her just as she is to me. I told Fran how strong she, Sam, his wife, and their whole family are. She is sad, admitting that Sam might not win this battle. I understood. I wanted to scream at cancer, "Damn you!" But cancer is a phantom nemesis—in which direction do I scream?

I think of the words I use to describe Len's fight. The media, pamphlets, charities, and everyday speech we all hear and use have shaped my vernacular. Military words are used to describe a person's challenge with this dreadful, angry, and mean disease. Warlike rhetoric like fighter, battle, brave, warrior, or phrases like "you will conquer this disease" are familiar to us all. I've heard people say they have "battle scars" from radiation or surgeries. Brave, bald fighters show the world they are in a battle with this disease, stripped of their long locks, coiffed curls, or tidy tapered cuts. This disease is projected to affect almost a third of our population. So many cancer patients and their loved ones and friends want to scream out loud along with me, "Fuck you, cancer!"

I let Fran talk and express how she felt. She told me teaching mah jongg is so incredibly helpful to her. She is real, she is raw; yet she is still strong.

I looked into her eyes and told her, "I will pray for Sam's strength and health." I squeezed her hand again reassuringly.

"I will continue to pray for Len, too," she said back to me.

For a brief time, we were encapsulated in this cancer conversation. We were heart to heart, and although the diner had other people sitting in it, it felt like it was just the two of us there. We were two yogis, dealing with our loved one's cancers, brought together by *b'shert* for conversations like this, for moments of support like this, for love to be exchanged from one heart to the other.

As I drove home, I did so in silence. Instead of listening to Dr. Laura, I needed to pray, right here, right now.

With every fiber in my body, I asked God to please bless Sam, with strength, resilience, health, and love. I squeezed the steering wheel. I looked over at the passenger seat. Insecurity was sitting there. It invited Doubt and Fear to sit in the back seat. *Oh no, guys, sorry, but you can't stay.* I opened all four windows of the car as I drove onto the entrance ramp to the Long Island Expressway, heading east. The wind sucked them out of the car as I drove home, windows open the whole time, my hair whipping in the wind as I continued to pray for Sam.

Chapter 17

The High Holy Days

The Jewish High Holy Days of *Rosh Hashanah* and *Yom Kippur* were coming up in a few weeks. *Rosh Hashanah* is the Jewish New Year. It's a time of renewal and celebration. We eat *challah*, which is baked in the shape of a circle to represent the continuation of year to passing year. We dip apples and pieces of *challah* into honey to signify a sweet new year. Families go to temple, then have festive meals together to celebrate the year ahead of them. Then, ten days later, the atmosphere is no longer celebratory or cheerful. It becomes somber, as *Yom Kippur*, the Day of Atonement, shakes us into an awakening.

According to Jewish tradition, on *Rosh Hashanah*, God inscribes each person's fate for the coming year into the "Book of Life," and on *Yom Kippur*, the book is sealed. Jews also receive their judgment for the coming year hoping for health, wealth, success, longevity, happiness, and more. The days in between the two holidays are called the Ten Days of Repentance, or Days of Awe. This is a time of reflection for Jews. We are to undertake the attributes of repentance, prayer, and charity. We make donations to our synagogues during the *Yom Kippur* appeal. We ask for forgiveness from those we think we may have wronged. This is when the seats of synagogues around the world are filled to capacity, rows and rows of seats being added to opened ballrooms and social halls as filled chairs spill outside the walls of the synagogue. The chairs are filled because we're all human. We all do things for which we need to ask forgiveness. We pray collectively in repentance for acts such as lying, cheating, infidelity, slandering, stealing, mistreating someone—the list goes on and on.

As we gather on the holiest of holy days, *Yom Kippur*, we fast. By denying ourselves food and water, we create an opportunity for restraint. We submit ourselves willingly to withhold from these essential needs which nourish our bodies. For twenty-four hours the body is slowed down, altered, changing its biological rhythm. This day we nourish our souls with prayer. Space is created from the void of food and water. We are open. We are hungry. We are empty, and we repent.

This year, I was also scared. I was scared for my husband, our children, and myself. I was scared our foundation would crumble, leaving us in a state of uncertainty and instability. I was scared the cancer Len had would turn aggressive and cause him pain. I was scared of this "Book of Life" that God writes in. *B'shert* knows whose names are in the "Book of Life." Please, be kind to us, God. *G'mar hatima tovah*. May we please be inscribed in the "Book of Life." Grant us health, longevity, and prosperity. Please. Please. Please.

Rosh Hashanah

It was September 11, a day of remembrance for all Americans. It was also the day on which *Rosh Hashanah* fell in 2018. It was the Jewish New Year. My family and I dressed and got ready to go to services at temple. Len and the boys like to attend the family service, which is run by Rabbi Rachel, who is our religious school rabbi. A teen band accompanies her, and it is a service that is filled with music and prayers that are broken down for young children to understand. I go to this service because it is most palatable for Len and the boys. I personally get more spiritually out of the adult service, and sometimes go to that service after I attend the family service with the boys, but not this year. I saw a lot of my students and their families in this service. I saw friends, fellow board members, and acquaintances too, and there was excitement in the air as Judaism was electrified that day throughout our synagogue.

We took our seats, and soon afterward the service

started. I sang and prayed along with the rabbi and band. Len and Alex stepped out of the service to call and try to find Anton and his family. We had saved seats for them. Then it was time for the *Torah* service. This is when the rabbi carries the *Torah* around to the congregation, and we touch it respectfully with our prayer books and kiss it, bringing the love of *Torah* to our lips and hearts. I walked up to her and wished her a Happy New Year and touched the *Torah* with my prayer book.

The rabbi said, "Want to follow me up for your *aliyah*?"

"Excuse me?" I responded, surprised.

"Yes, I have your name and Len's to come up and say the blessing before and after I read from the *Torah*."

I froze. I missed the memo, literally. I wasn't aware I was included in the service, speaking in front of three hundred people. Remember, I have a fear of public speaking.

"Um, I'll meet you up there. Len stepped out and doesn't know the prayer, so I'll do it solo," I said with trepidation in my voice.

Gabriel was with me, and I asked, "Do you remember the *Torah* blessings from your *bar mitzvah*?" Maybe he could come up with me. That would help ease my fear.

He said, "Sorry, Mom, I don't. You will be fine. You are a Hebrew school teacher. You know these prayers," he said, trying to give me confidence.

Ok, I've got to do this myself. I sat down, whipped my prayer book open and practiced the two prayers over and over and over. I knew them by heart, but when fear kicks in, and I'm the only voice chanting in a room filled with hundreds of people, my mind doesn't always work as well as I'd like it to. The treasurer of the Sisterhood came over and said hello. I immediately told her how freaked out I was that I had to recite the *Torah* blessings.

"You'll be fine. You know the prayer, right?" she asked.

"Yes, I do, but I'm a wreck right now. I didn't know I was going to be doing this today. Do I look okay?" I asked nervously.

She sensed my panic and kindly rubbed my back. "You look beautiful, and you will do just fine."

I can do this. I hope I look okay. When I picked my dress out this morning, I didn't know I would be on display! What would I have worn if I did know? Stop asking a senseless question, I told myself! I was wearing a favorite dress, a purple cotton wrap-around Diane Von Furstenberg-style dress with purple high-heeled shoes. I adjusted the V-neck to make sure it wasn't too revealing. I saw the rabbi was almost done walking the *Torah* around the ballroom. I waited for her to motion me up. My heart was pounding in my chest. I was very cold all of a sudden. My foot was tapping on the floor nervously. I realized then that I was committed. She was expecting me. I was about to be called up in front of all of those people in this crowded and noisy room to face my fear. They were my students, their families, fellow board members, friends, my children, and my husband.

"I would like to welcome up Mrs. Fern Bernstein,"

the rabbi spoke into the handheld microphone.

I smiled and walked up to the makeshift *bimah* in my purple splendor and stood next to Rabbi Rachel, who was wearing a white pulpit robe for the High Holy Days. She instructed me to hold one end of the *Torah* scroll as she unwound it to the exact section she was looking for. I was smiling through my fear. I was on display. I was standing next to the rabbi educator who was also my boss, as she runs our religious school. *I have to do this and do it well*, I thought. She found her place in the *Torah*, recited my name in Hebrew, "*Ta'amod Freyda bat Eli Hessel v'Kayla*," and handed me the mike. I held it in my hand, took a deep breath, and started to chant the first line of the prayer. The congregation responded by chanting the second line. Then I continued chanting, reading the Hebrew from my prayer book.

Did they hear my voice shaking? My breathing was too fast, and I couldn't slow it down. I finally got to the last few words, *ha Torah*, ending the first prayer. I took in a deep breath. I needed to reset my breathing. I looked down at the Hebrew in the *Torah* as the rabbi held the *yad*, the pointer, to the section she was chanting. Human fingers do not touch a *Torah*. The oils can damage the ink and parchment paper. I didn't look up. I couldn't. It would make me too nervous seeing everyone seeing me. I was halfway through. I was almost done. The rabbi finished reading from the *Torah* and handed me back the mike. I chanted the second prayer, while silently praying I didn't mess up the tune and recite the first prayer again by mistake. A lot of people do that. A few notes in, I decided it was the right verse. My foot wanted to start tapping, but I controlled the urge. As I continued to chant, I finished with the word Amen, and the congregation joined me. Hallelujah! I did it! I helped the rabbi roll the *Torah* closed. I glanced at the door where I saw someone waving at me. It was Len. He was pounding his hand in the air silently mouthing my name. He was my cheerleader. He knows how hard it is for me to speak in public.

The rabbi told the room full of people my temple bio. "Mrs. Fern Bernstein is one of our fourth-grade teachers, the yoga teacher for the nursery school, a board of trustee member, and the Sisterhood president. We thank you for all you do here at Temple Beth Torah."

I went back to my seat, and Gabriel told me what a great job I did and gave me a hug. I sat down with relief. Then I got tapped on the shoulder. I turned around and the gentleman tapping me said, "These three girls will be in your Wednesday class."

I stood up and walked to the row behind me and shook the three girls' hands, and their parents' as well.

"So nice to meet you all. We're going to have a fun year together," I said with a smile and a wink.

I went back to my seat next to Gabriel. Len and Alex came back to join us a few minutes later.

"You did great," Len said. "I didn't know you were part of the service."

"Neither did I. I was a wreck," I whispered back to him.

"It didn't show," he reassured me.

I think he must be lying. How can all the physical things I feel while being so nervous not show?

The service was over. As we walked out, more parents came up to me saying I was their child's teacher this year. Classes started in a few days, and notifications of teacher assignments were sent home the week before. After the rabbi told the congregants I was one of the fourth grade teachers, parents and children could now place a face to the name. I was happy to meet my new students and so very thankful I made it through the *aliyah*. On our way out the door, we saw David. He was ushering. We all wished him a Happy New Year, and went to Anton's house for a celebratory meal.

Round Six

It was September and the last round in this treatment plan for Len. It was autumn again, a time of seasonal transition once more on Long Island. The leaves were starting to turn color, creating nature's art in the trees for our awaiting eyes. School had begun; Gabriel was now a freshman in high school, another autumn transition. September is a month that holds two special dates for me: Gabriel's birthday on the twenty-second, and our wedding anniversary on the twenty-fourth. They are both loving celebrations in my life, each marking another year of growth, change, and unfolding. Time exposes these progressions subtly. The sun and moon intrinsically know their routine. They create a continuous and seamless flow of day into night and back again as month melds into month and year slides into year. *Rosh Hashanah* had just ushered Jewish people all over the world into a new year. I was aware of and thankful for time. It is a precious gift. Thank you, God, *todah lecha Elohim*.

We arrived at the cancer center, and Len checked in. We then went to the waiting area near the lab. We took two seats together among the other cancer patients and their loved ones. The attendant called out the name Bernstein, and Len walked into the lab. I saw a new cancer tour go by. Another cancer patient, another life and family affected. I remembered going on a new patient tour with Len. We learned about the side effects of chemo, diet, and trying to stay as germ-free as possible. We received a folder with all this information, and we toured the chemo area. There were three other patients that day on our tour. One stood out because she was in her twenties. She had breast cancer and needed a mastectomy, chemo, and then reconstruction. When she and Len spoke, she sounded like she had accepted her difficult and challenging course of treatment and was ready for her fight with the disease. I noticed her warlike rhetoric—another soldier preparing for battle.

Len came out of the lab and joined me back in the waiting area. A few minutes later, the attendant took us back to the chemo room. I saw the spunky blonde nurse.

I hoped she was assigned to Len again. I was disappointed when instead a new nurse came into the room, one we hadn't met before. She was also lovely, however, and had a great bedside manner. Len asked for Allegra instead of Benadryl so he wouldn't sleep all day and be awake all night. A vampire's sleep schedule doesn't work for Len's human lifestyle. Another patient gave us that great tip. Next, Len asked the nurse if she could put the IV into his forearm, pointing to the spot the nurse used last month. She looked at his arm, searching for a vein but didn't feel comfortable doing it where Len requested. She said she had never done it there before and preferred to do her regular sites on the arm. She put the IV line in for Len. Another nurse took his vitals. Then it was buddy-check time. Name, check. Date of birth, check.

The Rituxan was started along with the saline. Len fielded phone calls from work, and I sat next to him working on my laptop. He didn't get sleepy; Allegra worked like a charm. The Rituxan was done in about two hours, and it was time for the Treanda. Len felt some discomfort as he usually did with the Treanda, so I ran my fingers up and down his arm, trying to distract him from the pain. The drip was finished in fifteen minutes, and then the nurse removed the IV. We walked to the car, and Len was awake, thanks to the Allegra. As we drove home on the Long Island Expressway, I put on some '80s music. Today went very smoothly. I was happy and relieved.

It was Friday morning. We made it. The last day of

the chemo treatment for Len had arrived. He couldn't sleep until 4:00 a.m. that morning. The steroid must have kept him awake. His sleep was turned upside down during these treatments. I woke at 6:05 a.m. and got Gabriel ready for school. Then I woke Len at 9:00 a.m.

"Last day of treatment, sleepyhead. Rise and shine. Let's do this!" I said with enthusiasm, as I rubbed his arm to wake him gently.

As we drove to the cancer center, I asked, "What are you thinking?"

"I'm thinking I hope this treatment works," he said as he sighed.

"It will," I said with determination.

We arrived at the familiar cancer center, except this time it felt different for me. Len checked in, and we sat in the waiting area. A few minutes later, we were called to the chemo area. The sliding door opened. We stepped into the world of treatment, hopefully for the last time. We were taken to a private room. Today we had another new nurse. I was disappointed because I saw the spunky blonde nurse again today and was hoping she would be putting the IV in for Len, hopefully for the last time. Instead, we had a different nurse who was lovely, but took two attempts to get the IV in. I had to leave the room because it was hard for me to see Len squirming and making uncomfortable noises as she was trying to insert the needle. As I stood waiting in the hallway, I saw the young woman from our cancer tour walk by. She was transformed by chemotherapy; she had lost her hair and was wearing a scarf on her head. Under her shirt, I secretly knew that she was missing a breast. I sent her a prayer filled with health and strength.

Finally, the nurse had accomplished her task and Len had the IV in place. I walked back into the room with them. The buddy check was confirmed; the Treanda was running along with the saline. The burning sensation was uncomfortable, and the nurse slowed the drip down. I started running my fingernails up and down Len's arm, hoping to cause a distraction from the pain again. Twenty minutes later the machine beeped, and the nurse came in and disconnected the tubes and IV. He got his discharge papers and stood up.

I gave him a big hug and said, "Congratulations!"

He smiled with accomplishment and said, "Thank you."

As we were leaving, I saw the perky nurse at her desk. I went up to her and said, "Thank you for being the best nurse we had here. Your trick of placing the IV on the outside of the arm worked like a charm. No other nurse could do it. You should teach them how."

She thanked me and wished us well. Len and I walked out of the treatment center, hopefully for the last time, or at least for a very long time. We didn't use the valet today, and as we walked to the car in the parking lot, Len was full of accomplishment and hope.

As we drove home, I asked Len, "Do you want to get something special for finishing treatment?"

"No, but I think I'd like to book a trip to Italy for the boys and us."

I smiled. I would love to go to Italy, especially after learning about it from the audiobook I was listening to. It's on my bucket list. I would love to leave this cancer story behind us and jump into a story about health, travel, family adventure, and delicious Italian food.

We arrived home, and as I pulled into the driveway, Len said, "What a beautiful house we have!" as he gazed through the windshield.

"Indeed, it is. Out of the destruction of fire, came the beauty of this home. I think the fire of cancer will create beauty for you too. Look for it. It may take weeks or months to show, but something beautiful will come from this fire too," I said reflectively.

"Well said, Fern," Len responded as he nodded in agreement.

Earlier that morning, I plugged in the Echo by Amazon and got familiar with Alexa. Len and I were now both in the kitchen. I asked Alexa to play "Evergreen" sung by Barbra Streisand.

The guitar started the song off gently as Barbra hummed and then began to to sing the first two lines . . .

I asked Len softly, "Do you remember this song?"

"Of course, I do. It was our wedding song," he answered.

"May I have this dance?" I asked, extending my hand toward him, my palm face-up as Barbra's beautiful and graceful voice filled the kitchen, and loving memories of our wedding night flooded my heart.

"But of course," he placed his hand into mine.

As the song played on, we danced, our bodies pressed up close to one another. The last time we danced to this song was almost twenty-four years ago at our wedding. I whispered into his ear, "I love you, and I am so proud of you for finishing chemo and for being so brave."

"Thank you, I love you too," he whispered back.

We danced until the song ended.

My arms were wrapped around his neck, his around my waist. We swayed together listening to Barbra's melodious voice trail off as a piano and guitar accompanied her, the music softly surrounding us as we swayed on the kitchen dance floor.

"So much has transpired over these two decades. We raised three boys, survived one house fire, lost my mom, and just finished a chemo treatment. We're strong partners. Let's keep this dance going for another twenty years," I said lovingly.

"At least twenty more," he replied.

As we held each other in the kitchen, still embraced from our dance, now is when I would have kissed him on the lips, a lingering and sensuous kiss, but we can't kiss like that after chemo. It was streaming through his body, and dead cancer cells were hopefully being emitted. So I just hugged him extra tightly and gently kissed him on the cheek.

Later that day, I made my final Facebook post. I got creative and did a slide show of a few pictures, adding the theme song, "Gonna Fly Now," from the movie *Rocky*. The first picture read "Super Lenny" in bright yellow letters; the second picture read "It's a Knockout;" and the third read "Cancer is an ugly word, but you kick ass. You are awesome! You will beat this—fight on!" The last picture was a family snapshot of us all hugging while in Mexico. Let this be my last cancer post for Len. Please.

Reflection

The time in between *Rosh Hashanah* and *Yom Kippur* is one of reflection. Len was reflecting, but not due to the Jewish holidays. He reflected because of cancer and the treatment he just finished. He is agnostic; he has his doubts about God. He questions how God lets bad things happen to good people and questions how the Holocaust could have happened if there was a God to stop it. I can't answer those questions with answers that satisfy him. But I recently noticed that he was having a spiritual conversation with . . . something or some great source. Not everyone needs to have a formal name for God.

He asked me almost daily, "Why did I get cancer? What did I do wrong?" He was consumed with wanting to know the answer to his question. I gave him a myriad of responses: I do not think you did anything wrong. You are not being punished. You have cancer that is treatable. Your lifelong healthy eating habits and going to the gym regularly have helped you fight this disease. Before I met you, I never saw anyone include salad for breakfast! You have done so much right. You need to look at this differently. After months of these daily questions, I finally said, "Shift from questioning, 'Why?' to 'What can you learn from this experience?' Search for the good hidden within the bad. Look for a lesson in this challenging and scary situation."

I was thankful that he was reflecting. He was being introspective. He was searching. He was evolving. *Reflect, my love; it is so good for your soul.*

A Game of Reflection

Group Text: Leigh, Rose, Amanda, Phyllis
Me: Hi girls! It's a night game this week, 7:00 p.m. Who's in and who can host? Does anyone want to play in pajamas?
Leigh: I'm in! Pajamas? Why not!
Rose: Me too! PJ's sound cozy.
Amanda: I can host. PJ's sound perfect!
Phyllis: I can't play, sorry! Happy New Year everyone!
Me: Great! See you all Monday night for paja-mah-jongg! Thanks for hosting, Amanda!

We'll miss you, Phyllis. Happy New Year!
L'shanah Tovah!

We met at Amanda's house around 7:00 p.m. Her fluffy white dog greeted me at the door. I was wearing a white fleece pajama set with pink flowers. I had a cami on and left the top unbuttoned like a jacket in case I got warm. I usually sleep in a nightgown, so I don't own too many pajamas. The girls and I kissed hello, and we wished each other Happy New Year. Amanda was wearing a pajama top with Wonder Woman on it and the words: Be your own hero. The bottoms were black three-quarter leggings. Her socks were fuzzy and had little ears and eyes on them. Leigh was wearing a T-shirt she bought at Campowerment that read: Be good to people. She teamed the shirt up with printed leggings. Rose had on pink plaid cotton drawstring bottoms and a black cami. We were dressed all comfy and cozy for our night game, and took a seat at Amanda's mah jongg table, which she set up in her living room. She has a standard mah jongg set, and the four colored racks were placed in front of each chair. We took out our cards, mixed the tiles, and stacked our walls. Amanda had been playing mah jongg for over ten years and is very experienced and confident in her playing. She was East, rolled the dice, and started to deal out the tiles.

Leigh started telling us about a hard time she was going through. We all listened and chimed in with advice and support. One thing I'm clear about with mah jongg: it's therapy for each of us in our game. Even though that night I was sitting with a psychologist, a social worker/life coach, and another life coach who are trained professionals, I know that tables of other women sit together each week and help one another through their times of stress, sadness, and challenges, too—women with or without a college diploma or master's degree, varying certificates, or letters after their names. They are women who are just like you and me, from various backgrounds, towns, religions, ages, and occupations. Player profiles include grandmothers, gardeners, real-estate agents, retirees, homemakers, bakers, artists, accountants, translators, and teachers, to name only a few. The common threads are that we all love mah jongg, what happens around our tables and in our games, and seeing each other week after week.

Amanda had mentioned at our last game that she hula-hoops and recently needed to order another hula-hoop from Amazon.

"Did you get your hula-hoop?" I asked her.

"Yes, I did. After this game, I'll go get it and show you girls how I hula," she responded.

We continued our game. I was working on filling in a Winds hand. We chatted away as tiles were picked and discarded, Jokers were replaced, and we vied for the winning hand, hoping for luck along with our skill and poker faces, until Rose smirked when a tile was put down that she obviously needed. I'm glad I'm not the only one who can't contain herself at certain moments of gaming frustration. We all like to win. We're in it to win it, and there's a thrill in calling out

"Mah jongg!" Leigh picked the next tile and did just that.

"Mah jongg!" she called out. She exposed her winning tiles. She played a Quints hand.

We all exposed our hands and examined each other's attempts for mah jongg.

"Now I'll go get my hula-hoop and show you girls my special skill," Amanda said.

She returned with her hula-hoop and stepped into it. She started gyrating, and the hoop started rotating around her small waist.

"I won a contest in fourth grade. I hula-hooped for over an hour," she said proudly as she continued to move and groove.

We all sat in our chairs watching her hula-hoop. I thought to myself, *how amazing is this?* Here's a woman in her fifties doing something from her childhood that she loves and never outgrew or gave up. We all clapped and cheered her on! We all have special superpowers, tricks, or hobbies that make us unique.

"I love playing Frisbee, and can throw one about one hundred feet straight to the person I'm playing with," I said proudly.

"I went through four years of sleep-away camp without letting people know my real name," Leigh confessed with a smile. "I told everyone my name was Eileen."

We burst out laughing.

Rose chimed in, "I can do a split. I'm still very flexible despite the damage chemo did to my nerves and joints.

I'm also a philatelist. I have an extensive stamp collection," she smiled coyly.

This is what mah jongg is all about. It's four women getting together to play a game, connect, have fun, eat, drink, reflect, and that night, reveal something unique about ourselves. We aren't judgmental, but accepting of each other, our humanness and womanliness. Bonds form and friendships bloom around mah jongg tables. It's the relationships we form when we play together that leave us wanting to come back to play again and again.

What's happening at mah jongg tables right here in my Long Island town is happening at tables in towns all over the world. There is a World Mah Jongg Organization located in Beijing, and there is also a European Mah Jongg Association. Mah jongg sisterhoods are forming every day, and classes are being taught at synagogues, community centers, churches, libraries, and through adult education programs. If you haven't ever played, try a class and see if you like the game. Join or create a sisterhood of mah jongg players in your neighborhood. You too can call out: 2 Bam, 4 Crak, Flower, and South, and feel the thrill of calling out "Mah jongg!" I love my mah jongg sisterhood, and I love this game.

Chapter 18

Yom Kippur

The Day of Atonement arrived. It was *Yom Kippur*, the day the "Book of Life" is sealed. Len and Alex were fasting. Gabriel wanted to give up eating lunch as this was the first year he could fast since becoming a *bar mitzvah*. I don't fast. I stopped when I was pregnant and never resumed the ritual. Rabbi Rachel posted on Facebook a great idea the other day. She suggested if you can't fast by giving up food, choose something else to give up for twenty-four hours: technology, listening to music, wearing makeup, watching television, or something that breaks you away from your everyday routine and creates a void. I thought about this and decided I would fast from technology.

We went to the family service, then headed home to prepare for the break-the-fast meal, which we were hosting. We were having thirty guests over. My father was making a cameo appearance from New York City, Len's brother and family were coming, and Rose, Leigh, Delilah, and their families, too. A lovely couple from temple that I had become friends with joined us, and Gabriel's piano teacher, Lena, and her daughters came as well. Lena had become a recent widow. I introduced her to Delilah a few months before when Lena's husband was diagnosed with a degenerative lung disease. Delilah helped Lena through the eventual passing of her husband, and she has helped Lena with her transition into the widow world.

Having a house full of people, I planned ahead, and I hired a party helper for dinner—someone to help Len and me set up the food, clear plates, set up coffee and dessert, and help to clean up after the meal. What woman can host a thirty-person break-the-fast dinner at her home with sanity? Len and I started to set up the food, buffet style, in the kitchen. We had the standard break-the-fast meal of bagels, tuna salad, egg salad, whitefish salad, lox, and about ten side dishes to accompany the salads. The party helper was running late, and I decided to text the owner of the company, glad to have my phone back in use after giving it up for twenty-four hours. Guests were starting to arrive. Maybe the helper got lost. I was mistaken. I found out the person wasn't lost, but in the hospital and unable to come. I missed his phone call while I was fasting from technology. I texted the owner back to please send a replacement ASAP! ASAP never happened, but girl power sure did. My girlfriends jumped right in to help. We finished setting up all the food on the spacious center island, buffet style, and we arranged the plastic utensils, cups, and plates by the drinks on the smaller island counter. Mission accomplished.

Alex and Jared picked my father up from the Long Island Railroad station nearby. He made a grand theatrical entrance as he always does.

"Hello! *Good Yuntif!* The Renaissance Man from the East Village has arrived!"

He was resplendent, dressed in his standard attire and accessories. He was wearing black slacks and a white button-down dress shirt, with a bright yellow tank top visible underneath. He donned his customary accessories: a gold Jewish Star of David; multi-colored Mardi Gras beads; a lanyard holding his train pass, identification, and Metro card; a neck-tie which had a collage-like repeated picture of us from my wedding day; his NYU yellow baseball cap; a standard watch on his right wrist and the watch with Hebrew letters on his left wrist; along with the rubber bracelets; *and* orange socks. He was an eyeful. Everyone greeted him with hellos. He was the star of the show. This quirky character wasn't a paid actor. He was my father, my personal entertainer of drama and comedy.

"Where's Miss Flower Child?" he asked into the crowd as he entered the kitchen.

"Hi, Dad! Welcome, I'm so glad you are here with us. She will be here later with her husband," I said as I hugged him hello.

"What a fabulous turnout you have here, Fern! Such a mix of well-dressed, good-looking, educated, professional suburbanites!"

"Yes, Dad. You could say that about my friends," I responded, hoping he would behave socially. It's generally a crapshoot.

"I brought a joint if anyone wants to smoke with me later," he whispered as he winked at me.

"I'll ask around. Thanks, Dad," I said through clenched teeth. *Oh boy . . .*

I baked fresh *challah* for dinner, and my dad led us in the *motzi,* center stage as he sliced the bread. Dinner is served! We filled the seats in the dining room, kitchen, and had our outdoor seating area available for guests to sit and eat at as well. Everyone ate, those who fasted filling the void of hunger with the sustenance of food. Once dinner was winding down, I started the coffee brewer to serve thirty-six cups of piping hot coffee. The girls and I put the food away in containers as Delilah washed the overflowing sink of dishes. We prepared all the desserts on the center island, and then I asked everyone to please come into the kitchen. I had a few things to say. I asked Len and Gabriel to stand next to me.

As the guests filled the kitchen, I said, "I want to thank you all for being here tonight. As you know, Len finished chemo last week, and I want to make a toast to him for his bravery, determination, and strength through these six months. We will see the oncologist next week and set up a PET scan in about six weeks." I raised my glass in the air. "May the results show us that the cancer is shrinking, or maybe even in remission. May Len have a long and healthy life. We will be celebrating our twenty-fourth wedding anniversary on September 24, and I want to wish you an early happy anniversary, Len."

Everyone in the room said, *"L'chaim!"* which means "To life!" and we all gave Len a round of applause. Next, I turned to Gabriel as I lit a candle on a cupcake for him. His fourteenth birthday was in a few days. We all sang "Happy Birthday to You," and Gabriel blew out his candle while making a wish. We ate delicious desserts and drank hot coffee as the night wound down. My friends were amazing helpers and came to my aid, just like I would do for them in a pinch. After the last guests left, I got my dad set up in the guest bedroom, and exhausted, I called it a night.

The next morning, after Gabriel left for school and Len and Alex left for work, my dad and I spent some time talking. He appeared in his yellow tank top and tighty-whities. He said, "Good morning, my biological daughter!" as he joined me in the kitchen.

He has been saying that since I was a teenager. I often wonder if he has an adopted daughter somewhere.

"Morning, my biological father. I hope you slept well." I played along with his familial banter.

"Yes, yes thank you. Len looks good! Let's hope the scan is too," he said in a more serious tone.

"Yes, I pray it will be, Dad. I'm realistic; I know not all of the twelve spots of cancer will be gone. I'm hoping they all have shrunk, though, in response to the chemo, and I hope at least some have gone away completely. I'm most worried about the ones near his eyes." I took a deep breath and asked, "Coffee?"

"I would love some coffee, my dear," he responded.

We talked about my mom and Greenport. I told him how much Len and I love going to Greenport and how it's Len's dream to get a house out east. If his scan is good, he wants to start to look for a summerhouse there. I shared how sad it was for me that our house on Inlet Lane that my grandfather built was sold. Then I almost fell over from what my dad said next.

"I want to give you some money for a house. I want to do it while I'm alive and soon, so Len can start to enjoy it."

I asked, "Dad, are you kidding?"

"No, Fern! I'm serious. No kidding around! Let's make this happen! This will make your mother smile up in heaven," he said with emotion. "I've helped your brother and his family for many years. Now I want to do something for you and your family."

"Thanks, Dad," was all I could muster up at the moment. I had to absorb this offer and let it sink in. He had disappointed me in the past with offers he had rescinded.

Later, I dropped my dad off at the train station and called Len to tell him the news. I spent a lot of time reflecting on my dad's offer that day. I never thought he would make a suggestion like this. Had he softened in his twilight years? Did he realize the mistake he and my mother made all those years ago, selling a waterfront property that was a gem and a family treasure? What has caused this change? I was curious, yet cautious. I would start a house search and see how this unfolded, if—no, *when*—Len's scan results are good.

I said to my mom, silently, "I'm coming back home, maybe not to the same house that your father built, but hopefully to the same town. And I will continue your love for this special area on the east end of Long Island with my family. Promise you, Mom."

The Dragon Shirt Game

On Thursday, the day after *Yom Kippur*, Sarah texted Leigh and me wishing us both Happy New Year and saying that she was off a few days next week and wanted to get together. I texted back asking if she could play mah jongg with us. She was in! Leigh and I were very excited to both see and play mah jongg with Sarah.

About a week before, I received quite an unusual shirt from Len's mom included in a care package of various sundries. She knew I played mah jongg and must have thought

I would like this unique shirt when she bought it for me. I looked at it and burst out laughing along with Len when I took it out of the bag. The shirt was cotton, a light powder blue color with whipstitching around all existing edges—arms, hem, and collar. It had brown wooden buttons that would button the shirt closed *if* it fit me. The tag read, "Large" under "Made in the Philippines." Although I am petite, my chest size isn't. I couldn't close the buttons, but that was okay. I really couldn't wear this in public anyway. Let me continue.

The whipstitch is a darker blue, which matches patches of blue crochet near the collar. Interesting combination. The highlights of the shirt are two large Chinese dragons embroidered in a blue thread with fiery red tongues and red hats—yes, hats—which have blue plumes coming out of them. Although I truly appreciate my mother-in-law's generosity and thoughtfulness, at the same time I'm baffled by some of the things she sends. I decided to be funny and wear the mah jongg shirt along with a pair of earrings she sent me from her recent trip to Europe. The earrings were cobalt blue tassels made out of yarn. I didn't have anything to wear with them, and thought they would look interesting with the dragon shirt.

Humor and laughter are wonderful commodities, and I thought it would be fun to see the girls' expressions when they walked in and looked at me. Sarah and Leigh are all too familiar with the interesting gifts my mother-in-law has sent over the years. We took a picture one summer game wearing Russian winter hats she sent in a recent care package along with other sundries of interest: bug spray, soaps, Band-Aids, tissues, canned salmon, a bright orange wrist watch, and of course, staple care package must-haves—toothbrushes and toothpaste.

Group text: Sarah, Leigh, Delilah
Me: Morning girls! I'll see you a little later for mah jongg!
Sarah: Can't wait!
Leigh: Me too!
Delilah: See you all soon!

I got Gabriel ready for his bus, and once he left, I practiced yoga, did my morning meditation, took a shower, dressed, and accessorized. I set up the round mah jongg table and put four chairs around it in the mah jongg/meditation room and turned on the salt lamp, the pink Buddha lamp, and electric candles. I put out snacks and drinks for the girls, and before I knew it, there was a knock on the door. Delilah had arrived. I'd noticed the past few months she was looking more vibrant; there was a spark I detected. She was putting effort into her health with exercise and diet. She had lost the weight she had gained over the past few years. Her slim figure had returned, and although we

are technically middle-aged, I noticed she was aging gracefully into her fifties. I was happy she looked so well.

"Interesting shirt," she said with a puzzled look on
her face.

"Guess who sent it to me?"

"I've got one guess. Len's mom," she answered, smiling.

"Exactly! I thought it was so mah jongg-appropriate
for our game," I said and smiled back at her.

Sarah arrived next. We gave each other a tight and
lingering hug hello.

"Wait a second, your mother-in-law must have sent
you that shirt, and those earrings, too!" she observed,
laughing.

"Bingo!" I said and laughed back.

Leigh came in a few minutes later. She knew my fash-
ion style and looked at me as she tilted her head and said,
"There is no way you bought that shirt. Was it a gift from
Len's mom?"

I nodded my head yes. They know me too well and
know my mother-in-law's gift choices very well, too.

The girls all hugged hello, and we gathered in the mah
jongg/meditation room. I got my black velvet bag and took
out the two containers holding the racks and tiles. We
each chose a chair and settled in for game time. Each of us
took a rack and put our card in front of it. I took the two
containers housing the tiles and spilled them out onto the
table. The clickety-clack sound reverberated through the
room. We turned the tiles face down. Manicured fingers

painted dark grey, burnt orange, and two French manicures started mixing the tiles. We stacked our walls, and
as host, I started out as East. I rolled the dice. One landed
showing a two, the other a six. I counted out eight pairs
and placed those tiles aside for the last wall of the game. I
dealt out thirteen tiles to each of these special ladies and
fourteen tiles to myself. We passed through the Charleston,
then optioned across from each other. We organized our
tiles and searched for a hand. I decided to try something
different—a hand in the 3 6 9 section. I started the game
by throwing the first tile.

"Vest," I called, in a Russian accent, placing the West
tile on the table.

"In honor of your mother-in-law," Sarah said with
a smile.

The girls love when I imitate her accent. I have mastered the accent after all of these years.

Delilah picked a tile from the wall. The conversation
started to flow as the game progressed. Mah jongg is a left-
brain, right-brain symphony. It's one side focused on an
analytical assignment, while the other side is focused on
congenial conversation. Delilah picked and threw. Sarah
picked up a tile from the wall and updated us on her work,
family, and the new dog she is fostering and most likely
adopting. It's a goldendoodle that a rabbi and his family
couldn't keep. She discarded a tile.

"It's a great fit for your family. The dog knows all the
Shabbat prayers and is a member of the tribe," I joked.

She already had an older goldendoodle at home, and they seemed to be getting along really well. Conversely, Leigh had an animal story to share too. She had to put her ragdoll cat to sleep a few days before. She shared her sadness with us. This is what happens at our mah jongg games. We share our lives with each other; the good times, the happy times, the bad times, and the sad times. My heart was happy that Sarah had joined us for today's game, bringing her warmth, dynamic personality, and friendship back to the mah jongg table. Leigh and I miss her at our regular games.

Leigh called mah jongg on her next pick. We exposed our hands and showed each other what hand we were playing.

We put all the tiles in the center of the table and started to mix them up again to start the next game. Clickety-clack. We then stacked nineteen pairs of tiles down our walls. Delilah rolled the dice and dealt the tiles. We each racked our tiles and started to group them. I had two possible hands to play and was having trouble deciding which one to pursue.

I told the girls, "I'm stumped. What would Fran tell me to do?"

We all chuckled at this, as Fran had taught us all how to play mah jongg. After we played the first left in the Charleston, I decided to stop the Charleston to see if I could optimize one of the two hands.

Delilah laid the first tile out to start the game, "9 Dot."

Leigh picked a tile from the wall and discarded.

"Call," Sarah said, picking up the tile and making an

exposure on her rack. She discarded a tile.

It was my turn to pick. I held a 4 Bam in my hand. I felt the etched number four and the four slim bamboo reeds in the center of the tile. Bams represent strength and solidarity to me. I think of my friends sitting around my mah jongg table. We are four strong pillars for one another. We are four friends playing a Chinese game together here on Long Island, but we're also playing through the game of life at the same time. Mah jongg has created a safe and sacred space for us. It is the common thread of Monday gatherings, either by day or by night. The women I share this game with are all special to me. Friendship is a gift, but true friends are a treasure. Conversations around our mah jongg tables have created intimacy through trust and honesty, dared vulnerability, and exposed realness. Friends often hold up mirrors for us to glance into long enough to show us glimpses of ourselves we might have otherwise missed. They are gatekeepers into sisterhood and female-bonded love. These three women are all my kitchen friends, women I share the most with. Even though I don't get to see Sarah regularly anymore, certain friendships are like putting on an old worn glove. There is a comfort; there is remembrance and warmth from years of togetherness. Since my family is so small, I cherish my friendships and the importance they hold in my life. I am lucky to have such wonderful friends. I am thankful mah jongg has created the weekly opportunity for these friendships to deepen, to create consistency and sisterhood.

It was at Sarah's pool club five years ago where the big mah jongg idea started. Sarah was one of the original four. Leigh and I miss her a lot. We saw each other weekly for almost three years at our games. Sarah has one of the biggest and most giving hearts. She is smart, outgoing, a doer, and a pillar of strength. She is a powerhouse of a person and someone I'm lucky to call my friend. It was *b'shert*. We were meant to meet five years ago at our temple. Through common interests and volunteering at the temple, a friendship blossomed. We met at a caregivers committee meeting. That is one of our strong common bonds in our friendship, caring for others. We sit on the board of trustees together at temple. Like attracts like.

That one hot and humid August day at Sarah's pool started my idea about mah jongg, and what a great idea it was! That idea led me to write this book. Was that *b'shert* too? Yes, I think it was. By now, you are familiar with this Yiddish term and how it has affected my life. We can all think of situations where *b'shert* brought certain people into our lives at a precise time, maybe at an exact moment, which we can definitively remember. Is it *b'shert* that our parents are our parents? Is it *b'shert* how we chose our careers, or how they found us? Is it *b'shert* how we chose our job, our house, our spouse or partner, our family, and friends? Were you mystically meant to learn and play mah jongg? Was there a magical magnetic pull to buy and read this book? I believe the answer is yes.

Chapter 19

The Check-Up

We saw the doctor for the post-treatment appointment in October. Alex dropped Len off at the cancer center on the way to work, and I met him there after I got Gabriel ready for school and on the bus. I joined him in the examination room where the nurse was taking information and running vitals. The doctor came in.

"Len, how are you? I haven't seen you in three months! You are supposed to come in between treatments to see me."

"Sorry, doctor. I've been feeling well and really didn't see a need to come in, since my counts didn't drop after the treatments," Len responded with conviction.

"We make the rules here, not the patients," he responded with a slight edge. "Let's see your counts today."

The oncologist reviewed Len's blood counts and seemed satisfied. He palpated around Len's body and then dropped a bomb.

"So, things look good and so do you. You tolerated the treatment very well with only a few side effects and your mid-treatment MRI looked like it was definitely working. I'm suggesting two years of maintenance immunotherapy every two months," he said, very matter-of-factly.

Len was shocked. He looked incredulously at the doctor.

"What are you talking about?" he questioned.

My chest tightened. I had read on the Facebook groups that some lymphoma patients do maintenance after their treatments are completed.

"It's not a bad thing, Len. We find it extends remission for lymphoma patients. That's a good thing. We want the longest remission, and, maybe," he puffed up his shoulders and widened his eyes, "you will stay in remission for two years. At that time, for many patients, it means you have a very low percentage of cancer coming back."

Len and I looked at each other—he with surprise, me with understanding. I nodded my head at him to do it.

"Should we schedule an appointment to see the eye specialist after the upcoming PET scan?" I asked.

"That would make sense, since you had cancer near both eyes. He will send me his notes after seeing you," the doctor responded.

Len and I nodded our heads at the doctor, taking in his instructions and the news of "maintenance."

The nurse scheduled his first maintenance treatment six weeks out. Timing was essential, they said. Len agreed to it. I drove him to work in Queens after the appointment was finished. He was disappointed. He thought he had reached the finish line. He did; it was just the first finish line, we realized. He kissed me goodbye, and I headed back to the Long Island Expressway to drive home. I listened to the ending of the *Eat, Pray, Love* audiobook. It had taken me almost four months to finish listening to it, as I split my drive time between Dr. Laura, this audiobook, and music. I was happy to discover this book and her story have a happy ending. Elizabeth fell in love again and experienced adventure, self-recovery, and self-discovery through her year of traveling. Oh, I hoped my story would have a happy ending, too. I hoped Len's cancer shrank in size and location number, would stay indolent, or maybe, just maybe, go into remission.

After the audiobook ended, I put on a Christian music station. I needed some uplifting and inspirational music. I decided, on the ride home, I was overdue to see the spiritual medium I get readings from. I decided to make an appointment with Etta-Lyn within the next few days. As I drove home, my car was filled with a variety of ethereal passengers. I always save the front seat for God. In the back seat were Worry and Hope. They started to argue like siblings.

"Maintenance! That means the cancer is still there," Worry said in a bratty tone.

"Maintenance is there to make sure the chemo and immunotherapy work longer in his body," Hope said smartly.

"Not so!" yelled Worry.

"Is too," responded Hope with strength, perseverance, and calm in her voice.

"Is not!"

"Is too."

"Is not!" Worry started to wrestle with hope.

"Enough, my children," God said to them both. "Worry, you are creating a commotion and unnecessary distress for my child, Fern. You will need to leave now."

I'm not sure what happened next. Maybe God climbed or floated into the back seat and absorbed Worry, or threw her out of the car somehow. I didn't feel her presence in the car or in my mind any longer. What I did feel were peace and protection. I believe everyone has three parents, two earthly and one heavenly. God parents us in mystical and magical ways. My faith is strong and always there. God knows that. My family ties are very strong with this ethereal parent. Hope sat content in the backseat, and I was feeling calm, hopeful, and protected driving east on the Long Island Expressway back to my home. I smiled. I am a child of God.

Pre-Scan Game

Group text: Delilah, Rose, Leigh, Amanda
Me: Hi ladies! Who's in for Monday's game
and who can host?
Delilah: I can't play, sorry.
Rose: I can play and host, 11:30 a.m., ladies!
Leigh: I'm in. I may be a few minutes late
though.
Amanda: I can play! Yay!
Me: Great! See you then, ladies! Delilah,
we'll miss you.

We gathered at Rose's house. The fall had fully arrived here on Long Island. The leaves are telling, revealing fall's palette of vibrant and warm colors. Each color is distinct; individual, but fleeting. They go through a metamorphosis from a rich and lively green to a fiery red, burnt orange, or mustard yellow, slowly losing color and vitality, fading into a hollow, murky, lifeless brown. The leaves' colors change with each passing hour and day, until they surrender and drop to the awaiting bed of earth below them. As I drove along the tree-lined streets, I saw the leaves dance and skip on their angular edges as the wind and cars blew them around in their final display before they were raked away from sight.

Rose's home was decorated with Halloween-inspired webs, skulls, skeletons, and ghouls. She recently had a dress-up Halloween party that Len and I attended. I dressed as a genie, and he was dressed as a pimp. I remember secretly granting myself a wish that night, feeling the costume give me the confidence and power to do so. My wish was, of course, for Len to please have the cancer go into remission. Len was the only person who didn't drink at the party. He is constantly trying hard to eat mindfully, to exercise, and honor his body. I have always admired that about him. Since his cancer diagnosis, he is even more diligent.

We gathered in Rose's living room, enjoying the festive decorations as we each took a seat around the square mah jongg table. Amanda recently left her temple job and was focusing on her coaching career so she could now join us for day games too. We opened our cards, placing them in front of our racks, and we started to mix the tiles, their click-clack sound creating Mah Jong Monday magic. We stacked the tiles along our racks, nineteen pairs long. Rose was East, so she rolled the dice and started to deal. We racked our tiles and got to work grouping suits and numbers together, trying to create a hand. We started the Charleston and optioned across.

"So, ladies, today I am seeing Etta-Lyn, the spiritual medium I get readings from, at 3:30 p.m. Also, Len is getting his post-treatment PET scan later today," I told them.

They were intrigued about the spiritual medium and hoped that I would hear helpful and hopeful information from Etta-Lynn. I hoped so too. I had booked the appointment over six weeks before. Then Len scheduled and rescheduled his scan three times, finally keeping the appointment the very same day and time I was seeing Etta-Lyn. I didn't tell Len I scheduled an appointment with her. He doesn't believe in people speaking to spirits. He grapples with the existence of God, so how could he accept the existence of spirits and the ability of a human to somehow speak with them?

"That's a busy day," Amanda said. "Praying the scan is good and showing positive results."

"Me too," Rose said. "I know how hard these scans can be. I'll be praying for you guys."

"Oh, me too, Fern. You guys have been through a lot, and I only wish for good results," Leigh said lovingly.

"Thanks, ladies, that means a lot to me. Do you think we could take a minute and do a group prayer? I know whatever the results are . . . they are already, but it would help me to feel better."

"Don't say that, Fern," Rose urged. "Remember, I had a lot of people pray for me before my surgery. My tumor markers were off the charts, and I was given a dire prognosis. The doctor said that it was a medical miracle that the tumor was contained with no metastases. Prayer does work!"

"I do believe in prayer, ladies. I pray all the time," I said, with hope and conviction in my voice.

I extended both of my arms out. We linked hands around the table, creating an unbroken chain.

It turned into a prayer circle as I said these words: "Please, God, let Lenny's scan results be good. Please let the cancer be smaller, some spots gone, or maybe . . . even in remission. Let him have the courage to get through the scan easily, and please give us the strength to handle the results, whatever they are."

We all squeezed our hands, and everyone said, "Amen."

"Thank you, girls. I'm blessed to have each of you in my life," I said gratefully.

We were linked just like a chain. We all took a deep breath in and dropped our hands as we exhaled, all of us moved deeply by the experience. This was a soul-stirring Mah Jongg Monday for me. Not only did we sit around the table to play and socialize, but today we also prayed. Holy moments can happen around a mah jongg table too. We finished four games, and it was time for me to head home for Gabriel and get ready for my spiritual reading.

Spiritual Reading

I turned spa music on as I drove to Etta-Lyn's, hoping to get my head in a meditative groove. I had the feeling of fluttering butterflies in my stomach that I needed to calm. I arrived at her house at 3:30 p.m. She greeted me at the door, and we gave each other a big hug hello. I had become very fond of Etta-Lyn the past four years, and in awe of her special gift. She opened the basement door, and I headed down to the spiritual space I had come to feel welcome and comfortable in. I took my seat in the high-backed fabric armchair. Piano music was playing softly, and I smelled either incense or maybe Etta-Lyn had just smudged the room with sage. I sat in anticipation of messages from the "other side," specifically about Len's health. I've had Delilah's husband Robert come through, David's wife, my mom, one grandmother, both of my grandfathers, a friend's sister, Archangels, and a constellation of spirit guides.

I wondered whose spirit would be here today. Etta-Lyn took her chair and brought it to the side of the worktable. She had a mini tape recorder on which she tapes the sessions, then transfers them to CDs so clients can listen to the readings again in their car or at home.

She clicked the "on" button and placed it down on the desk. She took a deep breath in and then a long exhale.

"I'm feeling my lungs filled with fluid or something. Is there someone here on earth or who has crossed over recently that is or was suffering from a lung issue?"

This is crazy! Could it be?

"Yes, my son's piano teacher lost her husband from a degenerative lung disease."

"I feel like it's a recent crossing," she said.

"Yes, he died a few months ago," I responded.

"Tell her he says she made all the right decisions although they weren't easy."

"Ok," I whispered back.

"He had an intubation tube?"

"I don't know."

"He says he didn't feel it; he had started to cross over. He wasn't in pain."

I nodded my head in understanding.

"Were his hands turning blue?"

"I'm not sure," I responded.

"His father was waiting on the other side to greet him."

"Oh my God, yes. Lena told me he died of the same disease."

"What's with toenail polish?" she asked.

"I don't know."

"That's ok. It's a validation. Ask your friend. Is there a daughter?"

"Yes, three."

"He is saying to watch the youngest one."

"Ok, I'll tell her."

"The letter A keeps coming up. Is there an Ann maybe?"

"I'm not sure."

"Ok. He is thanking you for being her friend and helping her through this time."

I nodded my head. I felt humbled.

"Who's here? Move over please."

I watched her as she navigated through quiet conversations that are not privy to my ears.

"I feel nauseous, my bones hurt," she said. "Is Len having chemo?"

"He has recently finished. Please don't hold back any information you get."

"I won't," she nodded. "My head hurts. Now I'm

seeing a scan that is showing a red mass in the brain."

My chest tightened. No, please no.

Wait! There must be some kind of crossover of information, I thought to myself.

"Len is getting a scan, but I have two friends, and each of their fathers has a brain tumor."

"Ok. Validation please."

I sat in the chair uneasily.

"Does Len have a foot problem?"

"Yes. He needs to see a podiatrist."

"That was a validation. Ok, guys let's get this stuff straight. She's here for Len. When is the scan?"

"Now."

"Right now?"

"Yes, he had to reschedule it a few times; this is the date and time he picked," I swallowed hard.

I felt a little guilty being there while Len was in a tube at the cancer center. *We were both in our own portals right now,* I thought to myself. Alex had driven Len and would stay with him until he went in for the scan, so I decided to keep the appointment with Etta-Lyn. I would pick him up after the scan. The timing was coincidental. Or was it *b'shert?*

"Ok. This is good. I want you to go be with Len right now and bring me back answers," she said to a spirit somewhere in the room.

She obviously wasn't talking to me. I waited, holding my breath. This was crazy! And it got crazier!

"Jesus is here."

"Excuse me?"

"Jesus."

"As in Jesus Christ?" I asked incredulously.

"Yes. I often don't announce it. There is no religion in the spirit realm, Fern, just love."

"I get that, I do. Please tell him I am honored."

"He hears you and is touching your arm."

"Which one?"

"Your right. He always stands to the right."

I offered my arm into the air a little; I wanted to be inviting and respectful. I was in awe!

"Green light. He's giving a green light. Now there is a male figure standing next to him, wearing a T-shirt that says 'safe.' Len is going to be ok. I have such clarity. Wow. Thank you," she said to the spirit, undetectable to my senses.

I gasped in relief, "Thank God, all gods."

I registered Etta-Lyn was having a moment of her own with the clarity she just experienced. This was beyond amazing to me!

"The other two men with brain tumors, it's not good. One will be going fast."

"Yes, the doctors said within another month or so."

"Well, glad we got that squared away! There was a little confusion," she said.

I was so relieved! I couldn't believe the spirit of Jesus Christ was at my reading. I was so honored, blessed, and humbled.

"Can I ask spirit a question?"

"Sure."

"I'm almost done writing a book. Any input from them?"

"You have chosen someone to send it to for a professional edit?"

"Yes."

"She is going to tear it apart a little."

"Ok. I'm expecting to make changes."

"Pick your cover carefully."

"Ok."

"You are going to make coins."

I looked at her, not exactly understanding.

"You will sell many copies and make money."

I smiled.

"Your mom is here. She is saying the book will be continued, a sequel. She is standing right behind you, touching you on the head."

My chest filled with love. I reached my hand back, hoping my mother's spirit could touch my hand. I didn't feel anything but held it there for a few seconds more, imagining her touch as I closed my eyes for a few fleeting seconds.

"What are you wearing of your mom's today?" she asked.

I smiled and glanced down at the smoky topaz ring and the gold bangle bracelets that were both hers. "These," I said pointing to the special jewelry.

"That was a validation about your book. Good stuff," she said.

The hour was up. The portal closed. Etta-Lyn turned off the tape recorder and transferred the reading onto a

CD. I paid her for this incredible service and gift she had just provided for me. We walked up the stairs and gave each other a warm hug goodbye. As she opened the door, we were greeted by a clear blue and sunny sky. Clarity, I had it too. I turned the car on and reflected on the information I just heard. I needed to call Gabe's piano teacher, Lena, tomorrow and tell her that her husband's spirit was at my reading. I put the CD into the player in my car and decided to listen to it again as I drove to pick Len up from his scan. I met Jesus. I was so very humbled and felt so incredibly blessed.

Chapter 20

PET Scan Results

Tuesday arrived. We were probably going to hear from the oncologist today with the results from the PET scan. I would need to be patient. I knew that first the radiologist had to read it, then make a report and forward it to the doctor. I hoped Wednesday would be the latest we would have to wait. My day was busy, which I was thankful for. I went to the Jewish Tangents class at temple in the morning. The mental stimulation was good for my head and occupied my thoughts. I taught yoga at 2:00 p.m. in the preschool, another distraction I was happy for. I enjoy teaching preschoolers yoga and have fine-tuned my craft.

I have select songs that help the children stay interested and connected to the poses I'm showing them. I teach them *pranayama* by blowing into pinwheels. When they blow air into them, they can see their breath in action. They have learned many *asanas* or poses: butterfly, downward dog, mountain, bridge, tree, dancer, bow, cat, cow, and cobra. It fills my heart with pride when I call out a pose, and the little yogis get into position. I'm glad I can plant the seeds of yoga into their growing minds and bodies. I teach them calming words to say if they get upset and finger movements to help with concentration and focus. They like *savasana*. They lay their little bodies on their yoga mats. Some try so hard to keep still while others can do it with ease. I put on relaxing music and say a guided meditation for them, teaching them they all have a special light within themselves. I explain this light is filled with love, health, goodness, and kindness. I remind them it is their job to share this light with their families, friends, teachers, and pets. I further explain that by sharing their light, they add more light to our world. I'm shaping little yogis, and it is truly a special experience for me.

Yoga class was over; it was now 3:00 p.m. Neither Len nor I had heard from the oncologist. Once home, I decided to call the doctor's secretary.

"Hi, this is Len Bernstein's wife, Fern, calling. Len had a PET scan yesterday, and we're waiting for the doctor to call with the results please," I said to the nice voice on the other end of the phone.

"Ok, Mrs. Bernstein, I'll e-mail the doctor to get in touch with you or Mr. Bernstein."

"Thank you very much," I replied.

I changed out of my yoga clothes and back into my regular clothes to teach in the religious school. I live in black leggings, it seems. I put a pair on along with a grey collared shirt with a big pink heart on it. That heart set off my accessorizing. I went to the armoire and chose a diamond heart ring to wear on my pointer finger, a sterling silver ring with the word "love" written in script on the other pointer finger, and my grandmother's diamond ring for my ring finger. I wore a Swarovski heart necklace, CZ studs, and a diamond bracelet of interlocking hearts. I was so adorned; I felt nothing negative could penetrate this protective aura of love and bling. I was teaching at 4:30 p.m., so I packed my work bag and got Gabriel set up with homework and piano practice for the time I would be away.

I arrived at work, signed in, and greeted my fellow teachers, the rabbis, cantor, and children passing in the busy hallways. As my students filtered into the classroom, I welcomed them each with a big smile and hello. They took a seat and unpacked their backpacks. I checked their homework and sat with the students at their table and handed out the do-now worksheet for them to work on. I brought my phone with me to the table in case the doctor or Len called me. I gave the class a few minutes to fill in the review sheet, and then we began to go over it together. I asked Sydney to start the review by saying the letters and vowels she saw.

"I see a *Shin* with an 'ah' vowel, a *Bet* with an 'ah'

vowel, and a *Tav*. It sounds out *Shabbat*," she said with confidence.

"Excellent, Sydney," I said with enthusiasm.

My phone rang.

I looked down.

It's Len calling.

My chest tightened.

"Children, this may be a very important phone call, and I have to pick it up. Please sit quietly for me," I told them.

"Hello?"

"Hi. I just heard from the doctor."

"Ok," I said, bracing myself. His voice didn't give me any clues.

The children were staring at me and sitting so quietly as I listened. I was thankful. They saw my eyes fill with tears. They were concerned. I nodded my head at them, trying to convey I was really okay, even though I may not have looked it. I was processing what he had just said.

"I love you, and I'll see you at home. I'm teaching right now and sitting with my students. Bye," I said quietly and hung up. I flipped my attention back to my students. "Thank you for sitting so nicely, class. That was my husband Len calling. It was indeed a very important phone call. My husband just got great news from his doctor and called to share it with me," I told them.

The class started clapping.

My heart was overflowing with happiness and gratitude. My students were *mensches*, children of integrity and honor and so emotionally intelligent, knowing they needed to sit quietly and that whatever he was telling me was very important and clap-worthy.

I took a deep breath in, filling my chest with air, and released worry, despair, and fear out of my body.

I looked at the children and said with a big smile, "Okay, let's get back to work. Justin, please sound out the next Hebrew word."

We finished Hebrew and then had music together. Class ended, and we walked to the sanctuary for dismissal. I saw one of my colleagues and shared the great news with her. She was the first adult person I told.

"Len called me while we were in class. The doctor called him with results. The scan doesn't detect *any* cancer! All twelve spots are gone," I shared, sounding almost incredulous.

She gave me a huge hug and said, "*Mazel tov!* That is amazing news!"

"Thank you!" I said as we embraced.

I walked up to Rabbi Rachel and shared the news with her, adding that Len called me during class.

"I had to pick up in front of the children. They saw my eyes get teary. In case any parents call you, this is why," I explained to her.

"Fern, this is the most wonderful news!" She hugged me. "You made my day! Did you tell Rabbi Susie?"

"Not yet. I will, though!"

I walked out of the temple. It must be *b'shert*. Judaism

is where my faith stems from; this is exactly where I was meant to hear the great news—in my temple, my house of prayer. Thank you, God, for this blessing. I walked to my car and silently told my mom the news; I called my dad, and I started a barrage of texts to Jared, Alex, my brother, Rabbi Susie, Cantor, and my mah jongg friends: Leigh, Delilah, Rose, Amanda, Sarah, and Phyllis. Then, I texted Holly, Fran, David, and all my other close friends and family. When I got home, I told Gabriel the great news in person.

"Dad is cancer-free, Gabriel!"

"That's so amazing!" His voice cracked in adolescent hormone-induced discord.

We hugged each other in celebration.

Len arrived home around 8:00 p.m. I greeted him at the door with a big hug and an even bigger smile.

"God gave me a second chance at life today," he said with gratitude.

"Indeed, God did. Don't squander this gift, Len. Make some lifestyle changes. You've been talking about changing your hour-and-a-half commute in each direction to work by finding a warehouse here on Long Island."

"Yes, I plan to start looking for a warehouse next week. I also want to contact Habitat for Humanity and get involved. I need to give back," he said, humbled.

"Those are great ideas," I said in agreement, my heart bursting with joy and relief. This was a transformative moment. He saw the need to both take care of himself better, as well as to give back to the community.

He was now asking a new question. In place of why did he get cancer, he was asking what can he give back to society? I knew the fire of cancer would create beauty for Len. He just discovered the beauty of self-care and volunteering to help those in need. I am certain more beauty is in store for him.

Len was tired, both emotionally and physically, and decided to go upstairs to take a shower. He needed to rest and surrendered into the femininity and comfort of our four-poster bed draped in cream-colored chiffon. It is like a mother's womb—warm, encapsulating, and nurturing.

I decided to make my final post to this cancer story on Facebook:

"Extra! Extra! Read all about it! Len is cancer FREE! Remission was his mission. We thank all of our friends and family for your prayers, support, and love. Len is one happy, blessed, and very lucky man today."

I took a picture of the following quote and added it under my wording: "Only God can turn a mess into a message, a test into a testimony, a trial into a triumph, a victim into a victor."

I'm not sure who wrote this, but it resonated with me, and I love it. It sounds a lot like something Joel Osteen would say in one of his sermons. I'm not sure if it has a connection to any one religion, but I'm sure of this. There is a God out there, and whatever you want to name Him or Her, I know this source is an energy made and filled with love, purity, and light. It is my God, your God, and our

God. God was kind and generous to my husband today. *Todah raba*—thank you.

It was late, and I was tired when I finished the Facebook post. I washed off my makeup, put on moisturizer, brushed my teeth, put on my nightie, and lay down in my princess bed. My prince was asleep next to me. I gazed at him and wished him a peaceful night's sleep. I closed my eyes. *Laila tov*—good night.

The next few days were an emotional rollercoaster for me. I was beyond relieved and happy that Len's PET scan showed there was no cancer in his body, but I also felt like I needed to keep looking over my shoulder. I felt unsettled. *How long will the cancer be gone?* I had scheduled an appointment with Holly, my life coach, timing it so I would have the scan results to discuss with her. When she opened the door to welcome me into her home, she gave me a huge hug.

Holly loves candles and lit one, which filled the entrance hall with a warm and delicious pumpkin spice smell. We settled on her comfy couch and started talking. I explained that despite feeling relieved, I was also feeling unsettled and cautious. I also explained my feelings of being disappointed that I didn't hear from some family members after they heard the scan results from Lenny.

"I'm hurt they didn't call or even text me to share their relief and happiness about his results or even acknowledge the results," I said incredulously. "I would have reached out to them to show my support."

"Fern, you are the type of person who is emotionally

intelligent, empathic, and you are deeply considerate and compassionate. Unfortunately, not everyone vibrates on your level. People express themselves in different ways, and not always through a connection."

"It doesn't take away the fact that it hurts and is disappointing."

"Luckily, you have so many friends who care deeply about you and your feelings," she said, reframing the situation.

I smiled at her. "You are right, and I am grateful for them. I didn't use my coaching tool in this situation, and it's my favorite one."

"Now let's talk about your feelings of being unsettled and cautious. Acknowledge those feelings and ask yourself how you can feel more settled. Understand that some things are out of your control. Live in the moment of feeling this relief and happiness and try to let go of an attachment to any final outcome that will hold you back from experiencing the joy, relief, and satisfaction, which is here *right now*."

I sighed. "You are right again. I can't control the future. I need to be in the moment and soak up all the goodness right now."

This was a session where I was glad Holly had a social work degree. This was more than a coaching session for me today.

I filled Holly in on my spiritual reading with Etta-Lyn, including that Jesus was there. I'm still so in awe about that! Holly especially liked the part of the message from my mom that my book will make coins and be continued.

Writing is what initially motivated me to start life coaching with Holly. Not only did I finally get a story written, but I reaped so many other benefits along the way in coaching. I've learned a lot of tools and expanded myself personally and professionally from these golden rules and tools. I left Holly's feeling better, more focused on the positive, and being in the here and now.

Saturday night, we went to a steakhouse in Jericho to celebrate Len's great scan results. He likes this restaurant, but it's not one of my top picks. I don't eat meat, so a steakhouse doesn't even make my list. It's a noisy restaurant, but luckily we were seated in a private room, and were able to have a quieter space to celebrate. Steaks filled the table as I filled up on vegetables and a shrimp dish. We were a family celebrating the feelings of relief, happiness, and togetherness. We are in "the now," I reminded myself.

"Fern, could you please text or e-mail Jim's wife for me? I haven't heard from him since late August. I've sent him a few texts since then. I'm worried about my friend," Len said to me.

"Ok. I better do it now, so I don't forget."

I took my phone out of my purse and emailed her, asking how they both were. I didn't mention Len's scan results as Jim and his wife were still pursuing other naturopathic treatments, and I wasn't sure what shape Jim was in or the status of his cancer. I finished the e-mail and pressed the send button.

My friend Joni surprised me and had dropped off an apple pie earlier to celebrate our good news, so we didn't order dessert and planned on having pie at home instead.

Joni showed me the gift of friendship, kindness, and support. She often texted me to ask how Len was doing or if I needed anything. These random acts of kindness didn't go unnoticed. I have learned through Len's cancer journey just how kind and supportive some people can be, and I've learned some disappointment as well.

After pie, Len started looking into flights for Italy. We were planning to go in April during Gabriel's school vacation. As I lay in bed, I took out my iPad and started Googling vacation spots in Italy. I drifted off to sleep with thoughts of Italy filling my mind and the sweetness of apple pie filling my belly. *What a dreamy vacation it will be.*

On Sunday, Gabriel's piano teacher was scheduled to come for their lesson. Afterward, she wanted to hear the CD from my reading with Etta-Lyn. During their lesson, I headed upstairs to my bedroom. I tapped the e-mail button to see if any new houses were listed in Greenport. Instead, I found a reply from Jim's wife.

Hi Fern,

Really nice to hear from you. Jim would give me updates on Len, and I know chemo was difficult but helping. Devastating does not even describe this, but my sweet, precious Jim died . . .

I don't remember the rest of the email, because I burst out crying. He was my husband's good friend through a challenging time. They had hiked together, eaten together, shared conversations, infusion time, and cancer treatment ideas together. Now he was gone; just memories were left.

Luckily the piano music drowned out my crying, and Len didn't hear me. I got myself together and knew I had to face the music, to go downstairs and tell my husband that his friend had lost his battle with cancer. I mustered up my courage and determination, walked down the staircase onto the main floor and into the kitchen where Len was doing work at the table. I put my hand on his shoulder, pursed my lips as emotion flooded my body again. I couldn't open my lips, or it would pour out of me and onto him, drowning him with sadness, grief, and despair.

He looked at me, seeing I was shaken to my core.

"What's wrong? Fern, speak to me!"

The flood gates opened as tears streamed from my eyes, and I cried out the sad and heartbreaking words, "Lenny, Jim died."

He closed his eyes tightly and lowered his head to the table. He was hit hard, knocked down by the blow of sadness that death creates.

"I'm so sorry," I whispered, tears still rolling down my face.

"He was like a brother to me. This isn't fair. He shouldn't have died. He fought so hard, doing all the things the clinic told him to do. He was a fighter, damn it," Len said through clenched teeth.

He was devastated. His uplifted mood from his test results was wiped away, being replaced with feelings of sadness, loss, and survivor's guilt.

"Fern, if he died, I will never live long with this disease."

"Stop it! Every cancer is different. Every patient is different. Every case is different. You are strong and healthy. Believe that to your core! Fill every cell with that information! Be strong in your convictions!" I ordered him.

He felt defeated. I felt helpless. Gabriel's piano lesson ended. He and Lena walked into the kitchen.

"Ready to hear the CD?" I asked her, trying to shift my mood by necessity.

"Absolutely," she replied.

We went into my car to listen to it. It was chilly, so I turned the heated seats on, then I slipped the CD into the player.

"Are you ok? You look like you have been crying," she asked.

"Thanks for asking. I just found out during the piano lesson that Len's good friend died. They became friends at the clinic in Arizona. I had to tell Len the tragic news."

"I'm so sorry, Fern."

How many times has Lena heard those three words after her own husband passed away? Now she is offering condolences to someone else, shifting from the receiver of sympathy to the giver of support and kindness.

"I'm so sorry, too. Ready to listen to Etta-Lyn?" I asked.

Lena taped the conversation onto her iPhone. She

listened intently, nodding her head as what Etta-Lyn said made sense to her. Yes, he had an intubation tube. Yes, his hands turned darker. Yes, his father would be there, greeting him as he had died over thirty years ago from the same disease. Yes, their younger daughter was pushing limits a bit. The letter A would be for their daughter, Abby. Yes, he would be thanking you for helping me through this time. The section where her husband spoke to Etta-Lyn ended as other spirits stepped forward for me.

"Wow! That is some crazy stuff! I want to listen to this again at home," Lena said.

"Listen to it at least two to three times," I suggested. "I was honored that your husband came to my reading."

Lena stepped out of my car and thanked me for sharing the reading with her. I went back into the house to make sure Len was ok. We talked for a while, and I listened to him reflect about the times he shared with Jim. There was nothing I could say to make him feel better, so I just sat and listened and held his hand.

Later I headed to the food store, still numb and saddened. Cancer creates this game. Len was invited by the result of a scan. His moves were strategic against this nemesis. His teammates were smart doctors, competent nurses, and miraculous medicines. Len was the obvious winner from the results of his scan. Then cancer had to haunt us days later with the news of Jim's passing. Is the game over? Only *b'shert* knows. Games are supposed to be fun, but not when lives are at stake. Mah jongg is nothing like this other game. I turned on the radio. Good. Dr. Laura's show is on. Let me listen to other people's problems for a while.

Post-Scan Game

Group text: Delilah, Leigh, Rose, Amanda
Me: Hey ladies! Monday is game day! Who's in and who can host?
Rose: I'm in. I'll host again, How's 11:30 a.m.?
Leigh: Thanks for hosting, Rose. I'm in!
Amanda: I have a conference. Sorry to miss playing with you girls.
Delilah: I'm in and will see you all on Monday!

Monday morning arrived. I was grateful it was the start of a new week. Sunday was a hard day after hearing about Jim's passing. I woke up early at 6:05 a.m. I went downstairs, turned on relaxing music, and made a pot of coffee. I then started to get Gabriel ready for school. As I made him his breakfast and packed up his lunch, we had morning talk-time. Our morning time together is special to me. I love helping him prepare for a new day. We are never rushed. I make sure of that. It's an opportunity I have to help set up his day positively and calmly. I hope this positivity lasts throughout his day in school. I know being a student can be hectic. As he walked out the door to wait for the bus, I said, "Wait a second, Gabriel."

He turned to look at me, "What?" he asked inquisitively.

"Tell me two things you are grateful for this morning."

He barely hesitated. "You, of course!"

"And the second thing?" (I knew I would be his first answer.)

He pointed upward, "That sky art with the beautiful pink sky with the swirly clouds."

That's my boy. I taught him to appreciate sky art when he was a toddler. I would show him the different colors in a sunset, the different shapes and striations clouds would form, or the God-like sunrays beaming through the clouds.

"That is a beautiful sunrise, Gabe." I smiled at him. "Thank you for being grateful for the beauty of the sky and for me, too. Know you are my angel and I am grateful for you, too. I love you. Remember to stay positive and to be grateful throughout your day."

"I will. Love you, too. Keep looking at the sky art," he said back.

The bus stopped in front of the house a minute later, and he hopped on. I sent him off with a prayer of safety and protection as I have done since the day he started taking a school bus.

I went back into the kitchen, started cleaning up, and then I began to make a vegetable soup, one of the few things I cook from scratch. Len came down the stairs.

"Morning. How is my wife on this Monday morning?" he asked, trying to sound jovial.

"I'm good, thanks. It's Mah Jongg Monday, so I'm excited to play and to see my girls today." I winked at him. "How's my cancer-free husband this morning?"

"Sad. My friend died," he sighed. The mood between us had changed.

"I know. It is very sad indeed. Jim meant a lot to you."

Alex came down, and thankfully he shifted the energy in the kitchen. The boys made some breakfast and then headed out to work. I focused on cutting the vegetables for the soup. I needed to occupy my mind. My thoughts were starting to run wild. I was beginning to wrestle with that existential question, *what is the meaning of life?* My flippant, unsolicited, rampant, and otherwise impetuous answer went something like this: Ups. Downs. Calm. Bumps. Smooth sailing. Tumultuous waters. Falling and getting back up. Failures. Successes. Love. Friends. Family. Highs. Lows. Disagreements. Resolution. Disappointments. Overwhelming joy. Hardships. Choices. Education. Obligation. Religion. God/no God. Sickness. Health. Travel. Sex, drugs, rock, and roll. Winning. Losing. Birth. Then Death. The good, the bad, and the ugly. Funny, that's Len's ringtone on his phone. Coincidentally, it was Jim's ringtone, too. Something they shared besides cancer and friendship.

I finished the soup prep and decided I would go upstairs and practice yoga. Vinyasa flow and detoxifying twists were what I needed. I finished a forty-five-minute workout and then meditated for ten minutes. I focused my intention on perseverance. I struck the side of the singing bowl gently with the striker, sending a clearing vibration throughout the room. I cupped my hands over my head, focusing on perseverance, letting it pour from the heavens above me into my hands and spilling over onto my whole body. I brought my hands into *Anjali Mudra* (hands in prayer) and placed them at my third eye. *May I be mindful to persevere through any challenging situation or thought today.* I brought my hands to my lips. *May I speak words of perseverance and positivity.* I brought my hands to heart center. *May my body be filled with perseverance. May every cell, organ, and organ system be healthy, and may my body be a vibrant vessel for my soul to reside in.* I bowed and sealed my practice and meditation. I was more centered. *Namaste.*

I checked my watch and saw it was time to get ready for mah jongg. God, did I need this game and my ladies today! Mah jongg had become an anchor in my life. It provides consistency and companionship, fun and friendship, mental stimulation and emotional satisfaction. Today, I needed it to be an escape for me.

I pulled into Rose's development. Leigh and Delilah were just getting out of their cars. We kissed hello, and the girls congratulated me in person for Len's great scan results. We walked into Rose's house together. She and her dog greeted us at the door and welcomed us in.

"I'm so happy for you and Len!" she said with a big smile.

"Ladies, I need some mah jongg therapy today," I said with a big sigh.

I filled them in on my rollercoaster ride of feelings after hearing of Jim's death.

"I'm trying to be in the now, to experience the relief and happiness the scan results provided us. This other news has shifted me into a sad and scary place."

"Fern, you need to see every cancer is different and can have different outcomes," Delilah said. "Len called me the other day and said he had a second lease on life. He was feeling it. This was just bad timing, hearing about his friend. Don't lose sight of Len's personal journey."

I shook my head, processing what she was saying.

"Know that you have friends that love you and care about you."

Leigh said. "It's natural, what you are feeling. Don't be hard on yourself. You and Len have been through a scary time, remind yourselves about that and validate those feelings."

"I know. I hear you. I saw Holly on Thursday, and I left feeling better, but that was before we learned about Len's friend dying. I think I just need to whine. Thank you, girls, for listening."

Rose was quiet, then said, "Fern, you are experiencing normal feelings."

I processed her clinical response.

"Thanks for letting me vent. I am so happy to have mah jongg today. It couldn't have been better timing. Ok, I'm ready to move on and play."

Rose rolled the dice and started to deal. We racked our tiles as game one started. We picked three tiles each and started the Charleston. I started filling in a hand in Consecutive Run with Dots. As the game progressed, I just needed a Flower and a 5 Dot to win. My mind was occupied and focused. Anticipation builds when you get so close to calling mah jongg. You don't have extra tiles to throw when you are two tiles away from winning, so playing defensively is both a challenge and a decision. You don't want to throw someone's winning tile when you see the exposures on their rack, and you have figured out what hand they are playing. On the next turn, I picked up a Flower. *Yes! I'm one tile away!* I threw a North. Rose picked a tile from the wall, racked it, then discarded. Leigh picked and threw. Delilah picked next. She racked the tile and discarded. I picked and threw. Rose called it and laid out an exposure, then discarded a 5 Dot.

"Mah jongg!" I called out with delight as I exposed my winning hand.

Everyone exposed their hands. We saw who was lucky and had a Joker, who was close to winning, or whose hand was dead. This is how we learn and grow as players. Each game we have the possibility to discover something new, to play a new or challenging hand, to take chances, and to learn from our mistakes. We also hope to be lucky and pick up a Joker or two from the wall or to replace one from someone's exposure. My mind was occupied, and I was thrilled not to be thinking of anything but mah jongg and having a great afternoon with my friends.

"Oh, I thought something was wrong," Leigh said shyly.

"What's that?" I asked.

"I was playing with a 2016 card!" laughed Leigh.

We burst out laughing along with her. We didn't notice the hand she showed us was from an old card. We hadn't memorized the card like some mah jongg mavens do. I admire those who can do that. My dyslexia makes that goal a hard one to achieve. Leigh bent down and reached into her purse, took out her mah jongg cardholder, and switched out the old card with the current 2018 card.

"I thought the hands looked a little different," she confessed.

"Well, at least you realized it," Delilah said, smiling.

"Remember when Amanda called mah jongg with the 2017 card?" I added. "We all make mistakes."

We played another four games. I won two games, and Delilah won two. One game was a wall game, where there is no winner. It was 2:30 p.m., and Delilah and I needed to head home for our kids. We helped Rose put the tiles back into the cases.

I said, "Goodbye, and thank you, girls, for listening to me earlier and helping me through this funk of feelings I'm dealing with." I blew them each a kiss. Through life's ups and downs the past five years, mah jongg has been a constant for me. Sometimes the players and locations change, but the good feelings of fun and friendship are always there on Mondays for me.

As I drove home, I decided to light a *Yahrzeit* candle

for Jim. Even though he wasn't Jewish, this was a way I could honor him and his friendship to Len. I pulled into the driveway and unlocked the door to the house.

"Hey, Gabe, I'm home!" I called out, not knowing his exact whereabouts.

"Hi, Mom, I'm in the kitchen," he responded, his cracking voice making me smile.

I gave him some of the soup I had made earlier and chicken fingers for a snack, and then found a *Yahrzeit* candle in the cabinet. I lit a match and brought the flame to the wick. I recited the *Kaddish* in Hebrew and closed my ritual by saying, "Rest in peace, Jim. You were a fighter, a great man, and a dear friend to Lenny."

I had e-mailed Rose after the game, asking if she was okay. She had been rather quiet. As I lay in bed later, I checked my e-mails and found her heartfelt response.

Dear Fern,

Today was our first time getting together for mah jongg since Lenny's "all clear" PET scan. I expected the conversation to be one of relief, excitement, and jubilation. So, I was disheartened and of course quite sad to hear about the passing of his friend who he went through alternative therapy with in Arizona. I was very quiet during that conversation. Although I didn't share this earlier today, I was brought back to the many people I befriended during my own chemotherapy protocol, which lasted over two years. I saw many people come and go at the cancer center. Sadly, many of them passed away. Some were my roommates during inpatient admissions; others were patients I chatted with during frequent day-long outpatient treatments. I remember feeling a myriad of emotions, and I don't need to try hard to imagine what Lenny might be feeling right now. It's called survivor's guilt, and no amount of cognitive restructuring saves you from feeling deep sadness, and a level of guilt that you survived and someone else didn't.

During this conversation, I often thought about Delilah. Of course, she loves Lenny very much and is genuinely thrilled about his news. Nonetheless, I wondered if she felt some sadness, and maybe even anger that her own husband didn't get a second chance like Lenny. Delilah and Robert had a love couples dream about. My heart breaks every time I see her. Her sadness and persistent grief permeate my soul and make me wish that I could make it better.

Needless to say, this wasn't the Mah Jongg Monday I anticipated, and I had quite a difficult time regaining my focus.

So, I sit here writing this with a slightly heavy heart, but I am also so happy for Lenny! I pray that the remission will last for years and years. But the other news I learned today makes me sad and *fearful, both for Lenny and selfishly for myself. This is a familiar feeling, one I've had for over twenty-five years, since the last day of chemotherapy. I will move forward from this as I have done in the past; living for today, mindfully adding positive and "happy-making" experiences into my life, and surrounding myself with people I love and who know how to love in return. I remind myself often—especially when fear and sadness creep in, as was the case today—that life isn't measured by the number of breaths we take, but by the moments that take our breath away.*

Love,
Rose

I sighed. Not only was Rose a gateway for me into Len's past and Russian world, but a gateway into the emotions of a cancer survivor. She articulated herself so clearly. I am blessed to have this unique friendship. I see how grateful and lucky she feels to be alive and how fear haunts her, too, even twenty-five years later. I needed to make a plan of how to deal with fear, as I saw it would make unannounced and unwanted visits. As I closed my eyes, I prayed for Len and Rose. I showered them both with rays of light filled with health, strength, love, and longevity. *Spakoynayi nochi*. Good night, my Russian friend and my Russian husband.

Chapter 21

Dr. Laura

I have an appointment to meet a realtor in Greenport. I'm sitting in my driveway and looking at the outside of my home in Melville. Mums of different colors line the three steps to the front doors. Tall corn stalks are tied with orange ribbon around the columns on either side of the steps. Autumn is in its full glory. I turn on contemporary Christian music and back out of the driveway. I turn the corner and drive past the area where the plane crashed a few months ago. Someone keeps putting flowers out, creating a memorial for the pilot who died there. A few American flags wave on small wooden posts among the flowers. I read online that the pilot was a Naval aviator and served our country. The burnt foliage is slowly starting to be erased as new green growth covers the charred vegetation. I send a prayer to the pilot as I always do when I pass this spot. Rest in peace.

Death reminds me of the fragility of life, as well as the blessings life has given me. Death makes me aware of the gift of time, which I am so keenly aware of since cancer knocked on Len's door. I think of Dr. Laura asking: what do I want to do between now and dead? It sounds harsh when she asks that of her callers, but it's such an intro-spective and important question to ponder. I think of my answer as I have an imaginary conversation with her.

"Well, Dr. Laura, I want to travel to Hawaii, India, Italy, and England." I tell her about the things I want to do. "I want to keep volunteering and adding love and light to my community, to keep teaching children yoga and religion. I want to keep learning, growing, and expanding my abilities as a wife, mother, friend, and fellow human being. I want to continue keeping my promise to Robert. I want to continue to raise my three sons and watch them become good, loving, and virtuous men. I want to help my dad celebrate turning eighty in April. I want to watch him enjoy the last part of his life and honor his wishes when he is ready to leave this earth."

(He insisted, "Remember my wishes, DNR! Do not resuscitate! No life support!"

"Yes, Dad, I promise.")

"I want to keep playing mah jongg. I want to be a supportive, loving, reliable, and honest friend. I want to keep writing and to publish at least one book that will make a positive impact on someone's life. I would love the opportunity to meet Oprah Winfrey and share a conversation with her about life. I want to age gracefully. I want to retire with my husband and see him enjoy the fruits of his hard work all these years. I want to look into his elderly eyes when we are old and grey together. I want to welcome grandchildren into our family and gaze into a newborn's eyes.

"And . . . I want to have a house in or near Greenport to enjoy with Len, our family, and friends."

I imagine Dr. Laura nodding her head yes at me with her big smile and saying to me, "Now go, be, and do those things, woman!"

Now I pose the question for you to ponder: What do you want to do between now and dead?

Carole Lane

I arrive in town early and park near the carousel. I decide to walk around town for a little while. I pass a restaurant where music is playing. As I get closer, I recognize the song by John Denver. "Take Me Home Country Road." I smile. Universe, I hear you. I stop into a few stores and buy myself a shirt and a ring, and a sweatshirt for Gabriel. I get an iced coffee at Aldo's Coffee Company on Front Street on the way back to my car. I check my phone for the address of the first house we were scheduled to see. I text the realtor that I am on the way. I like her and value her experience. She's lived out here a long time and knows information that helps Len and me in our house search. I wonder if she knew my mom. I will have to ask her.

We see two houses and have one last house to see. As I follow her in my car, we turn onto the street leading to the last house. I see the street sign reads Carole Lane. My mom's name was Carol, without the 'E.' My heart twinges. Maybe the 'E' is there to represent my dad's name, which is Elliot. Is this a sign to make me aware that they are coming together from both heaven and earth, trying to fix the mistake of selling our treasured waterfront home thirty-eight years ago? Is my mom guiding me to my own Greenport home? This way, daughter, turn here. I pull up to the small house, and the realtor wants to walk out back before going inside. I am stunned by the breathtaking view.

"This is called Hashamomuck Pond. It's about a mile long. You can launch a boat, kayak, swim, fish, and Jet Ski here. There's also a hiking trail," she said.

It is beautiful and tranquil. My mind imagines all those activities, so many of them the things I did with my mom as a child. Len loves going hiking with the boys and our dog. I can envision them taking hikes together. Then my eyes fill with tears as I notice the perimeter of the house and property are filled with Shasta daisies. Daisies were my mom's favorite flower. My dad used to bring her home daisies every Friday when they were married. I am overwhelmed with emotion and the universal signs glaringly making me aware that *this* is "the house." Are these signs *b'shert*? I humbly explain my emotional state to the realtor. She nods understandingly.

"Did you know my mom? Her name was Carol Levitch," I ask.

"No, I don't believe I know the name or have ever met her," she says respectfully. "Let's take a look inside, shall we?"

We walk inside the outdated two-bedroom, one-bathroom home, and my body is buzzing with the feeling that *this is it*. It is the opposite of my home in Melville, but this view trumps it all. Across the street is Town Beach with more beautiful views. I envision my dad walking with his beach chair across the street and settling in under the sun for a relaxing day at the beach. I tell the realtor I need to come back with my husband and my father. I can't wait to tell the girls about the house, the water view, the street sign, and the daisies on Mah Jongg Monday. I take pictures of the house and the magnificent view and plan to tack a few up on the board above my writing desk. I want to see it every day and envision this as my home. Please, *b'shert,* work your magic.

My True Home

I decide to drive down to Inlet Lane and pass by my old house, then drive to Gull Pond Beach. I park the car, take my boots and socks off, and walk along the water's edge down toward the jetty. Here I am, walking on the same beach I played on as a child, looking at the familiar view of Shelter Island and the calm Peconic Bay separating these two beautiful places. I glance to the right as I walk past my old house. It's time to let my sadness go. I inhale deeply, bend down, and scoop sand into each of my hands, and as I exhale, I turn and throw the sand into the water, throwing away my sadness and indignation. I put my feet and hands into the cold water, letting the remaining specks of sand fall back into the sea. Tears roll down my cheeks. I sit down on the cool, dry sand by the water's edge. My parents were human; they were flawed and made mistakes. I need to forgive them. A thought became clear all of a sudden. I've lived in a home, an apartment, and condo throughout my life in Cresskill, Greenport, San Francisco, Bayside, and Melville. These are just man-made structures. My real home, the home of my soul, is within my skin. My body is a gift from God.

I think of the beautiful practice Rabbi Susie does at the close of our *Torah* yoga class, and I start to do it right here on the beach. I place my hands on my face, covering my eyes. I feel my damp eyes closed beneath my fingers. I am thankful for the gift of sight, to see my loved ones, the beauty of people and places, to see the beautiful colors that exist in our world. I bring my fingers to my nose. I am thankful for the gift of breath and the ability to smell. I can smell the sea. I love the smell of certain perfumes and Len's cologne. I love the smell of baking chocolate chip cookies, which triggers memories of a happy childhood. I trace my lips. My tongue tastes the salty tears, or maybe it's the sea breeze carrying the salty mist that I taste. I am thankful for the ability to taste and chew my food to nourish my body. I am thankful for the gift of speech, to be able to ask for help, to offer help, to pray, to smile, and to say the words I love you. My hands cover each ear. I am thankful for the gift of hearing, to hear music, laughter, loving words, and sometimes to hear silence and to enjoy the peace in the quiet stillness. My arms cross and I caress my upper arms, and I let my hands slip to my forearms, and I clasp my hands. I am thankful for my arms to hug. My hands enable me to use utensils to eat, to write, to type and create art, to shake hands, to offer help, to hold the hand of a loved one, and they help me to pick and discard tiles in mah jongg. I bring my hands together and place one over my heart, the other hand following and resting on top of the other hand. I am thankful for my heart. Not only does it pump blood and oxygen throughout my body, but it is also the sanctuary within my body. It is the place where God resides within me. My hands rest on my lower belly. I am thankful for digestion and recreation, for nutrients to be processed in my body, for the ability to have created and birthed life, and for the pleasure that can be unlocked here. I run my hands down my thighs, knees, shins, and I hold my feet in my hands. I am thankful for the ability to walk, run, practice yoga, and to transport my body. My body is the vessel that houses my soul to walk this earth and learn soul lessons from the people I interact with and the challenges and experiences I encounter. This is my true home.

I sit in the sand, tears still wetting my cheeks. My body is my home. My soul resides in this vessel of organs, bones, and skin. Genetics painted my hair dark brown and my eyes blue. My skin is painted apricot and my lips a soft pink. These are the colors of my home. I decorate it like the rooms of a house, but instead of furniture, I decorate with clothes of different fabrics and colors, and I place shiny things on my ears, neck, and fingers. I paint my face with makeup like a painting on a wall is brought to life with color and brush strokes. I sit in the sand as an adult on the beach of my youth. My older self made the discovery that I needed to free my younger self from the bondage of indignation and sadness about losing my childhood summers and the home I can't go back to. Today, I let it go. The breeze gently blows around me.

I swear I hear my mother say, "I love you."

I close my eyes. I see her so clearly, smiling at me with her big beautiful blue eyes looking at me with adoration. I feel her love wash over me. I take a deep breath in and open my eyes. I sense I was smiling. The tears have dried up. I say out loud, "I love you too, Mom."

I walk back to the car and clean the sand off my feet, then put my socks and boots back on. I start the drive home, excited about the house with an incredible view. I head to the North Road, but turn into the cemetery on the way to visit my mom's ashes that are buried here. I rode through this cemetery on a bike as a kid with my brother, Soula, and her siblings. I walk under the tree where her ashes are resting in the earth. I sit on the ground and look up at the huge oak tree. I hear a bird chirping somewhere in its branches. I feel close to my mom here. Greenport is where she loved to be most of all. I thank her for teaching me the life lessons of love and admiration for nature and the sea, and I thank her for blessing me with creativity and patience. I see a deer and her fawn eating grass nearby in the cemetery. Was it *b'shert* showing me a mother and her child here right now in this place of remembrance? After a few minutes, they wander off; I stand up and walk back to my car and drive away.

I turn left onto North Road, passing the condo where we stayed a few months ago. I call my father and tell him about the house I looked at today and fell in love with. I tell him about the street sign and the daisies and that the view is breathtaking. He wants to come and see the house with Len. I look forward to great summers ahead filled with weekend retreats with my family. I plan to have mah jongg retreats with the girls, too. *One day,* I say to myself. *Remember patience.* I head onto the Long Island Expressway back to Melville.

L'chaim

My phone rings, and I look and see it is Delilah calling.

"Hi there," I say.

"Hi. Is this a good time to talk?"

"Perfect, actually. I was in Greenport earlier looking at

some houses, and I just got onto the Long Island Expressway. Everything ok?"

"Yes, thank you. Well, I have some news I want to share."

I've been waiting for this. You see, a few months ago I noticed something different about Delilah. She had shifted. Close friendships provide tacit signs and signals. I secretly picked up on them and had hopes that my special friend had met someone.

"So . . ." Her voice is full of joy and exuberance. "I reconnected with an old friend, a male friend more specifically, and there was a spark there for sure. For the first time since Robert died, I'm exploring the opportunity to be with someone new. I'm feeling hopeful and optimistic."

"I knew it! I'm so over the moon happy for you!" I exclaim. "Did you kiss?"

"Yes. Fern, it felt like a lightning bolt! It's so nice to hold hands and to feel someone's touch again. It's been so lonely for me."

"This is epic! I'm smiling ear to ear right now—you just can't see," I say to my love-struck friend.

"Robert set me free. He told me before he died that he wanted me to go out and find happiness in the future. He told me to find someone who makes me laugh and who makes me happy. I told him I could never replace him in my heart. He told me I needed to find someone to share the rest of my life with. I told him . . . maybe one day."

"He loved you and knew one day you would be ready.

You will never replace him or the love you shared, but instead, find someone who will fill a different place in your heart and share a different part of your life. You deserve happiness, love, and companionship," I reply.

"Thank you, Fern. It feels so good to be able to share this with you. I'll tell the girls on Monday at mah jongg."

We finish our conversation and hang up. I am so incredibly happy for her. Delilah has found her way out of the darkness of loss and mourning and is rejoining the world once again with renewed hope. Despite a broken heart, she has made peace with the pieces of her broken heart and broken life.

Things are good with my widowed friends. I had lunch with David a few days ago at the diner. He has been in a committed relationship for over a year with a Match .com match. Over lunch, he, too, said how lonely he was after his wife died. David and Delilah are true survivors. Lena, Gabriel's piano teacher, said she just joined a dating service. She, too, is ready to leave behind mourning and step into life renewed. She is signed up to take Fran's beginner mah jongg class in a few weeks.

Sam and his devoted fiancé married, and he is focusing on his health, well-being, and enjoying being a newlywed with his beautiful and loving wife. His recent scan results were thankfully and amazingly clear. His mom, Fran, is staying strong and positive and continues teaching mah jongg. Rose is cancer-free and back to kickboxing, working, and leading a full life. Len is cancer-free and feeling strong and vibrant. He starts the first maintenance treatment in a few days.

Me? I'm focusing on being present, remembering what my life coach said. And right here, right now, I've got Hope, Health, and Happiness in the back seat of my car, and my constant companion God right next to me in the passenger seat. I feel really good about the way 2018 is coming into its final month. I am excited about the house I saw today with the amazing water view. I am feeling filled with hope and gratitude as I look forward to 2019. I look forward to continued health and remission for Len. I look forward to another year filled with Mah Jongg Mondays and seeing my special friends every week at our games.

I feel like celebrating all of a sudden. I imagine a glass filled with wine. I raise it into the air, toasting all the mah jongg players out there, "Here's to you, to me, to your group of players and mine, and to games and games of mah jongg for us all!" Then I raise the imaginary glass a little higher, toasting the fighters, the survivors, my beloved family and friends affected by cancer, and to the memories of Robert and Jim. I say the Hebrew word, *"L'chaim*—to life!" Just as the wine is sweet, so is life, so very sweet . . . if only for right now.

Book Club Questions and Discussion Ideas

1. What was your initial reaction to *Mah Jongg Mondays?* Did it hook you immediately or take some time to pull you into the story?

2. Which parts of the book stood out to you and why?

3. Describe the author's writing style and storytelling ability.

4. Did you relate to any character in the story?

5. What themes did you find in the story? How did they relate to each other and the story?

6. Do you play mah jongg, canasta, or bridge? If yes, did you relate to the author's description of sisterhood? If you play poker, did you relate to a brotherhood feeling?

7. Do you have any situations or experiences where you felt *b'shert* occurred in your life? Please share.

8. What life challenges have you had to face? Were there certain people who helped you through those challenges?

9. As Dr. Laura asks: "What do you want to do between now and dead?"

10. What were your takeaways from the story?

11. Would you recommend this book? Why or why not?

If you enjoyed my story, please make your feelings known by writing a review on the Amazon, Goodreads, or Barnes and Noble web sites. Your support would be much appreciated. Thank you!

Acknowledgments

With heartfelt gratitude and appreciation, I thank the following people for helping me on my author's journey and for supporting me as I brought my story from the 'whoosh' of an idea, onto the page, finally into a readable book and hopefully into readers' hearts.

First I want to thank Barry Levy, who is not only my beloved family member but also a talented author. You helped me step into the writer's arena with confidence and gusto.

I want to thank Brooke Warner, from Warner Coaching. You are a memoir and writing expert, and I have learned a great deal about writing from your online classes. I appreciate your guidance and for choosing an editing team that helped me keep my voice as I navigated towards publishing my first book.

To Jody Siegel—it was *b'shert* we were to meet at Temple Beth Torah. Little did I know that when we first met a few years ago, you would be part of Gabriel's *bar mitzvah* ceremony, your voice adding to the beautiful service along with Cantor Sarene's. Then you added proofreading power to my book after publication, with your background in journalism, desktop publishing, and as an English teacher with a discerning eye. I am grateful for your skill, patience, and attention to detail in both English and Hebrew.

My thanks to Jessica Bell, from Jessica Bell Designs. Your creativity, talent, and patience brought the vision of my story onto the cover of the book.

Thank you to Blair Billings, for taking photographs of me for the front and back cover of this book and for the website. Your photographic eye is superb as are your touch-up skills. The photo shoot was fun, and I felt like a star for an hour!

With heartfelt thanks to Linda Zagon, an avid book reader and reviewer with a kind and giving heart. You gifted me with your time during countless phone calls where you guided me, helped me make connections and gave me confidence when I needed it most.

With gratitude, I thank Karen Gooen. Our love of mah jongg and writing brought us together. Your experience as a fellow author has helped me tremendously. You took my hand and offered me your time, advice and experiential wisdom.

To my new and fun-filled friend Ahuva Ellner, I thank you for your support, pizazz, and interest in my book-writing endeavor.

To my niece, Lauren Rock, thank you for always supporting my ideas, writing, and dreams. We have a very special bond, and I cherish our times together. Love you lots!

Thank you to my Beta readers: Alana Klaben, Jiya Kowarsky, Barry Levy, Mollie Mandell, Fern Rubin, and Joyce Tisman. Your time spent reading, discussing and analyzing the story is greatly appreciated.

I am filled with gratitude and appreciation for Roz. You are a techno wiz and helped me navigate through Word, Grammarly, transferring documents and being a proofreading powerhouse. You went above and beyond with your help, and I am blessed not only with your friendship, but also with your dedication to my book. May you be blessed with continued good health.

To George Lancer, I am grateful for your time and help with my website. You are not only a great neighbor and dog walker, and one of Len's very good friends, but you are also a website wizard.

My transcendent thanks and gratitude to Etta-Lyn Cavataio. Your gift and ability to connect with other-worldly beings has me awestruck. You have connected me to family members on the other side and made me aware of angels, guides, and other special helpers guiding me on my earthly path. You are a mystical gift in my life.

My life has been blessed by two great rabbis. I thank

you both for giving me the knowledge and confidence to become a temple lay leader and religious school teacher. You both have nourished my Jewish soul with your love and teaching of Judaism.

I thank Rabbi Susie Heneson Moskowitz for teaching me about the strength of a woman through Judaism. Your Tuesday Tangents classes opened my mind to Mussar, Rosh Chodesh and a multitude of topics and holidays. Your Torah yoga classes have not only enhanced my practice, but have helped me incorporate Judaism and spirituality when teaching my children's yoga classes in our temple nursery school.

Thank you to Rabbi Todd Chizner, for being my other great teacher of Judaism. You helped bring the rituals, history, and adventure of Judaism and the study of Torah into my life.

Thank you to Dr. Dean Telano, Ph.D., E-RYT 500, RCYT, RPYT, Dip AH, for blessing and guiding me on my yoga certification journey. I am filled with gratitude, and I am in awe of your knowledge.

My deepest appreciation and gratitude to Holly Boxenhorn, my life coach over the past six years. You gave me the wind beneath my wings to fly and write and to reach the finish line—a published book! I have learned so much from you! You are a true professional and a gifted and special life coach. I'm so glad *b'shert* brought us together.

Thank you to my mah jongg loving friends: Amy, Diane, Eileen, Paula, Robin, and Roz, who bless my

Mondays with friendship, laughter, gaming, fun, and love. Your friendship and support have helped me through the tough journey of Len's cancer, and each of you adds your light and love into my life. I love you ladies and look forward to many years filled with Mah Jongg Mondays!

Thank you to Fern Rubin, my dear friend, mah jongg teacher, and a fellow woman warrior. You have blessed my life with friendship and helped me learn a game that has changed my life in such magical ways. I admire and respect your perseverance through Steve's battle with cancer. May he be blessed with health, happiness, and a long and loving marriage.

Thank you to my father, Dr. Elliot Levitch. Your support during the book writing process means the world to me. Yes, you tell me you are crazy, eccentric and sometimes "whacked-out." But you are my dad, and I accept your craziness and eccentricity. It's who you are and what makes you uniquely you. You are my intelligent and cultured East Village Renaissance father. I love you and all of your craziness, Dad.

I want to thank my three amazing sons: Jared, Alex, and Gabriel. You are all my cheerleaders and my loves. You are each a gift to me in your own individual ways. You taught me what unconditional love is all about. I love each of you with all of my heart and soul.

Thank you to my hero and husband Len. You have blessed me with a beautiful life. Your patience and support during the writing process have been a tremendous source of strength for me. Many mornings you would wake up and see me sitting at my desk, my fingers dancing on the keyboard. This book endeavor and the publishing process is another new path we are venturing down together. We've been through so much on our journey in marriage and parenting. You have shown me what a strong man and hero is as you have navigated our family through the ups and downs of life and through the challenges we have faced, including your fight with cancer. I admire and I am in awe of you. A house in Greenport is waiting for us. I just know it. May you be blessed with health and a long, loving, happy and successful life. I love you always and in all ways possible.

This memoir is in memory of my beloved mother, Carol Newman Levitch. You raised me well, Mom. You didn't have the easiest life, but you made the best from the life you had. Thank you for being my mother and teacher and for the beautiful and fun-filled summers in Greenport that you created for us.

Lastly, I thank God. You have blessed me with an abundance of love and blessings—too many to count. I won't forget my promise to you. *Todah lecha Elohim.*

About the Author

Fern Bernstein is a first-time author, her debut memoir titled *Mah Jongg Mondays*. She is a 200 RYT Yoga Instructor specializing in teaching children. She also is a religious school teacher and loves learning and teaching about Judaism. She lives on Long Island with her handsome and charming husband and her three incredible sons. You can find her on Mondays sitting around a mah jongg table with her friends, and all other times she can be found at www.fernbernstein.com.

Connect with Fern on Instagram at: fernlovesmahjongg or on Facebook at Mah Jongg Mondays.

Made in the USA
Coppell, TX
10 November 2023

24065897R00218